"With today's debates raging between science and religion, students are more concerned than ever about how to understand the Bible's creation texts. Leonard not only masterfully navigates these issues with scholarly precision and refreshing insights, but he also offers a robust theology of creation that provides meaning and direction for his readers. Through illuminating comparisons between biblical and ancient Near Eastern creation accounts that are meticulous yet accessible, Leonard asks the right questions and gives answers that both respect modern science and account for the Bible's ancient contexts."

—Kevin D. Chau, Senior Lecturer of Hebrew, University of the Free State

"Since the rediscovery of the ancient Near East, students and scholars of the biblical world have noted copious connections between the texts preserved in scripture and those from surrounding cultures. In a clear and conversational tone, Leonard demonstrates that the latter do not merely inform our understanding of the Old Testament, they provide the literary backstory necessary for fully appreciating the profound nature of the biblical creation story. *Creation Rediscovered* not only acquaints readers with the fascinating thought world behind Genesis, it also informs and models a faithful approach to reading the Old Testament. As such, this volume makes for an ideal supplementary textbook for introductory courses on the Hebrew Bible or hermeneutics."

—Kyle R. Greenwood, author of *Scripture and Cosmology: Reading the Bible between the Ancient World and Modern Science* and editor of *Since the Beginning: Interpreting Genesis 1–2 through the Ages*

"I enthusiastically recommend Jeffery Leonard's *Creation Rediscovered* to scholars, clergy, and thoughtful laypeople. This beautifully written and profound reflection on the creation stories of the Bible takes us to their important backstory and to Jesus, with important implications for our lives today."

—Tremper Longman III, Distinguished Scholar and Professor Emeritus of Biblical Studies, Westmont College

T0051477

"*Creation Rediscovered* is an uncommonly sophisticated book. It is at once a work written for a popular audience and a substantial scholarly contribution. Availing itself of the full range of ancient Near Eastern evidence and informed by the best critical scholarship, it is filled with detailed analyses that shed new light on the meanings of the biblical texts explored. Its lucid explanations demonstrate well that these texts were full participants in the thought world from which they emerged. The book also shows that, though the ancient creation accounts are sometimes strange, they need not be judged obtuse or outmoded. Through deft analogies to the modern world, Jeffery Leonard expertly guides the reader to deeper understandings of the biblical texts and their enduring significance for Christian thought and practice. The synthesis Leonard has produced is a remarkable accomplishment—erudite and eminently readable."

—Jeffrey Stackert, Associate Professor of Hebrew Bible, The University of Chicago

"Another book on the Bible, creation, and science? Yes, and a very good one—and one that covers much more besides. On every page, Jeffery Leonard displays deep learning and a deft pen, thorough control of the biblical and ancient Near Eastern material (not to mention pop culture), and pedagogical genius as he covers a veritable A-to-Z on creation in Genesis 1 and beyond (and behind and before): from Arcturus and astrophysics to Baal and Baruch, Copernicus and Calvin, on through to Galileo and genre, Marduk and Michelangelo along with the New Testament and Paul, *Toy Story* and *tiqqun*, Ugarit and Mr. Zuss, to name a few. The result is no mean feat: with Leonard as our guide we really do find new meaning in an ancient story. Rediscovered indeed!"

—Brent A. Strawn, Professor of Old Testament and Professor of Law, Duke University

Creation
Rediscovered

—

JEFFERY M. LEONARD

Creation
Rediscovered

—

*Finding New Meaning
in an Ancient Story*

an imprint of Hendrickson Publishing Group

Creation Rediscovered: Finding New Meaning in an Ancient Story

© 2020 by Jeffery M. Leonard

Published by Hendrickson Academic
an imprint of Hendrickson Publishing Group
Hendrickson Publishers, LLC
P. O. Box 3473
Peabody, Massachusetts 01961-3473
www.hendricksonpublishinggroup.com

ISBN 978-1-68307-234-8

Printed in the United States of America

First Printing — March 2020

Library of Congress Control Number: 2020934804

In loving memory of my grandmother,
Johnnie Frances Shepherd

He will wipe away every tear from their eyes.
Death shall be no more,
neither shall there be mourning or crying or pain,
for the first things have passed away.
And the one seated on the throne said,
"Behold, I am making all things new."

(Revelation 21:4–5)

. . . and there was no more sea.

Revelation 21:1

Contents

Preface

When a study ventures into an area as fraught with controversy as the doctrine of creation, it may be helpful to clear the air at the outset over the who, what, and why of the study:

This is a book that emerges from a deep love for the Scriptures and for the God who authored them. It proceeds from a conviction that the essential doctrines of the Christian faith are true: That a loving and sovereign God reigns over the creation that is his handiwork. That Jesus is God incarnate and Savior through his death on the cross and resurrection. That the Bible is God's Word and humanity's only authoritative guide to matters of faith and practice.

This is a book written primarily for those who share these convictions. While I hope others will find it helpful, I recognize that most of the people who wrestle with the doctrine of creation do so because they want to hold on to the truths of orthodox Christian belief even as they are confronted by the competing claims of science.

This is a book about biblical interpretation. While I love science and marvel at the seemingly endless discoveries it produces, the real impetus of this book is not scientific. It aims rather to look again at the Bible's creation texts and to consider whether the way these texts have been read has not needlessly created conflicts between the Bible and science.

This is a book that considers not *whether* the Bible is true—I take this as an article of faith—but *how* the Bible is true. It considers how we are meant to read the texts we find in the Bible, not whether those texts are ultimately trustworthy and authoritative.

This is a book that is written first and foremost for students, pastors, and educated laypeople. While I trust that the scholarship it contains is both comprehensive and compelling, I have felt it best to keep most techni-cal matters and bibliographic references in the notes that accompany the text. In addition, I have not hesitated to use illustrations from sources such as movies, television, or books where I thought they might make a dense subject more understandable.

Most of all, this book is written for fellow travelers in the faith who want to take seriously the biblical text while at the same time appreciating science's exploration of what we consider to be God's creation.

Acknowledgments

In one respect, a scholar's indebtedness to others is obvious: it is manifest in the allusions, quotations, and citations that fill the pages of that scholar's work. Less obvious but more important are the debts owed to those whose names are not always found in a footnote or a bibliography. High on the list of those to whom I find myself indebted are the teachers without whose patient guidance I would never have been able to find my life's calling: *My parents, Jim and Cheryl*, who served as my first and best Bible teachers and whose support for me and my family has always been unwavering. *Bryan Widbin*, whose love for the Hebrew Scriptures proved irresistible to me and whose passionate embrace of both scholarship and faith gave me the courage to follow the same path. *Marc Brettler*, whose demand for rigor as a teacher was at once intimidating and invaluable and whose support as a mentor and friend has been a blessing. *David Wright*, whose patience rivaled that of Job as he kindly walked me and my fellow grad students through the exotic worlds of Israel's neighbors. *Tzvi Abusch*, whose sensitive attention to the text remains a model for approaching literature from both Israel and Mesopotamia.

Alongside these, I am also indebted to my editor, *Jonathan Kline*, a wonderful scholar in his own right, who was kind enough to approach me several years ago with an invitation to do this study. Without his wise counsel and patient encouragement, this project would likely never have come to fruition.

I am, as ever, indebted to *my wife, Michaela*, and *my two sons, Samuel and Elijah*. My wife has been a constant source of love and support through the seemingly endless gauntlet of college, seminary, grad school, job search, tenure, and more. My sons are never far from my mind as I think through issues such as those laid out in this book. Helping them love God with all their hearts and all their minds remains my highest goal as their father.

Lastly, I remain deeply indebted to *my grandmother, Johnnie Frances Shepherd*, to whose memory this book is dedicated. I have studied the Scriptures in ways she could not, but I will never know them as profoundly as she did. The bitter trials that accompanied her last years on earth are never far from my mind when I read the Scriptures, whether their words are the cry "Why is light given to one in misery, and life to the bitter in soul?" (Job 3:20) or the hopeful confidence "Death will be no more; mourning and crying and pain will be no more" (Rev 21:4). Her influence on those around her, both in her life and in her death, could never be measured.

Abbreviations

General Abbreviations

*	marks a Hebrew verbal root
BCE	before the Common Era
ca.	circa
CE	Common Era
cf.	compare, see also
ch(s).	chapter(s)
esp.	especially
MT	Masoretic Text
no.	number
p(p).	page(s)
pl.	plural
Qoh	Qoheleth (Ecclesiastes)
v(v).	verse(s)

Bible Translations

ASV	American Standard Version
CSB	Christian Standard Bible
ESV	English Standard Version
HCSB	Holman Christian Standard Bible
JPS	*The Holy Scriptures: According to the Masoretic Text*
KJV	King James Version
NAB	New American Bible
NASB	New American Standard Bible

NIV	New International Version
NJPS	*Tanakh: The Holy Scriptures: The New JPS Translation according to the Traditional Hebrew Text*
NKJV	New King James Version
NRSV	New Revised Standard Version
RSV	Revised Standard Version

Journals, Series, and Reference Works

AB	Anchor Bible
ABD	*Anchor Bible Dictionary*. Edited by David Noel Freedman. 6 vols. New York: Doubleday, 1992
AnBib	Analecta Biblica
AnOr	Analecta Orientalia
BASOR	*Bulletin of the American Schools of Oriental Research*
Bib	*Biblica*
b. Pesaḥ.	Babylonian Talmud, tractate Pesaḥim
BRS	Biblical Resource Series
CAD	*The Assyrian Dictionary of the Oriental Institute of the University of Chicago.* Chicago: The Oriental Institute of the University of Chicago, 1956–2006
CBQ	*Catholic Biblical Quarterly*
COS	*The Context of Scripture.* Edited by William W. Hallo. 4 vols. Leiden: Brill, 1997–2017
CTJ	*Calvin Theological Journal*
Diatr.	Epictetus, *Diatribai*
Ep.	Seneca, *Epistulae morales*
EvQ	*Evangelical Quarterly*
HTS	Harvard Theological Studies
ICC	International Critical Commentary
JANER	*Journal of Ancient Near Eastern Religions*
JANES	*Journal of the Ancient Near Eastern Society*
JAOS	*Journal of the American Oriental Society*
JBL	*Journal of Biblical Literature*
JHI	*Journal of the History of Ideas*
JHNES	The Johns Hopkins Near Eastern Studies
JNES	*Journal of Near Eastern Studies*
JQR	*Jewish Quarterly Review*
JSOT	Journal for the Study of the Old Testament

JSOTSup	Journal for the Study of the Old Testament Supplement Series
KTU	*Die keilalphabetischen Texte aus Ugarit*. Edited by Manfried Dietrich, Oswald Loretz, and Joaquín Sanmartín. Münster: Ugarit-Verlag, 2013. 3rd enl. ed. of *KTU: The Cuneiform Alphabetic Texts from Ugarit, Ras Ibn Hani, and Other Places*. Edited by Manfried Dietrich, Oswald Loretz, and Joaquín Sanmartín. Münster: Ugarit-Verlag, 1995 (= *CTU*)
LCL	Loeb Classical Library
LHBOTS	The Library of Hebrew Bible/Old Testament Studies
MC	Mesopotamian Civilizations
NAC	New American Commentary
Or	*Orientalia* (NS)
OTL	Old Testament Library
Phaen.	Aratus, *Phaenomena*
Presb	*Presbyterion*
RB	*Revue biblique*
RHPR	*Revue d'histoire et de philosophie religieuses*
SBTS	Sources for Biblical and Theological Study
ST	*Studia Theologica*
SVF	*Stoicorum Veterum Fragmenta*. Hans Friedrich August von Arnim. 4 vols. Leipzig: Teubne, 1903–24
TDOT	*Theological Dictionary of the Old Testament*. Edited by Johannes Botterweck and Helmer Ringgren. Translated by John T. Willis et al. 8 vols. Grand Rapids: Eerdmans, 1974–2006
TynBul	*Tyndale Bulletin*
UT	*Ugaritic Textbook*. Cyrus H. Gordon. AnOr 38. Rome: Pontifical Biblical Institute, 1965
VT	*Vetus Testamentum*
VTSup	Supplements to Vetus Testamentum
WBC	Word Biblical Commentary
WTJ	*Westminster Theological Journal*
ZAW	*Zeitschrift für die alttestamentliche Wissenschaft*
ZNW	*Zeitschrift für die neutestamentliche Wissenschaft und die Kunde der älteren Kirche*

Introduction

It is the summer of 2016, and I am backpacking through the wilds of Yosemite National Park with my brother and my two sons. At the end of a long day of ups and downs, still struggling to acclimate ourselves to the noticeably thinner air our lungs are breathing high up on the North Rim, we arrive at our first night's camp. Dropping our packs and leaving the duties of setting up camp and cooking supper for later, we hurry to the rocky outcropping that sees Snow Creek Falls plunge toward the valley below. There, standing on the edge of the rocks, we look up to see one of the most glorious sights in all of Yosemite, indeed in all of the world: sunset on the face of Half Dome. It is a mesmerizing sight, a riot of oranges, yellows, and purples that captures the eyes and won't let go. Seeing that incredible mountain, bathed in the day's last rays of sunlight, one thought springs continually to mind: There has to be a God. There just has to be a God.

Students of the Bible will recognize in this experience more than just a mild case of too much John Muir and too little oxygen. Recognizing the *creator* in the works of *creation* has a long pedigree in Scripture. The songwriter who penned Psalm 19 insisted, "The heavens declare the glory of God, and the firmament proclaims his handiwork."[1] In a similar vein, the apostle Paul instructed the Christians in Rome that "since the creation of the world, his invisible attributes—his eternal power and divine nature—have been understood and seen through the things he has made" (Rom 1:20). Sunset on Half Dome is just one example of a widely shared theological tenet: We see something of God when we see God's handiwork in creation.

Unfortunately, "widely shared" is a term that can only rarely be applied to beliefs about creation. More often than not, creation is a battlefield in which the pitched forces of competing sides—Darwinists and creationists,

young-earthers and old, figurativists and literalists—struggle for the upper
hand. Like most battles, this fight has tended to inflict a great deal of col-
lateral damage along the way. This is especially true for younger Christians,
who have often been put in the terrible position of feeling they have to
choose between the Bible they have come to know at home and church and
the science they have studied at school.

On the one hand, these are students who are passionate in their love
for the Bible and for the God it presents. They embrace the Bible's message of love and redemption and the vision of hope it offers for the future.
On the other hand, however, these students have also come to admire and
revel in the marvels of scientific discovery. These are students who want to
take both science and the Bible seriously, but they are being challenged by
voices on both sides that say this cannot be done: a choice has to be made.
What I will argue in this book is that the choice being forced upon us is a
false one. It stems both from science's abandonment of the proper limits of
its capabilities and from an insistence on the part of some that the Bible be
read in ways that would have been foreign to its original context. The tragic
results of these twin errors are not difficult to find. With science arrogated
to the position of sole arbiter of knowledge and truth, it has been asked
to give answers to life's most important questions, answers it is entirely
incapable of providing. At the same time, while the biblical authors cry out
to a modern world with just the sorts of answers it needs, their message is
almost entirely obscured by endless debates over matters that would have
held no interest to them at all. Surely there must be a better way of embrac-
ing both God's revelation in the wonders of creation and God's revelation
in the words of Scripture.

CHAPTER 1

The Copernican Moment

The year 1543 CE witnessed the death of one of that century's most important figures, the Polish polymath Nicolaus Copernicus. Like many of the leading lights of this period, Copernicus was a man of remarkably varied pursuits. He was at times a physician, an economist, a politician, perhaps even a priest.[1] It is for his work as an astronomer, though, that Copernicus is best remembered. Prior to Copernicus, it was widely believed that the earth remained stationary while the sun, moon, planets, and stars revolved around it. This made intuitive sense, of course, as the earth did not feel as if it moved, and the celestial bodies did seem to make their rounds overhead each night. The then regnant *geocentric* model had also been given what appeared to be firm scientific footing by the philosopher Ptolemy in his well-known treatise on astronomy, the *Almagest* (ca. 150 CE). As Copernicus combined meticulous observation of the movements of the solar system with more sophisticated mathematical formulae, however, he revealed various flaws in the Ptolemaic model, flaws that could only be remedied by positing that the earth orbited the sun, not the sun the earth. Word of this new *heliocentric* model spread quickly through the halls of Europe. Copernicus himself, though, was quite hesitant to circulate his findings too widely. Whether because he hoped to avoid ecclesiastical disfavor or just unwanted controversy, it would not be until 1543, the same year that he died, that Copernicus would finally publish the work for which he is most famous, *De revolutionibus orbium coelestium* (*On the Revolutions of the Celestial Spheres*).

Copernicus' description of the revolutions of the celestial spheres was itself revolutionary. Though various modifications and alternative proposals to the Ptolemaic view of the world had been offered through the centuries, none had proved as compelling as the Copernican model. Toward the end of the sixteenth century, the famous astronomer Tycho Brahe made one last attempt to keep the earth in place at the center of the universe, proposing a *geoheliocentric* model in which the planets orbited the sun and the sun orbited the earth. His argument that the earth was a "hulking, lazy body, unfit for motion" proved no match, though, for the steady swell of observation confirming the fact that, hulking or not, the earth did indeed move around the sun.[2] With Johannes Kepler's discovery (ca. 1609) that the planets moved in elliptical orbits and with Galileo Galilei's observations through the newly invented telescope (ca. 1615), Copernicus' heliocentric view of the solar system was firmly established.

Copernicus and the Church

One of the most disappointing aspects of the Copernican revolution is that as the scientific evidence for the heliocentric model grew stronger, the religious objections to the model grew increasingly intense.[3] When Copernicus' views first made their way to Rome in the 1530s, Pope Clement VII appears to have received them with interested curiosity, and in 1536, the Archbishop of Capua actually wrote to Copernicus, encouraging him to publish his findings. When Copernicus did finally publish his work in 1543, he dedicated it to the then current pope, Paul III. In the decades following Copernicus' death, however, sharp criticism would begin to emerge from both Roman Catholic and Protestant divines.

Perhaps because Copernicus initially remained in good standing with Roman Catholicism, the first criticisms of his views hailed from Protestant circles. The transcripts of Martin Luther's conversations at the dinner table known as the *Tischreden* (i.e., "Table Talk") note that the views of "a certain new astronomer who proved that the earth moves, not the heavens, sun, and moon" were raised on one occasion. Luther is said to have described both the views and the one from whom they originated in dismissive terms:

> But that is how it goes nowadays. Anyone who wants to be clever must not let himself like what others do. He has to make something of his own, as this fool does, who wants to turn the whole of astronomy upside-down. Even if these things are confused, I still believe the Holy Scriptures, for Joshua commanded the sun to stand still and not the earth.[4]

Luther's fellow reformer Philipp Melanchthon offered a more extensive critique of Copernicus in his *Initia doctrinae physicae* when he argued:

> The eyes are witnesses that the heavens revolve in the space of twenty-four hours. But certain men, either from the love of novelty, or to make a display of ingenuity, have concluded that the earth moves; and they maintain that neither the eighth sphere nor the sun revolves. . . . Now, it is a want of honesty and decency to assert such notions publicly, and the example is pernicious. It is the part of a good mind to accept the truth as revealed by God and to acquiesce in it.[5]

In one of his letters, he went so far as to suggest governments should suppress such views:

> Certain people believe it is a marvelous achievement to extol so crazy a thing, like that Polish astronomer who makes the earth move and the sun stand still. Really, wise governments ought to repress impudence of mind.[6]

Calvin's assessment of Copernicus' views has been the subject of some controversy. On the one hand, it has now been definitively demonstrated that Calvin did not utter (or write) the oft-quoted demand, "Who will venture to place the authority of Copernicus above that of the Holy Spirit?"[7] On the other hand, it is also clear that Calvin held to the geocentric view and, at least on one occasion, directly condemned those advancing its heliocentric rival. Calvin's geocentrism is evident throughout his commentaries. In his commentary on Ps 93:1, for example, he argues:

> The heavens revolve daily, and, immense as is their fabric and inconceivable the rapidity of their revolutions, we experience no concussion—no disturbance in the harmony of their motion. The sun, though varying its course every diurnal revolution, returns annually to the same point. The planets, in all their wanderings, maintain their respective positions. How could the earth hang suspended in the air were it not upheld by God's hand? By what means could it maintain itself unmoved, while the heavens above are in constant rapid motion, did not its Divine Maker fix and establish it?[8]

Here Calvin emphasizes the movement of the heavens ("the heavens revolve daily," "the rapidity of their revolutions," "in constant rapid motion"), in contrast to the stationary aspect of the earth ("suspended," "unmoved").

Similarly, as he discusses the account in Joshua 10 of the sun and moon standing still, he remarks:

> As in kindness to the human race he [God] divides the day from the night by the daily course of the sun, and constantly whirls the immense orb with indefatigable swiftness, so he was pleased that it should halt for a short time till the enemies of Israel were destroyed.[9]

Again, Calvin's emphasis is on the rapid movement of the heavens ("constantly whirls," "swiftness"). His condemnation of those who would place the sun at the center of the solar system is evident in a sermon he delivered on 1 Corinthians 10:19–24:

> We will see some who are so deranged, not only in religion but who in all things reveal their monstrous nature, that they will say that the sun does not move, and that it is the earth which shifts and turns. When we see such minds we must indeed confess that the devil possesses them, and that God sets them before us as mirrors, in order to keep us in his fear. So it is with all who argue out of pure malice, and who happily make a show of their impudence. When they are told: "That is hot," they will reply: "No, it is plainly cold." When they are shown an object that is black, they will say that it is white, or vice versa. Just like the man who said that snow was black; for although it is perceived and known by all to be white, yet he clearly wished to contradict the fact. And so it is that there are madmen who would try to change the natural order, and even to dazzle men's eyes and benumb their senses.[10]

While he does not mention Copernicus by name—neither here nor elsewhere in his voluminous writings—it is clear that Calvin's invective is directed at least toward supporters of the Copernican model. The force of his language—"deranged," "monstrous nature," "the devil possesses them," "malice," "impudence," "madmen"—would set him comfortably alongside Luther and Melanchthon in his rejection of this new model.

Catholic opposition to Copernicanism took longer to develop but ultimately proved to be more forceful. When Galileo began to write in support of Copernicus and the heliocentric model, he quickly drew the attention of the Inquisition.[11] Cardinal and Inquisitor Robert Bellarmine first issued a warning to Galileo concerning his views, and in 1616 a committee formed by the Inquisition to review Galileo's beliefs more thoroughly concluded that heliocentrism was to be condemned outright. Bellarmine himself delivered the Inquisition's orders that Galileo not hold, teach, defend, or discuss such views, and subsequently the Congregation of the Index banned books and letters that espoused the Copernican system. Galileo was eventually tasked by Pope Urban VIII with outlining the arguments for and against the Copernican system, but his views (and tone) were not well received.[12] In 1633, the Pope summoned Galileo to Rome, forced him to recant, and put him under house arrest for the last years of his life.

Over time, opposition to the Copernican model faded, especially as the system proved to be so useful for generating calendrical observations. Official sanction of heliocentric works remained elusive, though. Indeed, as late as the early nineteenth century, the chief book censor for Rome, Filippo Anfossi, continued to resist the publication of or granting of the papal imprimatur to textbooks espousing the heliocentric view. In the end, it took the direct intervention of the Inquisition and Pope Pius VII in 1822 to ensure that books teaching the movement of the earth could be given the imprimatur. It was not until 1835 that the previously banned works by Copernicus and Galileo were dropped from the *Index*.[13]

Lessons Unlearned

There are lessons for both science and religion in the fits and starts of the Church's acceptance of Copernicus' heliocentric discovery. Sadly, though, it appears that both camps have often learned the wrong lessons from this key moment. For many, the Copernican revolution has become the example par excellence of religion's attempt to obscure and suppress the light of scientific discovery. Religion, they contend, wants nothing more than to preserve its power over the masses and so is all too happy to undermine the progress of science when it feels its position threatened. The Church's treatment of figures like Copernicus and Galileo left it wide open to these sorts of charges.

Unfortunately, science's victory over the religious objections to Copernicus' model was so thorough that it also tended to produce negative effects within science itself. So badly did the Church respond to the controversy that many came to arrogate science to the position of sole arbiter of human knowledge. This is a mantle science is incapable of bearing. As the British scientist and theologian John Polkinghorne has observed:

Science's success has been purchased by the modesty of its explanatory ambition. It does not attempt to ask and answer every question that one might legitimately raise. Instead, it confines itself to investigating natural processes, attending to the question of how things happen. Other questions, such as those relating to meaning and purpose, are deliberately bracketed out. This scientific stance is taken simply as a methodological strategy, with no implication that those other questions, of what one might call a why kind, are not fully meaningful and necessary to ask if complete understanding is to be attained.[14]

The tools of the scientist are wielded with marvelous precision when directed toward questions of *what* and *how*. They are almost entirely ineffective when turned toward matters of meaning and morality, purpose and principle. Science can tell us how a human heart works; it cannot tell us whether it would be immoral to stop that heart from beating. It can tell us how a giant sequoia grows to such astonishing size; it cannot tell us whether or when it would be wrong to cut it down. Rather than admit, however, the limitations of science's proper field of inquiry, a growing chorus of voices has preferred instead to deny the existence of any reality lying outside its observational powers. Matters related to God and the spiritual are deemed not to exist simply because the tools of science are not suited to considering their existence. It is as if science, having been cast in the role of a hammer, should deny the existence of anything not presenting itself as a nail.

But if devotees of science have drawn poor lessons from the Copernican affair, so too have we, their counterparts in religion. We see aspects of this already in Galileo's defense of his own views to the Grand Duchess Christina in 1615. In his letter to the duchess, Galileo focuses especially on the manner in which the Bible ought to be read when it touches on matters of science.[15] He goes to great lengths to affirm the veracity of the Scriptures. With regard to Copernicus, he argues that "he did not ignore the Bible, but he knew very well that if his doctrine were proved, then it could not contradict the Scriptures when they were rightly understood." Galileo affirms that, if his own beliefs were to disagree with the assertions of Scripture, they too would have to be regarded as erroneous and heretical, "since the Bible cannot err." He insists, "It is very pious to say and prudent to affirm that the holy Bible can never speak untruth—whenever its true meaning is understood." And with regard to ideas found in "the books of the sages of this world," he maintains, "Anything contrary to the Bible involved [i.e., espoused] by them must be held undoubtedly false and should be proved so by every means possible."

Galileo was at pains to argue that science would not contradict the teaching of Scripture *when the Scriptures were properly understood.* To interpret the Scriptures properly, however, he insisted that two important issues must be taken into account. In the first place, he maintained that the Bible often speaks in language that cannot be understood on a strictly literal level. After affirming that the Bible "can never speak untruth," Galileo goes on to say:

> But I believe nobody will deny that it is often very abstruse, and may say things which are quite different from what its bare words signify. Hence in expounding the Bible if one were always to confine oneself to the unadorned grammatical meaning, one might fall into error. Not only contradictions and propositions far from true might thus be made to appear in the Bible, but even grave heresies and follies. Thus it would be necessary to assign to God feet, hands, and eyes, as well as corporeal and human affections, such as anger, repentance, hatred, and sometimes even the forgetting of things past and ignorance of those to come.

Even more importantly, he suggests that the language of the Bible often condescends to the level of its readers: "These propositions uttered by the Holy Ghost were set down in that manner by the sacred scribes in order to accommodate them to the capacities of the common people, who are rude and unlearned." Galileo insists that the authors of Scripture did, in fact, understand the true nature of the universe but hesitated to reveal this to the common people lest it foster doubt or mistrust. He argues:

> If the sacred scribes had had any intention of teaching people certain arrangements and motions of the heavenly bodies, or had they wished us to derive such knowledge from the Bible, then in my opinion they would not have spoken of these matters so sparingly in comparison with the infinite number of admirable conclusions which are demonstrated in that science. Far from pretending to teach us the constitution and motions of the heavens and the stars, with their shapes, magnitudes, and distances, the authors of the Bible *intentionally forbore to speak of these things, though all were quite well known to them.* (emphasis mine)

He then quotes with approval Augustine's sentiments in this regard: "Hence let it be said briefly, touching the form of heaven, that our authors knew the truth but the Holy Spirit did not desire that men should learn things that are useful to no one for salvation."[16]

While there is an element of truth in Galileo's protestations, the issues he highlights understate the reckoning Christians needed to have with the manner in which they read Scripture. It is true that the Bible often uses non-literal language; more important, however, is the larger recognition that the Bible is fundamentally misunderstood when it is read solely through a historical lens. To read Scripture properly, we must recognize that *the Bible is not just history*.

Further, it is doubtless true that there is an element of condescension in God's provision of his Word to humanity. It is not at all clear, though, that this accommodation extends to the relationship between the "sacred scribes" who penned the words of Scripture and the readers who received it. We ask too much of the biblical authors when we suggest that they did indeed understand the scientific structure of the universe and that they chose to shield their readers from this knowledge. The authors' knowledge of the world was as limited as that of their hearers because God chose human beings to record Scripture. To read Scripture properly, we must recognize that *the Bible is not just divine*.

The Bible Is Not Just History

One of God's most remarkable gifts to humanity is that of language. While a great many species of animals have systems of communication, the linguistic abilities we possess as humans are truly astonishing. We speak, we write, we sing, expressing thoughts that range from simple statements to complex figures of speech to the most abstract of ideas. Equally as impressive as our abilities for producing speech, however, are our abilities to discern the meaning in the speech we hear and read. From the subtlest of clues, we know almost immediately not just what is being said but *in what category* a certain saying belongs. We distinguish jokes from tall tales from historical accounts from instruction manuals in an instant and without needing explicit directions for doing so. We possess a high level of what we might call *genre competence*.[17]

Genre competence comes so naturally to us that we are usually blissfully unaware of its working behind the scenes to give us the "rules" that help us understand a book we read or a movie we watch. Our ability to tell what *kind* of text we have before us (whether that "text" is a book, story, movie, television program, etc.) is what tells us what *kinds* of things can happen in that text. We know intuitively that the castaways from the *Swiss Family*

Robinson will survive and even thrive; we know the same will not be true of the castaways in *Lord of the Flies*. We are not at all surprised when a young boy is eaten by a shark in the movie *Jaws*; we would be shocked, outraged even, had little Russell plummeted to his death in the movie *Up*. So keen is our genre competence that we can even distinguish between the rules for the book and film versions of the same story. The genre of Michael Crichton's novel *Jurassic Park* is such that the death of the park's founder, John Hammond, at the hands (or rather teeth) of a pack of dinosaurs hardly raises an eyebrow. As the story is retold in Steven Spielberg's movie of the same name, such a scene would be hard to imagine.

It actually takes a great deal of effort to fool us when it comes to the genre of a text. In 1985, *Sports Illustrated* convinced the famous writer George Plimpton to pen a story about an astonishing pitching prospect in the New York Mets organization. Hayden Siddhartha "Sidd" Finch was said to be part yogi, part French horn player, and part baseball pitcher. And what a pitcher! With a heavy hiking boot on his right foot, an entirely unconventional windup, and no warm-up at all, Sidd Finch was said to be able to throw a baseball with uncanny accuracy at nearly 170 miles per hour. Mets fans could hardly believe their luck in landing such a prospect. News crews were sent to interview the young man. The then commissioner of Major League Baseball, Peter Ueberroth, was questioned about the safety of even letting Finch pitch. For a brief moment, the entire baseball world was abuzz over Sidd Finch. Only one thing stood in the way of Finch's rise to baseball stardom: he didn't exist. *Sports Illustrated* had persuaded Plimpton to write the story as an April Fools' Day joke, a joke he coyly hinted at in the acrostic subtitle of his article: "He's a pitcher, part yogi and part recluse. Impressively liberated from our opulent life-style, Sidd's deciding about yoga—and his future in baseball." As some careful readers noticed, the first letters of these words spell out, "Happy April Fools' Day—ah fib."[18]

It is a rare occurrence when a story manages to take in its hearers and trick them concerning the story's genre. A few horror movies have had middling success in doing so, and Orson Welles' *War of the Worlds* radio broadcast managed to misdirect quite a few listeners, though even here the tales of widespread panic have been greatly exaggerated.[19] For the most part, though, we are just too competent at discerning genre to be fooled with any great success. This is not to say that genre competence comes entirely naturally; it is actually a learned skill. When we are children, we do not really understand the rules of a particular genre in the same way we do as adults. Most of us who are parents have had the experience of smiling at our children's deeply felt concern over whether Woody, Buzz, and the gang might really be incinerated in *Toy Story 3*, whether Boo might actually be squished by the trash compactor in *Monsters, Inc.*, or whether the monster at the end of this book in *The Monster at the End of This Book* will truly turn out to be a *monster* at the end of this book. We smile because we know as more experienced viewers and readers that those are possibilities that would break the rules that guide these sorts of "texts." As the proud survivor of countless Cub Scout and Boy Scout campfires, I can personally attest that a ghost story told at the former is received quite differently than one at the latter. What might make a ten-year-old Webelos blanch only makes a fifteen-year-old Scout laugh. Over time, kids learn the rules and know what kinds of dangers in stories are real and what kinds are imagined.

It is not only actual children, though, who sometimes lack the genre competence of adults. In a sense, we all become children when we venture over into the literary worlds of *other cultures*. For Western audiences, an unexpected dance number in the middle of a Bollywood film might bring smiles to our faces, but it might also leave us a bit perplexed as to why it is there and what sort of film it belongs to. We might find a fable from China or Japan entertaining, but we might also struggle to understand what lessons it was meant to teach. As the products of cultures that may be foreign to us, these texts present challenges we rarely face in our own literary world. Many of us have had the experience of trying valiantly to tell a joke to a person from another culture only to watch the joke die slowly and painfully for want of laughs. It dies because it wasn't understood or, more importantly, *because it was not perceived to have been a joke at all.*

What we sometimes miss in this dynamic is the fact that the Bible is also the product of a foreign culture. While we might feel an affinity for the characters of the Bible because we know their stories so well, the truth is that we share very little in common with the culture of those characters. They may be our spiritual ancestors, but they are separated from us by great gulfs of time and space. The foreignness of the biblical world ought to serve as a caution to us that the finely honed skills of genre competence we possess in our own culture may not be as sharp when we read texts from the Bible. Our literary categories may be different from those of the biblical authors, and our talent for placing a text in one category or another may not work as well when reading their works.

As an illustration of this idea, we might consider the story of the Rich Man and Lazarus found in Luke 16:

> There was a rich man who was dressed in purple and fine linen and who feasted sumptuously every day. And at his gate lay a poor man named Lazarus, covered with sores, who longed to satisfy his hunger with what fell from the rich man's table; even the dogs would come and lick his sores. The poor man died and was carried away by the angels to be with Abraham. The rich man also died and was buried. In Hades, where he was being tormented, he looked up and saw Abraham far away with Lazarus by his side. He called out, "Father Abraham, have mercy on me, and send Lazarus to dip the tip of his finger in water and cool my tongue; for I am in agony in these flames." But Abraham said, "Child, remember that during your lifetime you received your good things, and Lazarus in like manner evil things; but now he is comforted here, and you are in agony. Besides all this, between you and us a great chasm has been fixed, so that those who might want to pass from here to you cannot do so, and no one can cross from there to us." He said, "Then, father, I beg you to send him to my father's house—for I have five brothers—that he may warn them, so that they will not also come into this place of torment." Abraham replied, "They have Moses and the prophets; they should listen to them." He said, "No, father Abraham; but if someone goes to them from the dead, they will repent." He said to him, "If they do not listen to Moses and the prophets, neither will they be convinced even if someone rises from the dead."
>
> (Luke 16:19–31 NRSV)

When we read this story, one of the first questions that ought to come to mind is whether it is meant to be understood as a parable or as a historical account. Several pieces of evidence point in the direction of historical account. Most notably, there is the fact that the story includes a proper name, Lazarus. Nowhere else in the Gospels does Jesus give a name to one of the characters in a parable. We find *a certain priest, a certain man, a sower,* and other generic titles, but never a person with a name. Our story also refers to an actual historical character, Abraham, who welcomes Lazarus into paradise and speaks to the rich man who is being tormented. This again is unprecedented in Jesus' parables. Lastly, it bears pointing out that neither Jesus nor Luke explicitly says the story is a parable. As Luke has preserved the account, Jesus simply launches into the story without any introduction at all.

While these clues may point toward a historical reading of the story, there is even more evidence on the parabolic side of the ledger. Like other parables, the story of the Rich Man and Lazarus is so clearly intended to serve a didactic purpose. Its instructions on the need to care for the poor could hardly be more clear, and an additional lesson is also embedded in the parable. When Jesus tells his hearers that those who will not listen to Moses and the prophets will not be convinced even if someone rises from the dead (v. 31), he is, of course, warning them that even his own resurrection will not be enough to convince them.

Again, like other parables, this story revels in hyperbole, the use of exaggeration for effect. The rich man is not just rich; he wears luxurious clothes and feasts sumptuously every day. Lazarus is not just poor; he longs even for crumbs and is beset by dogs that come to lick his sores. The fate of the rich man is not just losing his wealth but agony in flames of torment, and when he asks for aid, he asks only that Lazarus dip his finger in water and touch his tongue. This kind of hyperbole is reminiscent of parables like the Good Samaritan, in which those most expected to help, the priest and the Levite, callously pass by the wounded man, while the most unlikely of characters, the Samaritan, offers him extravagant care. We find the same sort of exaggeration in other parables as well. In the parable of the Lost Sheep, the shepherd inexplicably abandons the ninety-nine to search for the one. In the parable of the Lost Coin, the woman ransacks her house searching for a coin of quite modest value. Especially hyperbolic is the parable of the Prodigal Son, in which the son quickly squanders all of his fortune and is reduced to such poverty that he longs for the shoots the pigs eat and is willing even to become his father's slave (Luke 15).

Even apart from its hyperbole, the language of the Rich Man and Lazarus sounds parabolic. The story's opening line, "There was a certain man . . . ," strikes the ear in the same way we might hear the line "Once upon a time . . . ." This is not to say that the story here should be taken as a fairy tale, which would be another genre entirely, but rather that it fits with a kind of conventional introduction to a parable. One thinks of Nathan's parable, delivered to David after his affair with Bathsheba, which begins, "There were two men in a certain city, one rich and the other poor . . ." (2 Sam 12:1), or Isaiah's parable of the vineyard, which begins, "There was a vineyard that belonged to my beloved . . ." (Isa 5:1). The parable of the Good Samaritan opens in similar fashion ("A certain man was going down from Jerusalem . . ."; Luke 10:30), as do the parables of the Prodigal Son ("A certain man had two sons . . ."; Luke 15:11), the Great Dinner ("A certain man gave a great dinner . . ."; Luke 14:16), the Dishonest Manager ("There was a certain man who was rich . . ."; Luke 16:1), the Ten Pounds ("A certain man of high status . . ."; Luke 19:12), and the Wicked Tenants ("A certain man planted a vineyard . . ."; Luke 20:9).[20] Finally, we should note that the context of our story in Luke is rich with other parabolic material. The parables of the Lost Sheep, the Lost Coin, the Prodigal Son, the Dishonest Manager, and our own story are all gathered into this stretch of material now labeled as Luke 15–16.

The evidence for reading the story of the Rich Man and Lazarus as a parable is ultimately far stronger than the evidence for reading it as a historical account, which is why scholars from across the theological spectrum interpret the story in this way.[21] The incorporation of personal names and historical figures in the parable does raise interesting possibilities, though. Might there be other texts in the Bible that follow this same pattern? We might think, for example, about the book of Job. Job shares all of the parabolic characteristics of the Rich Man and Lazarus, the Good Samaritan, and the Prodigal Son. The book's didactic purpose is evident as it wrestles with the problem of suffering and explores how humans ought to respond to their creator when faced with that suffering. The book also makes generous use of hyperbole. Job is not just an important man but "the greatest of all the people of the east" (Job 1:3). He is not just a good man but one accounted by the narrator and by God himself (twice!) as being "blameless, upright, fearing God, and turning away from evil" (1:1, 8; 2:3). He is a man who offers sacrifices for his children even when there is no evidence that they might have sinned (1:5), a man who continues to worship God even in the midst of terrible suffering (1:20; 2:10). And how he suffers! In the course of a single day, Job loses all his oxen, his donkeys, his sheep, his camels, his servants, and even his children. Shortly thereafter, he loses his health as well. He is reduced to sitting on the ground in silence, scraping his sores with a potsherd, unrecognizable to his friends who have come to comfort him.

The language of Job also points toward a parabolic reading. It begins with a phrase reminiscent of our other parables, "There once was a man in the land of Uz . . . ," and as the narrative progresses, it uses heavily stylized language to recount its story. Note, for example, the extraordinary use of repetition in the narration of the two encounters between God and the Satan in Job 1–2:

First Encounter (Job 1)	**Second Encounter (Job 2)**
⁶And it happened one day that the sons of God came to present themselves before YHWH, and the Satan also came in the midst of them.	*¹And it happened one day that the sons of God came to present themselves before YHWH, and the Satan also came in the midst of them* to present himself before YHWH.
⁷And YHWH said to the Satan, "Whence *have you come?" And the Satan answered YHWH, and he said, "From going to and fro on the earth, and from walking up and down on it."*	*²And YHWH said to the Satan,* "From where *have you come?" And the Satan answered YHWH, and he said, "From going to and fro on the earth, and from walking up and down on it."*
⁸And YHWH said to the Satan, "Have you considered my servant Job? For there is no one like him on the earth, a man blameless and upright, who fears God and turns away from evil."	*³And YHWH said to the Satan, "Have you considered my servant Job? For there is no one like him on the earth, a man blameless and upright, who fears God and turns away from evil.* He still persists in his integrity, although you incited me against him, to destroy him for no reason."
⁹And the Satan answered YHWH, and he said,	*⁴And the Satan answered YHWH, and he said,*
"Does Job fear God for nothing? ¹⁰Have you not set a hedge around him and around his house and around all that he has, on every side? You have blessed the work of his hands, and his possessions have increased in the land.	"Skin for skin! All that people have they will give to save their lives.
¹¹*But stretch out your hand now, and touch* all that he has, *and he will curse you to your face."*	⁵*But stretch out your hand now and touch* his bone and his flesh, *and he will curse you to your face."*

¹²*And YHWH said to the Satan,*
"Behold, all that he has is in your
power; only do not stretch out your
hand against him!"

And the Satan went out from the
presence of YHWH.

⁶*And YHWH said to the Satan,*
"Behold, he is in your power; only
spare his life."

⁷*And the Satan went out from the*
presence of YHWH.

We see a similar kind of repetition in the reports of the attacks on Job's live-stock and children as verse after verse begins with the language "While he was still speaking, another came and said . . ." and ends with "I alone have escaped to tell you" (1:15, 16, 17, 19). There is also the extraordinary problem of imagining Job, his three friends, Elihu, and God taking turns declaiming thirty-nine chapters of complex and difficult poetry back and forth to one another in the midst of Job's desperate suffering.

A great many lines of evidence point toward our understanding the book of Job as something like a parable. As in the case of the Rich Man and Lazarus, the fact that the book includes named characters like Job, Eliphaz, Bildad, Zophar, and Elihu would not undermine this categorization, nor would even the possibility that the book might include historical figures. We have little way of knowing whether a historical person named Job existed. Even if this were the case, though, his appearance in the book that bears his name no more requires that the story be regarded as a strictly historical account than does Abraham's appearance in the Rich Man and Lazarus. We should also be open to the possibility that the book of Job lies somewhere between history and parable. It is entirely possible that there was a person named Job, and that he may have suffered in extraordinary fashion. What we have in the book of Job, though, would not be a strict historical account of his experiences but a heavily stylized adaptation of his story told to highlight specific theological themes. In this case, the book of Job would be neither entirely history nor entirely parable.

I recognize that suggesting the book of Job may be a parable-like story will immediately set off alarm bells for some readers of Scripture. Perhaps the most common objection is this: If we take Job as a parable, are we not venturing onto a slippery slope where a great many passages in the Bible could be read as parables? Where do we draw the line? While I appreciate the weight of this objection, if we step back for a moment, is it not the case that Job either *is* or *is not* a parable irrespective of our views of the book? Whether Job was written as a parable or as a historical account, it remains a parable or historical account whether we correctly recognize it as one or not. The genre of the book of Job is not dependent on our correctly recognizing it. I would argue that Job is a parable or parable-like story based on generic clues in the way the story is told. If that leads to reading other portions of the Bible as parabolic as well, it would only be because the other passages in question also present themselves with parabolic features.

Embedded in this objection, though, is another issue. It assumes that historical accounts are ultimately more valuable and "true" than non-historical genres like parables and that we therefore demean Scripture when we recognize portions of it as belonging to categories other than history.[22] This seems a terribly odd view to hold for those who subscribe to the teachings of Jesus, the master parable-teller. It is perhaps understandable, though, if we take into account the biases of our own culture. Ours is a culture that lends great weight to historical accounts and historical accuracy and tends to look askance at the truth claims of genres that do not fit into the historical category. When we relate an improbable story and want to assure our hearers that the story really did happen, we can do so by saying two simple words: *true story*. But think of the implications of these two words: A *true* story for us is a story that really happened. So, what is a story that did not really happen? False. The same could be said of words like *fiction* or *myth*. In our culture, it is hard not to hear the word *fiction* and think *untrue*, or worse, *lie*. When we hear the word *myth*, we almost instinctively think of something that is just *made up* and therefore *not true*. But, would the authors and readers of the Bible have shared this view? Is it not at least possible that the biblical authors might have been comfortable with the idea of conveying true ideas through non-historical genres? This certainly seems to have been the practice of Jesus himself when he used non-historical stories to communicate the truths of his message.

This is a point that can hardly be overstated: When we take our culture's views of whether so-called "fictional" genres such as parable, myth, or legend can be used to communicate truth and impose them upon the Bible, it is difficult to see how we are thereby honoring Scripture. Would it not dishonor Scripture to force its texts into genres they were not intended to fit? It is interesting, at least, to see that this problem tends to work in only one direction. While we might be scandalized to see a passage we believe to be historical treated as fiction, we likely would not feel the same scandal were a fictional passage like a parable to be treated as history. At the heart of this double standard is our own cultural preference for historical texts over non-historical ones. But this is, it must be stressed, *our own* cultural preference.

So how does this relate to the Copernican and Galilean crises? Galileo was doubtless correct in suggesting that some passages in the Bible ought to be interpreted figuratively, not literally. But a proper reading of the Bible must take this idea one step further. It is not just the case that the Bible contains poetic passages that even we in our culture would recognize as figurative. We must also consider the possibility that even some passages we are culturally conditioned to think of as history—Job, for example—ought not to be read as historical accounts. It is not just that certain texts may contain figures of speech; *they may belong to non-historical genres altogether.* Among these texts may very well lie some of the biblical texts that discuss creation.

The Bible Is Not Just Divine

While the internet can sometimes be a wonderful thing, it can also bring out the worst in people. Make the mistake of delving into the comments section below an online article, and you may be reminded of the wise words of Obi-Wan Kenobi: "You will never find a more wretched hive of scum and villainy. We must be cautious." Whether the commenters are purported Christians gleefully wishing the flames of perdition upon their opponents or their counterparts mocking the Faith and the faithful, no good seems to come from these venomous exchanges. Attacks on the Divine pop up with inordinate frequency in these settings: "So, can God make a rock so big that he can't lift it? Can God make a square circle?" These and other similarly sophisticated criticisms of theism are not hard to find.

While these kinds of objections may tell us more about deficiencies in logic on the part of commenters than deficiencies in ability upon the part of God, they do raise an interesting question: Are there things that God cannot do? For those who believe in divine omnipotence, the answer would seem to be an obvious *no.* Further reflection, though, should tell us that there are quite a few things God cannot do. First and foremost, orthodox Christian belief would say God cannot *sin.* But there are other things besides just this. James tells us that not only is God unable to sin, he cannot even *be tempted* (Jas 1:13). If God is omniscient, then he also cannot *learn;* he cannot *not know* something. The divine attribute of *independence* would say that God is also incapable of *having a need.* Were God to need something, it would imply a deficiency on his part that could be resolved only by something outside of God. Thus, God cannot need food, drink, or sleep. Hunger, thirst, and fatigue are simply not possible for God. The upshot of all of this should be obvious: *Surely, Jesus cannot be divine.* After all, while the Bible makes clear that Jesus never sinned, it also portrays him as doing many other things God is simply incapable of doing.

Temptation

The authors of the New Testament are clear in their assertions that Jesus did experience temptation. Apart from the accounts of Jesus' temptation in the wilderness (Matt 4:1–11 // Mark 1:12–13 // Luke 4:1–13), we also have the testimony of the book of Hebrews: "For we do not have a high priest who is unable to sympathize with our weaknesses, but we have one *who in every respect has been tempted just as we are, yet without sin*" (Heb 4:15).[23]

Questions

Jesus also repeatedly asks questions in the Gospels, questions that are straightforward requests for information he does not already have. He asks the man possessed by an unclean spirit, "What is your name?" (Mark 5:9 // Luke 8:30). In the story of the woman suffering from hemorrhages, after perceiving that someone in the crowd has touched him, Jesus asks, "Who touched my clothes?" When the disciples are unable to answer, Mark tells us, "He looked around to see who had done it" (Mark 5:30–32 // Luke 8:45). Before he feeds the multitudes, Jesus asks the disciples, "How many loaves do you have?" (Mark 6:38 // Matt 15:33). When he only partially heals the blind man at Bethsaida, he asks, "Can you see anything?" (Mark 8:23). When he finds the disciples arguing with a group of scribes, he asks, "What are you arguing about with them?" (Mark 9:14–16). Upon discovering that it has to do with a child whom the disciples were unable to heal, Jesus asks the boy's father, "How long has this been happening to him?" (v. 21). Once again, after they journey to Capernaum, he asks the disciples, "What were you arguing about on the way?" (v. 33).

Learning

The Gospels also specifically tell us that Jesus learned. Luke records that Jesus "*increased in wisdom* and in stature, and in favor with God and people" (Luke 2:52). John adds, "Now when Jesus *learned* that the Pharisees had heard that Jesus was making and baptizing more disciples than John—although Jesus himself was not baptizing but his disciples—he left Judea and departed again for Galilee" (John 4:1–3). In a somewhat different sense, the author of Hebrews notes, "Although he was a son, he *learned* obedience from the things he suffered" (Heb 5:8). The Gospel writers even note that there is one thing specifically that Jesus does not know: the hour of his return. Both Matthew and Mark record, "But of that day and hour no one knows, not even the angels of heaven, *nor the Son*, but the Father alone" (Matt 24:36 // Mark 13:3).

Need

Jesus also suffered needs, the very needs we saw above that God cannot experience. We know, for example, that Jesus experienced *hunger*. Matthew tells us concerning Jesus' time of temptation in the wilderness, "After fasting forty days and forty nights, *he was hungry*" (Matt 4:2 // Luke 4:2). Jesus also experiences hunger in the story of his cursing the barren fig tree. Mark records, "On the following day, when they came from Bethany, *he was hungry*" (Mark 11:12 // Matt 21:18). Luke observes that Jesus ate food even *after* his resurrection: "They gave him a piece of broiled fish, and he took it and ate in their presence" (Luke 24:42–43). Jesus also experienced *thirst*. As he journeys with the disciples from Judea to Galilee, he famously asks the Samaritan woman at the well to give him something to drink (John 4:7). On the cross, Jesus says specifically, "*I thirst*," before drinking the sour wine offered to him and giving up his spirit (John 19:28). Jesus also knew *fatigue*. His conversation with the woman at the well was occasioned by his need to stop for rest. John records, "He came to a Samaritan city called Sychar, near the plot of ground Jacob had given to his son Joseph. Jacob's well was there, and Jesus, *tired out by his journey*, was sitting by the well" (John 4:5–6). Again, in the story of Jesus' calming the winds and the waves, we first find Jesus *sound asleep* in the stern of the boat (Matt 8:24 // Mark 4:38 // Luke 8:23).

If there is any lesson to be learned from this litany of temptations, questions, learning, and needs, it must surely be that Jesus cannot be divine. Jesus clearly does things that *God cannot do*. But, of course, there is another matter to consider: *Jesus is also human*. How Jesus' humanity and divinity coexist remains a matter impossible for us to understand fully, especially since the authors of the New Testament do not pause to give us a detailed explanation of this theological tenet. With Paul, we have to admit that on this side of the veil, "We see through a glass darkly." Only later will we see "face to face" (1 Cor 13:12). But if we cannot know everything about the manner in which Jesus' humanity and divinity coexist, we can at least affirm this: There was a cost involved in Jesus' condescending to become human. In his letter to the Philippians, Paul uses the notion of *kenosis*, or "emptying," to describe the sacrifice Jesus made in taking on human flesh:

> Let the same mind be in you that was in Christ Jesus, who, though being in the form of God, did not regard equality with God as something to cling to, but *emptied himself*, taking the form of a slave, being born in human likeness. And being found in human form, he humbled himself, becoming obedient to the point of death—even death on a cross.
>
> (Phil 2:5–8)

Paul argues that Jesus somehow set aside certain of his divine prerogatives as part of his incarnation. It is this act of self-sacrifice that enabled Jesus in his humanity to do things God as God simply could not do.

If we struggle to wrap our heads around these kinds of issues, we should know that we are not the first followers of Jesus to do so. Two early Christian groups, the Ebionites and the Docetists, illustrate the struggles individuals have faced in trying to understand who Jesus was.[24] The Ebionites were largely Jewish Christians, and their background in Judaism greatly affected their view of Christ and Christianity. They believed, for example, that Christians ought still to obey the Mosaic Law, and they held a dim view of New Testament authors who seemed to argue that they should not. Thus, James and Matthew were held in high regard by the Ebionites, while the works of Paul were not. When it came to their understanding of Jesus, the Ebionites had no trouble accepting the humanity of Jesus. Their commitment to monotheism, however, led them to reject the notion that Jesus was divine. The Docetists stood at the other end of the theological spectrum. As Greeks, they did not believe that Christians were under any obligation at all to follow the Jewish Law. As a result, they rejected New Testament works like James and Matthew and embraced those of Paul and John. As for Jesus, the Docetists accepted the belief that Christ was divine. What they could not countenance was the notion that he was human. Influenced as they were by Greek philosophical notions that regarded the material world as evil, the Docetists could not accept the idea that God could interact with the physical world in a manner as overt as the incarnation would require. The Docetists believed that the figure who appeared as Christ to the disciples was in fact only a projection of God's power, an emanation or phantasm, but not a real human. He did not eat or drink. When he walked, he did not leave footprints. Indeed, the word *Docetic* comes from the Greek term *dokeō*, which means *to seem* or *appear*. According to the Docetists, Jesus was entirely divine; he only *appeared* to be human.

It is my contention that many of us as modern Christians are really *closet Docetists*. All too often, we treat the humanity of Jesus as incidental when compared to his divinity. While we may not opt for beliefs as outlandish as the idea that Jesus did not leave footprints when he walked, we can be scandalized by Jesus' humanity in other ways. When the Gospels record that Jesus asked questions, we are apt to treat these questions as merely rhetorical. We struggle with the notion that Jesus genuinely *did not know* the answers to the questions, and we assume, consciously or unconsciously, that he asked them only for the benefit of those around him. When we hear Jesus' prayer in the garden, "Let this cup pass from me; yet not what I will but what you will" (Matt 26:39), we may be tempted to give less weight to the first part of this prayer than we give to the second. Jesus' willing submission to the Father does not bother us; the notion that Jesus so dreaded the cross that he was willing to forego his role as Messiah is much harder to accept. When we hear Jesus' cry on the cross, "My God, my God, why have you forsaken me?" (Mark 15:34 // Matt 27:46), we often minimize the full thrust of this lament. Rather than accept Jesus' words in straightforward fashion as meaning "God, I don't understand why you are doing this," we impose upon the text our conviction that Jesus really must have understood what was going on and known why the Father had to turn away from him.

At the risk of stirring up more controversy than I really intend to, we might consider for a moment the matter of Jesus' sexuality. The Scriptures give us no indication that Jesus ever married, and I see no reason to believe that he did. The question, though, is *could* Jesus have gotten married? Is there anything other than the practicality of his not wanting his mission to be compromised by the entanglements of marriage that would have prevented him from doing so? It is an interesting and difficult question, and I confess that my initial reactions against Jesus' marrying have nothing to do with practicality. They are rather a matter of my not wanting to consider the possibility that Jesus could have had sex. I am uncomfortable on a visceral level with the notion that Jesus could have noticed and been attracted to a beautiful woman who might have been in his audience. At the same time, though, I recognize that my discomfort with this subject is little more than a reflection of my own closet Docetism. There are aspects of Jesus' humanity that I hesitate to consider, even while I recognize that denying these aspects of his humanity undermines the pivotal moment in God's outreach to us as human beings, *the incarnation*. If Jesus could not have gotten married, if he never noticed that beautiful woman in his audience, then of what consolation is the assurance of the author of Hebrews that Jesus is a person "who in every respect has been tempted *just as we are*, yet without sin" (Heb 4:15)? If Jesus did not feel sexual attraction, how could he possibly know what it is like to have to resist such temptations? In fact, he must have experienced those temptations, but he mastered them without sinning. The problem lies not in whether Jesus could have experienced the challenges of normal human sexuality, but in whether admitting such a possibility pushes too hard against *our subtle undermining of his humanity*.

So, how does this relate to the matter of reading Scripture? It is interesting to note that Christians have traditionally recognized not one but two entities as being both human and divine. Both Jesus *and the Scriptures* have been regarded by Christians in this fashion. The Scriptures themselves and the Christian communities they produced affirm that the Bible is both a divine and a human work. But just as Christians can tend to be closet Docetists in their beliefs about Jesus, they can succumb to the same temptation in their beliefs about the Bible. In our eagerness to affirm that the Bible is the Word of God, an eagerness that I certainly share, we are apt to forget that the Bible is also a human work. Just as Jesus in his humanity could do things that God alone could not do, so the Scriptures in their humanity can do things we would not expect God's Word to do. Just as Jesus could hunger, thirst, learn, and grow tired, so the Scriptures can show the limitations of their humanity, *and they can do so while not jeopardizing in any way their status as being divinely inspired.*[25]

That the Bible assumes the limited scientific understandings of its day should not surprise us any more than it should surprise us that Jesus shared in our own human limitations. We should expect the Bible to share and even borrow from the stories of neighboring cultures, *as all human cultures do*. We should not be surprised when the human authors of Scripture approach matters from different points of view and even argue with one another at various points. Had we been in charge, perhaps we might have chosen a different method for giving the Scriptures to humanity. But then, our beliefs about God's wisdom and omniscience suggest that our method would of necessity have been the wrong one. For reasons we may not be able to divine, God chose to use human authors to convey his Word to humanity, and we go astray when we neglect and overlook this key aspect of Scripture.

To return to our earlier point of departure, it is not enough to suggest with Galileo that the authors of the Bible understood the true nature of the universe but shielded their readers from such knowledge so as to avoid confusing them. The Bible is human as well as divine—*by God's own intention*—and so it makes use of the science, the genres, the shared stories, and the limitations of its human authors. We misread Scripture when we fail to take these truths into account.

CHAPTER 2

An Undiscovered Country

Most of us can relate to the experience of pulling into the driveway and suddenly wondering just how we got there. We are alone in the car, sitting in the driver's seat; clearly, we did the driving. And yet, we have no memory at all of having done so. Sometimes this happens to us because we were doing something we definitely should not (like texting) or at least probably should not (like talking on the phone). But sometimes this happens just because we were lost in thought, daydreaming or mulling over one problem or another. Our body goes into autopilot, and some part of our brain kicks in and takes over the task of driving for us.

If we can do this with a task as complicated as driving, it should not be surprising that we can do this with other, simpler tasks as well. My students would say that it often happens to them while they are reading. We have all done it at one time or another. Our eyes are methodically scanning one line of a book after another when we suddenly realize we have *no idea what we are actually reading.* Our brains have slipped into cruise control, and though the images of words have passed through the lenses of our eyes and perhaps even ventured down the pathways of our optic nerves, they most certainly did not find a home in our brains. As we turn back page after page to find some passage we actually remember, we realize that we have read but not really read. This is often our experience in reading the Bible. Some passages are so foreign to us (think Leviticus or Ezekiel) that our eyes might glaze over after just a few verses. Others are so familiar (think Genesis, Psalm 23, or the Gospels) that we may not take the time to give the text our full attention. We read the words, mostly, but the words are really just skipping off the surface of our minds like stones skipping across water.

One result of this kind of unintentionally superficial reading of the Bible is our failure to appreciate just how foreign the world of the Bible is to our own. Because we are so intimately acquainted with its people and places—the Abrahams and Isaacs, Davids and Solomons, Jerusalems and Jerichos—we can lull ourselves into forgetting that to enter the Bible is to enter an undiscovered country, a world almost entirely different from our own. A couple of examples will suffice to illustrate the point.

David Remained in Jerusalem

One of the more ominous passages in the Bible is found at the beginning of 2 Samuel 11:

> Now it happened in the spring of the year, the time when kings go out to battle, that David sent out Joab and his servants with him and all Israel. They ravaged the Ammonites, and besieged Rabbah. But David remained at Jerusalem.
>
> (2 Sam 11:1)

Those familiar with the story of David will recall that this verse signals the king's terrible fall into adultery, murder, and eventually the loss of his own family. As we read this verse, though, the author intends for us to be struck by one glaring oddity: David's *army* went out to fight the Ammonites, but *David* stayed home. For the author, this was strikingly odd, unprecedented even. The David who had bested the Philistine champion, the David of whom the Israelite women had sung, "David has killed his tens of thousands"—this David did not stay in Jerusalem while his forces were engaged in battle. With his pregnant line "David remained in Jerusalem," the author impresses upon his readers just how very strange this was.

From a modern perspective, though, is this really odd? The author of 2 Samuel 11 could hardly conceive of a monarch who did *not* accompany his troops into battle. Today, we could hardly conceive of a head of state who *would*. It is difficult to imagine even a general today at the head of an infantry charge, much less a president or prime minister. Indeed, in the English and American tradition, the last sitting head of state to lead troops into battle was the British king George II, who did so at Dettingen in Bavaria *in 1743*. The biblical author found it odd that the leader of the people would not go to war; we would be astonished if they did. Yet, we

are so steeped in the language of the Bible that we hardly notice this ancient practice.

This is hardly the most unusual aspect of this ancient text, however.
While the biblical author might have been at pains to point out the oddity of
the king's not going to war, what is most shocking about this text is something
we hardly notice at all: *"In the spring of the year, the time when kings go out to
battle."* Like other ancient nations, Israel and its neighbors had a war season
that started when the weather cleared in the springtime. They thought nothing at all about the idea that at a certain season of year, it was time to ransack
enemy villages and pillage foreign towns. The author glides past this phenomenon as if it were little more than our thinking of fall as football season. Where
I live, in "SEC country," football is only marginally more important than religion and politics. Six months (or more) ahead of time, sports personalities on
the radio begin counting down the number of days left until football kicks off
again. Israel did not have football. Instead, the Israelites and their neighbors
counted down the days until "springtime, when kings go out to war." This was
a world so very different from our own, but our very familiarity with the Bible
can cause us to miss how foreign this world was.

The Heavens

The foreignness of the biblical world is not limited solely to its culture. It
is equally evident in the way biblical authors conceived of the structure of
the universe and especially in the way they describe the heavens. When we
think of the location of heaven—the divine abode, not just the skies—we
naturally think "up." If we had to point, we would point straight up. Today,
though, we mean this only in the most metaphorical of senses. We might
use the language of going *up to heaven*, but we don't really believe we could
construct some particularly speedy rocket, launch ourselves into space, and
finally arrive at a constellation that spells out, "Just five more lightyears to
heaven!" After all, what does *up* even mean when we live in a world that
is round? Going up for someone in America would be just the opposite of
going up for someone in China.

When we speak of heaven as up, we are speaking figuratively; the biblical
authors most certainly were not. When the ancient Israelites spoke of heaven
as God's dwelling place, they described it *and meant it* straightforwardly as
up. The prayer the Israelites are instructed to offer over their firstfruits of-
ferings in Deuteronomy includes the words, "Look down from your holy
habitation, from heaven, and bless your people Israel" (Deut 26:15). Later in

the same book, the people are assured that God's commandment is not hidden from them; they need never ask, "Who will go up to heaven for us and get it for us so that we may hear it and observe it?" (Deut 30:12). In a different context, God is said to take Elijah "up to heaven by a whirlwind" (2 Kgs 2:1, 11). In the book of Job, Eliphaz asks, "Is not God high in the heavens? See the highest stars, how lofty they are!" (Job 22:12). One of Israel's psalmists declares, "YHWH looks down from heaven; he sees all of humanity. From the place where he sits, he watches all the inhabitants of the earth" (Ps 33:13–14). In the book of Acts, Jesus is "lifted up" to heaven in a cloud, and the disciples are assured by the angels who appear in his wake, "Men of Galilee, why do you stand looking up toward heaven? This Jesus, who was taken up from you into heaven, will come in the same way as you saw him go into heaven" (Acts 1:9, 11). Even Paul describes his being "caught up to the third heaven," which he subsequently describes as "Paradise" (2 Cor 12:2–4).[1]

The biblical authors also differed from us in how they conceived of the other "heavens," *space* rather than the divine realm. To cite just one example, we find in the Gospels a description of terrible cataclysms that will accompany the return of the Son of Man:

> But in those days, after that tribulation, the sun will be darkened, and the moon will not give its light, and the stars will be falling from heaven, and the powers in the heavens will be shaken.
>
> (Mark 13:24–25 // Matt 24:29)

These descriptions fit perfectly with an ancient understanding of celestial bodies like the sun, moon, and stars. They diverge greatly, though, from what we now know about these entities. That the sun should be darkened is no problem. It is interesting, though, that the moon is also described as no longer giving "its light." The trouble with this, of course, is the fact that the moon does not actually give off any light of its own. It merely reflects the light of the sun.[2]

Much more problematic, though, is the description of stars falling from heaven. Because of their extraordinary distance from earth, even the brightest stars appear to the naked eye as little more than pinpricks of light in the night sky. Given this, it is easy to understand how meteors streaking across the heavens could be thought of by our ancestors as "falling stars." We know today, though, that *stars* and *falling stars* could hardly be more different. Stars, we have learned, are massive and ferocious bodies of which our own sun is only a modest-sized example. Even the smallest star so far discovered is larger than Saturn, a planet that dwarfs the earth in size.[3] The largest stars reach sizes so massive that even our own sun—itself nearly a million times larger than the earth—is vanishingly small by comparison.[4] The meteors we see as "falling stars," by contrast, usually range in size from grains of sand to small pebbles. The brilliant streaks they make across the sky result from the great speed at which they encounter earth's atmosphere, not from their great size. As with the notion of heaven's being *up*, when we speak of *falling stars*, we do so only metaphorically. The biblical authors did no such thing; limited as they were by the science of their day, they made no distinction between stars and falling stars.

My point in highlighting these differences between the conception of the universe in the biblical period and our own understanding today is not to cast aspersions on the intelligence of these ancient peoples. On the contrary, the feats of engineering, agriculture, and scientific observation accomplished by these ancients never cease to amaze. My point is rather that our familiarity with the biblical text and our deep love for that text can dull our appreciation of just how different the world and worldview of the text is from our own.

Creation

It would be surprising indeed to find that the foreignness of the biblical world stopped abruptly at the doorstep of creation. The biblical authors appear to have had quite different ideas than we do about the structure of the creation and the nature of the bodies that inhabit it. We should be open to the possibility that they also thought differently than we do when it came to telling the story of creation. The issues related to creation that concern us today in a world dominated by science may be different from the issues that concerned them. Just as importantly, we have to remain open to the possibility that our own intense familiarity with the Bible's creation accounts may have served to shield our eyes to just how foreign these ancient texts are. This is especially true given the important role these texts have played in the development of our theological understanding of God and his world.

Journeying into the Biblical World

In the chapters that follow, my aim is to help us explore the Bible's creation texts with all of their exotic differences intact. Here, we might compare ourselves to travelers preparing to visit a culture very different from our own. With a few travel guides in hand, we would learn a bit about the country's history and culture, master some important words in the native tongue, and ready ourselves for sights, sounds, and tastes that are unfamiliar but intriguing in their own right. Most of all, we would open ourselves up to the possibility of expecting the unexpected, trying to appreciate a world that has something new to offer us if only we will let it. When we venture back into the foreign country that is the biblical world, we should be prepared to undertake the same preparations. Before we impose our own cultural ideas and modes of thought onto the biblical text, we should try to understand how the biblical authors understood their world and the cultures around them. We should anticipate that they may have approached issues differently than we do, that they may have been concerned about different questions than we are, and that they may have told their stories of creation in ways that might turn out to be quite foreign to our own ways of thinking.

CHAPTER 3

Odd Creation Traditions

While the early chapters of Genesis contain the Bible's most famous creation traditions, by no means do they contain *all* of these traditions. Scattered throughout the Bible's poetic and prophetic books, we find a number of interesting and varied texts that revolve around this same creation theme.

Psalm 74

One of the Psalter's most interesting creation texts is found in Psalm 74. In vv. 16–17, the psalmist extols God's creative power:

> Yours is the day, yours also the night;
>   you established luminary and sun.
> You have fixed all the boundaries of the earth;
>   summer and winter—you made them.

Though it seems unlikely that this text draws directly upon Genesis 1,[1] it overlaps with much of its imagery. The creation of day and night, the establishment of heavenly lights and the sun, the separation of sky, water, and land to form the boundaries of the earth—all of these echo elements of this creation account (cf. Gen 1:5, 6–10, 14–18). The establishment of the seasons echoes themes from both the story of creation (Gen 1:14) and the story of God's re-creating the world after the flood (Gen 8:1–3, 22).[2]

What makes this text so interesting, though, is not its echoes of the Genesis creation account. It is rather the setting in which the psalmist places this creation. Verses 12–15, the lines that lead up to the psalm's description of creation, contain language that seems out of place for a creation text:

Yet God my King is from of old,
> working salvation in the midst of the earth.

You broke[3] the sea by your might;
> you shattered the heads of the dragons[4] in the waters.

You crushed the heads of Leviathan;
> you gave him as food for the creatures of the sea.[5]

You split open spring and wadi;
> you dried up ever-flowing rivers.

Of particular note is the connection the psalm makes between God's kingship, his creative work, and a battle fought against the sea and/or sea monster. The language of combat is especially evident in the psalmist's expressions "you broke up," "you shattered," and "you crushed." Less clear, though, is the entity God is said to be fighting against. There is the sea, of course, but we also find *dragons* and the *Leviathan*.

The Hebrew term rendered as *dragons* in some translations and *sea monsters* in others is *tannînîm*, plural of *tannîn*.[6] The meaning of *tannîn* varies from one passage to another in the Hebrew Bible. In some contexts, it appears to refer to just a serpent. Thus, as Aaron squares off against Pharaoh's magicians, his staff becomes a *tannîn*, as do the staffs of the magicians (Exod 7:9–12). The Song of Moses in Deuteronomy 32 berates the enemies of Israel whose "wine is the poison of *tannînîm*, the cruel venom of asps" (v. 33). The parallel between *tannînîm* and *asps* leaves little doubt that serpents are in view.[7] Finally, Psalm 91 assures those who take refuge in the shadow of the Almighty that they will be delivered from all harm: "On the lion and the asp you will tread, you will trample the young lion and the *tannîn*" (v. 13). Again, the parallelism in the verse suggests the serpentine reading.

Alongside these three passages in which *tannîn* refers to serpents, though, stand a number of passages in which a much more fearsome monster is in view. In the midst of one of his laments to God, Job asks, "Am I the sea or the *tannîn*, that you set a guard over me?" (Job 7:12).[8] How are we to understand Job's language? The connection with the sea is clear; indeed, the sea and the *tannîn* seem almost interchangeable.[9] In context, Job is asking God why he has trained his sights on him in the first place. Job cries out that he is so small that he does not understand why God would take notice of him even if he were guilty (cf. vv. 17–18, 20). To emphasize his insignificance, Job highlights the entities that lie at the other end of the spectrum of power from his own lowly estate. What he places at this other end of this spectrum, what he deems to be God's true cosmic antagonists, are the sea and the *tannîn*. The sea is personified here as something active that opposes God, and the *tannîn* in the passage can hardly be a mere snake. Even the largest of living creatures would not capture the *tannîn's* role as divine opponent.

The hostility between God and the *tannîn* is evident in Psalm 74 as well. In v. 13 of the psalm, we read: "You broke the sea by your might; you shattered the heads of the *tannînîm* in the waters." Here, *tannînîm* is again set in parallel with the sea, as both oppose God and are defeated by him. It is clear in this text as well that no serpent—indeed, no ordinary creature of any sort—would suffice to capture the cosmic nature of God's opponent. But if it is not a regular sea creature that the psalmist describes, what else could it be? We find a clue in the next line of the psalm, v. 14a: "You crushed the heads of Leviathan." The term *Leviathan* is derived from a Semitic root, **lwy*, meaning *twist* or *coil* and pointing toward the creature's serpentine nature.[10] This element features strongly in the literature of Israel's ancient Canaanite neighbors, where the Leviathan, known as *Lōtān* or *Lîtān*, is depicted as a monstrous, serpentine dragon. The biblical descriptions of the Leviathan fit this same pattern. The serpentine and dragon-like aspects of the Leviathan receive particular emphasis in Isaiah 27:1:

> On that day, YHWH with his hard and great and strong sword will punish Leviathan the fleeing serpent, Leviathan the twisting serpent, and he will kill the *tannîn* that is in the sea.

In the prophet's oracle, the Leviathan is cast as a serpent-like dragon whom God will defeat in the apocalyptic conclusion of the present age.[11]

It is possible that deep in the background of the conception of Leviathan there lies some natural creature or combination of creatures, perhaps a whale, crocodile, or sea serpent.[12] The features of such creatures have been almost entirely eclipsed, however, by the mythic features attributed to the beast both in Canaanite literature and in the pages of Scripture. Unlike any natural creature, for example, the Leviathan was often depicted by the Canaanites as having seven heads.[13] Careful readers will have noted that Psalm 74 offers a similar description. In v. 14a, God is said to have crushed the heads (plural!) of the Leviathan (singular).[14] The extended description of the Leviathan in the divine speech found in Job 41 [40:25–41:26] similarly sets the beast apart from any natural creature. Unlike both whales and crocodiles, which were regularly hunted in antiquity, the Joban Leviathan is depicted as utterly immune to human assault:[15]

Can you draw out Leviathan with a fishhook,
　　or restrain his tongue with a cord?
Can you put a rope in his nose,
　　or pierce his jaw with a hook?

　　　　　　　　　　　　(Job 41:1–2 [40:25–26])

Can you fill his skin with harpoons,
　　or his head with fishing spears?
Lay your hands on him; remember the battle;
　　you will never do it again!
Behold, any hope at all is false;
　　even the gods were overwhelmed at the sight of him![16]
No one is fierce enough to stir him up.
　　Who then can stand before me?

　　　　　　　　　　　　(Job 41:7–10 [40:31–41:2])

When he rises up, the gods are afraid;
　　at the crashing they retreat.
Though the sword reaches him,
　　it does not avail,
　　nor does the spear, the dart, or the javelin.
He regards iron as straw,
　　and bronze as rotten wood.
The arrow cannot make him flee;
　　for him, slingstones are turned to chaff.
Clubs are regarded as chaff;
　　he laughs at the rattle of the scimitar.

　　　　　　　　　　　　(Job 41:25–29 [17–21])

There is no one on land who can rule him,
　　a creature without fear.
He surveys everything that is lofty;
　　he is king over all that are proud.

　　　　　　　　　　　　(Job 41:33–34 [25–26])

And no wonder! Job's Leviathan is described not as a mere whale or crocodile or serpent, but as a dragon-like monster of mythic proportions. His back is depicted as armored with thick rows of scales:

> Who can strip off his outer garment?
> > Who can penetrate his double armor?
> Who can open the doors of his face?
> > Around his teeth there is terror.
> His back is made of rows of shields,
> > shut up closely as with a seal.
> One is so near to another
> > that no air can come between them.
> They are joined one to another;
> > they clasp each other and cannot be separated.
>
> > > (Job 41:13–17 [5–9])

The underside of the Leviathan is equally formidable:

> His underparts are like sharp potsherds;
> > he spreads himself like a threshing sledge on the mire.
>
> > > (Job 41:30 [22])

And unlike any natural creature, Job's Leviathan breathes fire:

> His sneezes flash forth light,
> > and his eyes are like the rays of the dawn.
> From his mouth go flaming torches;
> > sparks of fire leap forth.
> Out of his nostrils comes smoke,
> > as from a boiling pot and burning rushes.
> His breath kindles coals,
> > and a flame comes out of his mouth.
>
> > > (Job 41:18–21 [10–13])

Like the Canaanite *Lītān*, the biblical Leviathan is cast as a serpentine dragon unlike any natural creature. This was certainly the way the term was understood by the Jewish scholars who produced the Septuagint, an early translation of the Hebrew text of the Bible into Greek. These early Jewish translators rendered all but one of the Hebrew Bible's instances of *Leviathan* using forms of the word *drakōn*. This is the Greek word (and source of the English word) for *dragon* that is familiar to readers of the New Testament from its various appearances in the book of Revelation.[17] This characterization of the Leviathan sheds light on our earlier term *tannîn* in Psalm 74:13–14a. The parallel the psalmist draws between the *tannîn* and the Leviathan suggests that the *tannîn* should also be understood as a serpentine dragon. Confirmation of this understanding is found in the fact that the Canaanites also described their *tunnan*, the semantic equivalent of Hebrew *tannîn*, in terms identical to those applied to *Lītān* (Leviathan)—namely, as a twisting serpent with seven heads.[18] It is also noteworthy that the translators of the Septuagint rendered *tannîn* as *drakōn* (dragon) as readily as they did *Leviathan*.[19]

Though perhaps initially mystifying to us, the psalmist who composed Psalm 74 depicts God as fighting the sea and some multiheaded sea monster/dragon/Leviathan as part of, or as a precursor to, his creation of the world. It is this act of divine combat that provides the ground for God's being called *king from of old*. Clearly, we are a long way from the sort of creative work described in Genesis 1. Yet, the unusual creation imagery found here is not confined to just Psalm 74. Similar language is scattered across various parts of the Bible.

Psalm 89

Psalm 89 is a text that also combines imagery related to God's kingship, his battle with the sea/dragon, and his creation of the world. In vv. 5–8 [6–9], the psalmist extols God's incomparability in much the same way that Psalm 74 depicted God as king:

> Let the heavens praise your wonders, YHWH,
>> your faithfulness, too, in the assembly of the holy ones.
> For who in the skies can be compared to YHWH?
>> Who among the divine beings is like YHWH,
> a God greatly feared in the council of the holy ones,
>> and held in awe by all that are around him?
> O YHWH God of hosts,
>> who is as mighty as you, YHWH?
>> Your faithfulness surrounds you.

Of particular interest is the fact that the psalm depicts the God of Israel as being surrounded by other heavenly entities. Note the psalmist's language: *assembly of the holy ones,* those *in the skies, divine beings, council of the holy ones, hosts.*[20] It is not entirely clear whom the psalmist has in mind in these various descriptions. Our initial thought might be angels, but *angels* is the one term that is conspicuously absent from this passage. We can only say that God is depicted as reigning over some attendant gathering of heavenly entities. It may well be that the kingship described in Psalm 74:12 ("Yet God, my king, is from of old") is similarly intended to refer to his reign over heavenly beings and not just humanity.

Psalm 89 also focuses on an act of divine combat. Note vv. 9–10 [10–11]:

> You rule the raging of the sea;
>> when its waves rise, you still them.
> You crushed Rahab like a carcass;
>> you scattered your enemies with your mighty arm.

Verse 9 praises God for his defeat of the sea, but again, like the author of Psalm 74, the psalmist here connects this battle against the sea with a battle against some other entity: "You crushed Rahab like a carcass." The *Rahab* mentioned here is not to be confused with the Canaanite prostitute who rescued the spies in Joshua 2 (the two names are actually spelled differently in Hebrew). This Rahab is instead, like the *tannîn* and Leviathan in Psalm 74:13–14, a reference to a mythical sea monster or dragon. This is evident, for example, in the parallel treatment of Rahab and the *tannîn* in Isaiah 51:9b:

> Was it not you who cut *Rahab* in pieces,
>> who pierced the *dragon* [*tannîn*]?

In this passage, the battle against Rahab is applied to the sea crossing that was the pinnacle event of the exodus from Egypt. The dragon-like character of Rahab, however, is clear. The verb **rhb*, from which the proper name *Rahab* is derived, refers to *surging, storming,* or *pressing,* underscoring the connection between Rahab and the storms and surging waves of the sea.[21]

Most important for our discussion here is the fact that Psalm 89 also makes a connection between God's combat against the sea and Rahab, on the one hand, and his creation of the world, on the other. Thus, we find in vv. 11–13 [12–14]:

The heavens are yours; the earth also is yours;
>   the world and all that is in it—you have founded them.
> The north and the south—you created them;
>   Tabor and Hermon sing forth your name.
> You have a mighty arm;
>   strong is your hand, high your right hand.

Once again, the psalmist has connected notions of God's transcendence with his victory over the sea and sea monster and his creation of the world.

Job 26

Job 26 is yet another passage in which God's creation and his battle with the sea and sea monster are combined. In vv. 7–11, Job declares:

> He stretches out Zaphon over emptiness,
>   and hangs the earth upon nothing.
> He binds up the waters in his thick clouds,
>   and the cloud is not split open by them.
> He covers the face of the full moon,[22]
>   and spreads over it his cloud.
> He has described a circle on the face of the waters,
>   at the boundary between light and darkness.
> The pillars of heaven tremble;
>   they are astounded at his rebuke.

These verses contain various allusions to God's creative work. In v. 7, God is said to stretch out *Zaphon*—a term that can mean either *the north* or a particular *northern mountain*—over the *tōhû*, the same term used to describe the unformed, watery chaos of Genesis 1:2. The text then goes on to say that God "hangs the world on nothing." Verse 10 continues the description of God's creative work, as Job credits God with marking the horizon, the curved boundary between light and dark. Even the reference to "pillars" in v. 11 likely has in mind God's creative work, since elsewhere in the Bible it is on pillars that God is portrayed as having founded the heavens and earth (1 Sam 2:8; Ps 75:3 [4]).[23]

In the wake of this description of creation, though, Job's language turns in v. 12 to the now-familiar description of divine combat:

By his power he stilled the Sea;
>   by his understanding he struck down Rahab.
By his wind the heavens were made fair;
>   his hand pierced the fleeing serpent.

As in other passages we have considered, the poet here draws a parallel between the sea, Rahab, and the "fleeing serpent" (cf. Isa 27:1). It is against these forces of sea and sea monster that God battles as he creates. His divine power, understanding, wind, and hand are extolled as he brings order to these chaotic enemies.

Job 9

Another Joban passage linking creation with God's battle against the dragon is found in Job 9. In v. 8a, Job describes God as the one "who alone stretched out the heavens." In v. 9, he says that God is the one "who made the Bear and Orion, the Pleiades and the constellations of the south." Set between these two descriptions, in v. 8b, is Job's description of God as "the one who trampled the heights of the sea." Here, God's creative work is once again connected with his defeat of the sea. And just a few lines later, in vv. 13–14, the dragon Rahab returns:

God will not turn back his anger;
>   beneath him bowed the helpers of Rahab.
How then can I answer him,
>   or choose my words with him?

Following the pattern of the other texts we have seen, creation is seen as the outcome of a divine conflict that occurred at some point in the past.

Isaiah 51

As we saw in our discussion of Isaiah 27 above, the image of God's battle against the sea and sea monster can be transferred from its most common setting, creation, to other moments as well. In Isaiah 27:1, this imagery is transferred to a time of future apocalyptic judgment: "*On that day*, YHWH with his hard and great and strong sword will punish Leviathan the fleeing serpent, Leviathan the twisting serpent, and he will kill the dragon that is in the sea." In Isaiah 51, the prophet's description of a battle at creation blends seamlessly with his recounting of another battle at the sea, namely, God's parting the sea to allow the Israelites to escape from Egypt. In v. 9, we find the same kind of conflict language we have seen thus far:

> Awake, awake, clothe yourself with strength,
>   O arm of YHWH!
> Awake, as in days of old,
>   the generations of old!
> Was it not you who hacked Rahab in pieces,
>   who pierced the dragon?

The prophet refers to ancient times—"days of old," "generations long ago"— much like Psalm 74:12 does. Rahab is here, paralleled by our term *tannîn*, the dragon. Yet note the shift as we move to v. 10:

> Was it not you who dried up the sea,
>   the waters of the great deep;
> who made the depths of the sea a way
>   for the redeemed to cross over?

Here, the prophet treats the Israelites' exodus from Egypt as a new act of creation, this time of a people rather than the world.[24]

Conclusions

The roster of texts noted above is too lengthy for us to dismiss as some isolated obscurity buried in a poorly translated chapter of the Hebrew Bible. In one text after another, the same constellation of images emerges: God is hailed as an incomparable king. He is praised as the creator of the world. But he effects his creation through a victory over the hostile sea and its attendant sea monster, the dragon, Leviathan, or Rahab. These are creation texts, to be sure, but they are odd creation texts that appear to differ markedly from the "normal" story of creation found in the early chapters of Genesis. It is clear that something is going on behind the scenes here; the question is just what that something is.

CHAPTER 4

Creation's Backstory

If you have ever watched a movie as an adult that you once watched as a child, you have probably experienced those moments of amusement that come as you notice all of the things you missed the first time around. As a somewhat silly example of this, I have sometimes shown my students clips of the animated movie *Madagascar* to highlight just how often the movie slips in allusions they would not have recognized when they were kids. The movie begins with a rendition of the theme to *Born Free*, a film not coincidentally about lions being released from captivity back into the wild. Later, Marty (the zebra) walks through the streets of New York to the sounds of "Staying Alive," just as John Travolta did in *Saturday Night Fever*. As Marty and Alex (the lion) run toward one another on the beach in Madagascar, the anthem that plays in the background is none other than Vangelis' theme from *Chariots of Fire*, the movie that contains cinematography's most famous beach-running scene. The movie *Castaway* is hinted at not once but twice, first as Alex speaks to a volleyball (Spalding, not Wilson!) marked by his bloody paw print and then again as Melman (the giraffe) shouts Tom Hanks–style boasts for having started a fire by rubbing sticks together. The *Twilight Zone* episode "To Serve Man" is invoked as a panicked lemur holds up a volume bearing the title *To Serve Lemur* and warns, "It's a cookbook!" Perhaps most amusing of all is the nod to *Planet of the Apes* found in Alex's falling to the sand before his ruined "Beacon of Liberty" and lamenting in Hestonesque fashion, "You maniac! You burned it up! Darn you! Darn you all to heck!"

A "text" like *Madagascar* really operates at two levels. On the surface, there is the simple humor found in a conspiracy of lemurs set to flight at the barest mention of the word *fossa* or in the overly dramatic tone struck by Alex at the loss of his Beacon of Liberty. Beneath the surface, though, another level of humor is activated when one knows the *backstory* to these comedic allusions. It is this level that clarifies and explains the oddity of a lemur's inexplicably referring to a cookbook or Alex's suddenly dramatic pose. What is true of a work as accessible as *Madagascar* is certainly true of more sophisticated texts as well. The 1974 novel *Jaws* by Peter Benchley offers a spellbinding tale of the efforts to track down and kill a shark that has terrorized a New England resort town. Lurking behind *Jaws*, though, as its backstory, is the important American novel *Moby-Dick*. Beyond the obvious connection in both stories' being set in New England and centering on the pursuit of a great monster from the sea, it is also clear that Benchley's Quint, Brody, and Hooper are literary reincarnations of Melville's Ahab, Ishmael, and Queequeg. Like Ishmael, Sheriff Brody is a landlubber who only reluctantly sets out to sea and who, against all odds, remains as the voyage's last survivor. Like Queequeg, Hooper attempts to kill the beast with a harpoon (a bang stick in Hooper's case) but ultimately dies in the process. Most interesting, though, are the echoes of Ahab in Quint. As successive attempts to kill the great white fail, Quint becomes possessed by an Ahab-like obsession to kill the beast. It is this obsession that ultimately drives him to the same death suffered by Ahab: both captains die tangled in the lines of their own harpoons, dragged to the depths by the creatures they could not defeat.[1] To know the backstory of *Moby-Dick* is to gain new levels of understanding of what transpires in *Jaws*.

The roster of "texts"—whether novel, film, song, painting, or what have you—in which a particular backstory proves essential to understanding the story at hand is too long to rehearse. The tragic story of Cain and Abel forms a constant and indispensable backdrop to John Steinbeck's *East of Eden*. Simon's terrifying encounter with the Lord of the Flies in William Golding's novel by the same name draws heavily upon the Gospel accounts of Satan's testing of Jesus in the wilderness and of *Simon* Peter on the night he denied knowing Jesus (cf. Luke 22:31–32). Here, the backstory is especially significant when it is recalled that Satan is also known as Beelzebub—literally, "lord of the flies," in Hebrew. The musical *Westside Story* is a well-known retelling of Shakespeare's *Romeo and Juliet*. The Woody Allen movie *Crimes and Misdemeanors* hinges on an understanding of the book of Job. Francis Ford Coppola's *Apocalypse Now* is built upon the foundations of Joseph Conrad's *Heart of Darkness*. To grasp the import of Picasso's *Las Meninas*, one must first appreciate Velázquez's painting bearing the same name. In these and countless other examples that could be cited, it is the backstory that supplies the missing information that helps make sense of the work at hand.

As we saw in the preceding chapter, the Bible contains a great many passages that depart from our traditional understanding of biblical creation. With their references to the sea and sea monsters, their Rahabs and multiheaded Leviathans, their divine crushing and striking, these passages present a version of creation that can seem almost unrecognizable to readers steeped in the themes of the first chapters of Genesis. It is hard not to ask just what is going on in these passages. The key, I would argue, lies in our recognizing that behind these odd creation texts lie backstories, in this case stories of divine conflict told among Israel's ancient neighbors in Canaan, on the one hand, and Mesopotamia, on the other.[2]

Canaan: Baal vs. the Sea

As is often the case in matters archaeological, the discovery of the important Canaanite city of Ugarit took place entirely by accident. In 1928, a farmer plowing his field near Minet el-Beida, a small bay on the northern reaches of Syria's Mediterranean coast, happened to strike upon an ancient burial vault. The French authorities who were alerted to the discovery had the foresight to commission an archaeological expedition the next year to research the area. What this expedition uncovered would prove to be one of the most important finds in all of the ancient Near East.[3]

Working under the direction of Claude Schaeffer, the 1929 campaign first examined the tomb at Minet el-Beida and its environs and then turned to explore the mound, or "tel," of Ras Shamra a half-mile further inland. At Tel Ras Shamra, Schaeffer and his team found the remains of ancient Ugarit, a port city that had reached the apex of its importance and influence in the fourteenth to twelfth centuries BCE. It was here that they unearthed monumental temples dedicated to the gods Baal and Dagon, the so-called House of the High Priest, and some of the largest royal palaces in the ancient Near East. Even more importantly, they also found troves of clay tablets inscribed with a form of alphabetic cuneiform writing.[4] As this script was deciphered—a remarkable feat that the French scholars working on the project managed to accomplish in their very first season of digging—a wide variety of economic, ritual, and literary texts began to emerge. These texts and others that would be discovered in succeeding decades of excavation offered an unprecedented window onto the culture and religion of Israel's Canaanite neighbors.[5]

Of particular importance for biblical studies was the discovery of a series of mythic texts at Ugarit centered on the intrigues and conflicts of the

Canaanite pantheon and especially the god Baal. While Baal appears with some regularity in the pages of Scripture, only a rudimentary picture of the deity could be gleaned from the biblical authors' warnings against worshiping this foreign god. Inscriptions found in the Levant on a few buildings and sarcophagi, brief references to the gods of the Canaanite pantheon in treaties and letters, and various pieces of iconographic evidence provided scholars with some additional insight into beliefs about Baal, but still a great many gaps remained. With the discovery of the so-called *Baal Cycle* at Ugarit, however, a great many of these lacunae were filled in.[6] Most important for our purposes is the fact that this same Baal Cycle sheds invaluable light on the texts we considered in the preceding chapter. The Baal story forms part of the backstory of our odd creation texts in the Bible.

The Baal Cycle

The Baal Cycle begins with a conflict between Baal, god of the thunderstorm, and Yamm, god of the sea.[7] In the story's opening scene, the gods are gathered in the hall of El, head of the Canaanite pantheon, when messengers arrive from Yamm demanding that the gods hand over Baal to their master. While most of the gods cower before these messengers, Baal stands tall and rebukes the others for their cowardice. His protests have little effect, though, as El accedes to Yamm's demand and declares Baal to be Yamm's servant. He then instructs the craftsman god, Kothar-wa-Hasis, to build a palace for Yamm, a gesture apparently intended to recognize Yamm as king of the gods. Even in the face of Yamm's apparent coup and El's willingness to turn him over, however, Baal remains defiant. He swears that he will yet defeat this sea god.

Now it is Kothar-wa-Hasis' turn to lend assistance to Baal rather than Yamm. The craftsman god proclaims that Baal will indeed defeat his enemy, the Sea:

> Let me tell you, O Prince Baal,
>> let me repeat, O Rider on the Clouds:
> Now, your enemy, Baal,
>> now your enemy you will kill,
>> now you will vanquish your foe.
> You will take your eternal kingship,
>> your dominion forever and ever.

(KTU 1.2 IV, 8–11)

To aid Baal in his battle against the Sea, Kothar-wa-Hasis fashions two clubs for him: *Driver*, to drive back Yamm, and *Chaser*, to chase him from his throne. Baal strikes Yamm with the first club, but the sea god is not defeated:

> The club leapt from Baal's hand,
> > like a vulture from his fingers.
> It struck Prince Yamm on the shoulder,
> > Judge Nahar between the arms.
> Yamm was strong; he did not sink;
> > his joints did not shake,
> > his frame did not collapse.
>
> > > > > (*KTU* 1.2 IV, 15b–18a)

Baal then presses his attack with the second club, striking a mortal blow to Yamm's head:

> The club leapt from Baal's hand,
> > like a vulture from his fingers.
> It struck Prince Yamm on the skull,
> > Judge Nahar between the eyes.
> Yamm stumbled and fell to the earth;
> > his joints shook,
> > his frame collapsed.
> Baal captured and pierced Yamm;
> > he finished off Judge Nahar.
>
> > > > > (*KTU* 1.2 IV, 23b–27)

As Baal dismembers Yamm and scatters his remains, his victory is secure. "Yamm is dead!" declare the gods.

Baal's defeat of the Sea is celebrated with a feast on the heights of Mount Zaphon. One task still remains, however, before his conquest of the Sea can be considered truly complete: Baal requires a palace of his own. Enlisting the help of his sister, Anat, a terrifying warrior goddess in her own right, and of El's wife, Lady Athirat (Asherah), Baal makes his request known to El. The goddesses confront El over the dishonorable treatment Baal has received even in the wake of his newly acquired kingship:[8]

> Our king is Baal the Conqueror,
> > our judge who is higher than all:

his goblet all of us must bear,
    his cup we must bear.

. . .

But Baal has no house like the (other) gods,
    no court like that for Asherah's sons.

(KTU 1.3 V, 32–34, 38–39)

Moved by the goddesses' demand, El tasks Kothar-wa-Hasis with the job of constructing a palace for Baal on the heights of Mount Zaphon. Caravans of silver and gold, lapis lazuli, and the finest cedar from Lebanon arrive for the palace. Kothar-wa-Hasis sets these in place and then kindles a fire in the palace that burns for seven days and seven nights, until finally, at the end of the week, the flames subside to reveal the bricks of silver and gold that form the building blocks of the palace. It is from this palace that Baal sends forth the stormy elements for which he was revered among the Canaanites. As Lady Asherah exclaims:

Now Baal will provide his abundant rain;
    he will provide a greatly abundant rain in the downpour.
And he will give his voice in the clouds,
    flash his lightning to the earth.

(KTU 1.4 V, 6–9)

Enthroned above the defeated Sea, Baal thunders forth his voice, sends out his lightnings, and provides rain for the earth below.[9]

The Canaanite Story and the Bible: Battle with the Sea

Even this brief rehearsal of the Canaanite story of Baal sheds light on the odd creation texts discussed in the previous chapter. First and foremost is the connection between Baal's battle against the sea god, Yamm, and YHWH's own battle with the sea. These echoes resound with particular force as the Hebrew text of the Bible refers to the sea through a term it shares with Ugaritic, *yām*:[10]

You broke up *yām* [sea] by your might.

(Ps 74:13)

You rule the raging of the *yām* [sea].

(Ps 89:9 [10])

By his power he stilled the *yām* [sea].

(Job 26:12)

Am I *yām* [sea], or the Dragon, that you set a guard over me?

(Job 7:12)

Was it not you who dried up *yām* [sea],
    the waters of the great deep;
who made the depths of *yām* [sea]
    a way for the redeemed to cross over?

(Isa 51:10)

On that day, YHWH with his hard and great and strong sword will punish Leviathan the fleeing serpent, Leviathan the twisting serpent, and he will kill the dragon that is in the *yām* [sea].

(Isa 27:1)

The Canaanite notion of a battle between Yamm and Baal may ultimately have developed from the people's experience of the powerful storms whose winds, rain, thunder, and lightning stirred up the seas along the Mediterranean coast.[11] Both the Canaanites and the biblical authors came to regard these events as more than just natural phenomena, however; they saw them, rather, as displays of divine power.

The Canaanite Story and the Bible: Sea and Dragon

A second area in which the texts from Ugarit shed light on the Bible's creation texts is found in the connection the Canaanites drew between the sea and the dragon. In a passage from Tablet III of the Baal Cycle, Baal's sister, Anat, refers to her own part in the battle against Yamm:

Indeed I struck down the beloved of El, Yamm [Sea]!
    Indeed I finished off Nahar [River], the great god!
    Indeed I bound Tunnan [Dragon] and destroyed him!
I struck down the Twisting Serpent,
    the seven-headed monster.[12]

(*KTU* 1.3 III, 38–40)

As is typical in Ugaritic (and biblical) verse, Anat's speech is structured according to the conventions of poetic parallelism.[13] Here, poetic lines are divided into, usually, two or three parallel parts, called *cola*, with the meaning of the first *colon* being extended and clarified by the remaining, parallel cola. The parallelism in the first tricolon (the first three-part poetic line) of Anat's speech is particularly tight, as the goddess boasts, "Indeed I struck down ...! / Indeed I finished off ...! / Indeed I bound ...!" This parallelism extends into the latter half of each colon as well. Sea, River, and Dragon in these cola are apparently not meant to be understood as three separate entities but as three ways of describing one entity.[14] The close combination of Sea (Yamm) and River (Nahar) suggests that the Canaanites considered the influence of Yamm to extend beyond the sea to the rivers that fed it. These two together are then cast as a dragon (*tunnan*), a description extended in the following poetic line. In this succeeding bicolon, "twisting serpent" and "seven-headed monster" are set in parallel as further elaborations on the dragon-like character the Canaanites attributed to the sea. This is the same identification found in a separate passage from the Baal Cycle:

> When you struck down Lītān, the fleeing serpent,
>   when you annihilated the twisting serpent,
>   the powerful one who has seven heads.
>
>   (*KTU* 1.5 I, 1–3)

In this case, it is clear that "the twisting serpent" and "the powerful one who has seven heads" are further descriptions of "Lītān, the fleeing serpent" in the first part of the poetic line. This same connection is made again in an Ugaritic text known as *KTU* 1.83. In this text, a deity—perhaps the goddess Anat, though the text is too broken to be sure—battles against Sea and Dragon. The text credits this deity with fighting Yamm, setting "a muzzle on Tunnan," and boasting, "Toward the desert shall you be scattered, O Yamm! To the multitude of ḫt (?), O Nahar!" Again, these descriptions—Tunnan the dragon, Yamm the sea, and Nahar the river—are to be understood as complementary ways of understanding just one multifaceted divine opponent.[15]

The famous Tel Asmar seal from Eshnunna offers an iconographic parallel to Ugarit's textual descriptions of Baal's fight against the dragon. In this seal, which dates from ca. 2200 BCE, a deity is shown defeating a seven-headed dragon. At first glance, it appears that there are actually two deities fighting the dragon, one striking the dragon's head and the other its back. As Gary Rendsburg has pointed out, however, it is more likely that the "two" identical deities striking the dragon are meant to be understood as one deity striking the dragon twice.[16] The parallel with the Baal Cycle is particularly close, as the Cycle describes Baal's having first struck Yamm's back, with no effect, and then having struck his head with a crushing blow. In the seal, one iteration of the deity strikes the back of the dragon with no apparent effect. The other iteration of the deity, however, strikes the heads of the dragon, causing four of the dragon's seven heads to loll lifelessly in defeat. The close parallel between the narrative traditions preserved in the Baal Cycle and this seal suggests that it forms another piece of evidence connecting Baal's fight against the dragon with his fight against the sea.

Not to be missed in all of this is the extent to which the language of the Ugaritic texts overlaps with the language of the biblical texts we have already considered. There is the sea, of course, referred to as *yamm* in Ugaritic and *yām* in Hebrew, but we also find the extension of the sea's power into the river, *nahar* in Ugaritic and *nāhār* in Hebrew (cf. Pss 24:2; 72:8; 89:25 [26]; Jonah 2:3 [4]; Nah 1:4; 3:8; Zech 9:10). The Ugaritic scribes refer to their serpentine dragons via the terms *tunnan*, cognate to the Hebrew term *tannîn*, and *lîtān*, cognate to Hebrew *liwyātān* (Leviathan); and the imagery used in these texts to describe the dragons is remarkably similar to that found in the Bible. Isaiah 27:1, for example, refers to "Leviathan the fleeing serpent, Leviathan the twisting serpent," using Hebrew terms that are identical to the Ugaritic words for "fleeing" and "twisting."[17] Psalm 74:14 refers to the multiple heads of Leviathan, and images of the seven-headed dragon persist even into the New Testament (cf. Rev 12–13).[18]

The Canaanite Story and the Bible: Kingship

A third area of connection revolves around the issue of kingship. In the Baal Cycle, Baal's defeat of the sea is integrally tied to his rise to a position of kingship over the gods. As we saw above, it is after Baal's defeat of the sea that the goddesses declare, "Our king is Baal the Conqueror, our judge who is higher than all" (*KTU* 1.3 V, 32–33). A similar situation obtains in the Bible's own divine combat texts, as God's defeat or control of the sea is often linked to the proclamation of his kingship. As he introduces God's defeat of the sea in Psalm 74, the psalmist declares, "Yet God *my king* is from of old, working salvation in the earth" (v. 12). Psalm 93 makes a similar connection, as the psalmist proclaims in v. 1a, "YHWH is *king*, he is robed in majesty; YHWH is robed, he has girded himself with strength," and then goes on in the following verses to link YHWH's kingship with creation and his supremacy over the sea:

The world is established;
    it shall never be moved.
Your throne is established from of old;
    you are from everlasting.
The floods have lifted up, O YHWH,
    the floods have lifted up their voice;
    the floods lift up their roaring.
Mightier than the voice of mighty waters,
    mightier than the waves of the sea,
    YHWH on high is mighty!

(vv. 1b–4)

We find the same link in the related Psalm 95.[19] In v. 3, the psalmist declares YHWH to be "a great God and a great *king* above all gods." Then, in v. 5, he insists, "The sea is his, for he made it." Psalm 29:10 uses this language as well: "YHWH sits enthroned over the flood; YHWH sits enthroned *as king* forever." Though it does not use the title *king*, Psalm 89:6–8 [7–9] emphasizes the supremacy of God even in comparison to his heavenly host:

For who in the skies can be compared to YHWH?
    Who among the divine beings is like YHWH,
a God greatly feared in the council of the holy ones,
    and held in awe by all that are around him?
O YHWH God of hosts,
    who is as mighty as you, YHWH?
    Your faithfulness surrounds you.

Again, like various other passages we have seen, the psalm ties YHWH's supremacy to his rule over the sea in vv. 9–10 [10–11]:

You rule the raging of the sea;
    when its waves rise, you still them.
You crushed Rahab like a carcass;
    you scattered your enemies with your mighty arm.

The upshot of all of these passages is that both the Canaanites and the biblical authors made a connection between a deity's defeat of the sea and that deity's claim to kingship.

This connection extends even to the kingship that YHWH is said to confer upon human kings. In Psalm 89:20 [21], YHWH declares: "I have found my servant David; with my holy oil I have anointed him." In the verses that follow, YHWH goes on to swear that he will always stand with David, shielding him from the assaults of his enemies. In the midst of these promises, he says: "I will set his hand *on the sea* and his right hand *on the rivers*" (v. 25 [26]). The terms used here for "sea" and "river" are *yām* and *nāhār*, the same terms used in parallel in Ugaritic.[20] The prayer for Israel's king found in Psalm 72:8 uses similar language: "May he rule *from sea to sea* [*yām* to *yām*], and from *the River* [*nāhār*] to the ends of the earth."

The discovery of the Baal Cycle at Ugarit has opened an extraordinary window onto the Canaanite backgrounds of the biblical creation traditions we explored in the previous chapter. Although thousands of tablets have now been unearthed at Ugarit, however, one kind of text has continued to elude the archaeologist's spade: no account of creation itself has yet been found. The Canaanite texts from Ugarit detail Baal's battle with the sea, his rise to kingship, and the dragon-like nature of his opponents—all elements that correspond to the biblical accounts of creation discussed above. What these Ugaritic texts lack, however, is any indication that Baal was thought to move on from his defeat of the sea to the creation of the cosmos. As Mark Smith notes, "The Baal Cycle does not assert that Baal 'creates' or even 'arranges' the cosmos. It suggests, rather, that Baal is its preserver and savior."[21] There are hints, perhaps, in the construction of Baal's palace and in the provision of rain that it affords, of the creation motif of establishing the seasons. Providing seasonal rains is a far cry, though, from the sorts of creation accounts we find in biblical texts.[22] Taking this matter one step further, it is important to note that when creation is mentioned at Ugarit, it is attributed to El, not Baal. It is El, not Baal, who is lauded as "the creator of creatures," *bāniyu bunuwwati* (cf. *KTU* 1.4 II, 10–11; 1.6 III, 4–5), and as "father of humanity," *'abû 'adami* (cf. *KTU* 1.14 I, 36–37, 43). Yet even here, El's creative work is merely stated, not described.[23]

There is simply no evidence from the traditions found at Ugarit that a connection was made by the Canaanites between the defeat of the sea/ dragon (whether by Baal, Anat, or even El) and creation. While the Baal Cycle appears to provide the backstory for the Bible's imagery of God's battle with the sea and dragon, if there is precedent for connecting this battle with creation, it must lie outside of Canaan.[24] Interestingly, as we look further afield, we find that this is precisely the case: the connection between sea, battle, and creation is found in the creation story of ancient Babylon.

Babylon: Marduk vs. Tiamat

The nineteenth century was a golden age for the discovery of archaeological and textual remains from ancient Mesopotamia. One of the most famous texts discovered during this time of burgeoning exploration was the seven-tablet Babylonian creation epic known as *Enuma Elish*.[25] Enuma Elish is concerned first and foremost with the ascendancy of Marduk to the position of king of the gods, an elevation in status that went hand in hand with the growing importance of Babylon, the city for which Marduk was the patron deity.[26]

Like the Baal Cycle from Ugarit, Enuma Elish revolves around a conflict between a particular god and the sea. As we will see, though, Enuma Elish is far more extensive in its recounting of this ancient battle and in its description of the battle's aftermath. In the Babylonian story, when we go back to the beginning of everything—before there was heaven above or netherworld beneath, before there was land or sky or plant or person—there was only water. This water was not impersonal and lifeless, though; it was embodied in the form of a god, Apsu, and a goddess, Tiamat. At the beginning of everything, there was water and nothing more; there was Apsu, there was Tiamat, and that was all.

With nothing to separate Apsu and Tiamat, the waters of these two mingled, and it was from their "mingling" that the descendant gods were produced. The creation of these gods presented a problem for their primordial mother and father, though. Since as yet there existed only Apsu and Tiamat, the descendant gods had nowhere to live except in the watery matrix that was their parents. With their movements back and forth, the gods roiled and churned the waters of Apsu and Tiamat. Unable to sleep by day or by night, Apsu finally grew so distressed that he determined he would kill off the descendant gods. Fortunately for the gods, though, one wise and cunning deity, Ea, managed to thwart Apsu's plans before he could execute them. Ea crafted a spell and recited it over Apsu, putting him to sleep and then killing him before he could do the same to his divine descendants.

The boisterous actions of the gods grew even more intense after Apsu's death. Winds and waves churned the waters of Tiamat with such intensity that she finally decided to pick up where Apsu's efforts had left off. Tiamat was joined in her plans by some of the other gods who had also found it difficult to sleep. To these gods she added a host of vicious monsters who would aid in her attacks: the Hydra, dragons, giant serpents whose veins were filled with poison, and a multitude of demonic beasts. Finally, she elevated the descendant god Qingu to be both her husband and her military chieftain. Now, with her ranks complete, Tiamat drew up her forces for battle.

If the gods had been afraid when Apsu plotted against them, they were panic stricken by the threat of Tiamat's onslaught. Ea, the god who had single-handedly put a stop to Apsu, was terrified at the sight of Tiamat's advance. Seeing her might, he despaired that any god would be strong enough to defeat her. In a desperate attempt to conjure some strategy for taking on the Sea and her monstrous band of helpers, the gods gathered together in a divine assembly. There was only stony silence in their divine council, though, as one after another refused to venture out against Tiamat. It was then, just at the moment when all hope seemed lost, that one god did finally step forward. Marduk, the firstborn of Ea and a deity already regarded as mightiest of the gods, said he would take up the challenge.

Marduk's offer to fight Tiamat hinged upon one key demand: He would battle against Tiamat, but if he should prove victorious, he must be declared king of the gods. The gods were only too happy to oblige; after all, Marduk was already the wisest and mightiest among them, and he was a worthy choice to be king. Their decision made, the gods then began to prepare Marduk for the battle that lay ahead. Supplied with bow and club, thunderbolts and fire, the four winds, and a net, Marduk set his face toward Tiamat, sallying forth on his terrible chariot to join the battle. At the first sight of Tiamat, even mighty Marduk began to lose his nerve. As he regained his composure, though, he issued his challenge to her. He accused Tiamat of needlessly stirring up trouble against the gods, of acting arrogantly and aggressively toward her divine children. Marduk's accusations were too much for Tiamat. She was enraged by his invective and threw caution to the wind, charging at Marduk with mouth open, fangs bared. It was at that moment that Marduk sprang his trap. He spread out his net to encircle Tiamat, then he threw his fierce winds into her open mouth, letting their swirling blasts paralyze Tiamat as they roiled around inside her. An arrow loosed from Marduk's bow tore through Tiamat's flesh and pierced her heart. Finally, he took his terrible club and smashed his enemy's skull. Mighty Tiamat was dead.

Marduk's work was not yet complete, however. His battle won, he then began to fashion creation from Tiamat's corpse.[27] First, Marduk split Tiamat's body from stem to stern, dividing her corpse into two halves. One half he stretched overhead, so that Tiamat's hide formed a dome holding back the waters of her body as a great upper ocean. He then fixed gods as constellations of stars in the dome, adding the moon to light up the night and the sun to light up the day. From the other half of Tiamat's body, Marduk formed the land. He heaped up Tiamat's breasts to form mountains. He gouged out her eyes, letting the waters that flowed from them form the Tigris and Euphrates. He dug through her body to the waters below to form wells. He formed rain and wind, mist and cloud. Then, he created bonds to fix heaven and earth, the two halves of Tiamat's body, together. Finally, Marduk turned his attention to the leader of the rebellious gods, Qingu. He slit open his veins to drain his blood, and from this blood he fashioned humans to bear the toil of the gods.

With his creation of the cosmos complete, Marduk returned to the gods as a conquering hero. In unison, they declared, "Behold the king!" The most ancient of the gods proclaimed, "Formerly, Marduk was our beloved son; now he is your king! Heed his command!" As befits a text whose twin purposes were to chart the rise of Babylon and of Babylon's god, Enuma Elish ends with the construction of Marduk's temple in Babylon and a celebration of Marduk's glories. Marduk named his temple *Esagila* and decreed that it should serve as the gate between the gods above and the gods below, a fitting declaration since both the Sumerian and Akkadian names for Babylon, KÁ.DINGIR.RA[ki] and *bābilīm*, mean literally, "Gate of the Gods." The concluding celebration of Marduk is found in a list of fifty names that extol his incomparable nature. He is creator, commander, Lord of all the gods of heaven and netherworld.

The Babylonian Story and the Baal Cycle

Though the Canaanite Baal Cycle and the Mesopotamian Enuma Elish differ in many respects, the connections between the two are substantial enough that many scholars suggest they must derive from a common tradition. Even if this point of connection does not lie in a shared literary antecedent, it is clear that the two draw from a common reservoir of mythic traditions. Nowhere is this overlap more evident than in the motif of the divine battle against the sea.[28] At the heart of the Baal Cycle and Enuma Elish lie the accounts of Baal's fight against Yamm and Marduk's fight against Tiamat. In both cases, the protagonists in the accounts are gods of the storm. As we saw earlier, Baal was regarded by the Canaanites as the god of the thunderstorm, the deity famous for his thunderous voice and his arrow-like bolts of lightning. Marduk was also cast as god of the storm.[29] It is noteworthy as well that the antagonists in the two accounts are the ones who initiate the divine conflict. It is Yamm who demands that El turn over Baal to be his servant, thus provoking the ensuing battle. Likewise, it is Apsu and then Tiamat who attack the descendant gods and force the devastating response from Marduk.

A second connection between the Baal Cycle and Enuma Elish lies in the area of kingship. In both accounts, the conquering heroes are declared king of the gods. There are significant differences, to be sure, between the kingship of Baal and the kingship of Marduk, and we will have to consider the reasons for these differences below. For now, though, it is enough to note that elevation to kingship is a central theme of both traditions. Closely connected with this elevation to kingship is the construction of a temple for the victorious gods. When Baal has defeated Yamm, his victory is ultimately sealed through Kothar-wa-Hasis' construction of his great palace on the heights of Mount Zaphon. Marduk's victory and his kingship over the gods are affirmed as well in the construction of his Esagila temple in Babylon.

One additional connection, and an important one, is the link in both accounts between the sea and dragons. As we have already seen, the Canaanite traditions draw a connection between the sea god Yamm, on the one hand, and the sea monster Tunnan and dragon-like Lītān/Leviathan, on the other. A similar relationship with dragon-like creatures can be posited for the Mesopotamian Tiamat as well. Although Tiamat is said to create a variety of monsters to aid her, first in the list are always the Hydra, the dragon, and giant serpents, suggesting that these resemble the mother who gave birth to them (I.133–143; II.19–30; III.23–34, 82–92). Tiamat's dangerous maw and long tail only add to this connection (IV.65; V.59). The fact that Marduk uses a net to capture Tiamat, as one would a sea creature, also points in this direction.[30] Apart from these details in the text of the Epic itself, a variety of Mesopotamian cylinder seals and reliefs feature depictions of gods battling a dragon or standing over the dragon's defeated form. It seems likely that many of these are meant to portray Marduk and his nemesis Tiamat.[31]

The Babylonian Story and the Bible: Combat and Creation

Where the Baal Cycle and Enuma Elish part company is in the emphasis on creation that is evident in the latter but not in the former. Creation accounts typically include motifs related to providing for the continued care of creation, and the Baal Cycle does touch upon these, as the construction of Baal's palace appears to regularize the provision of seasonal rains. There is nothing in the Baal Cycle, however, that approaches the extensive description of creation found in Enuma Elish. Where we do find another link between the battle against sea and dragon, on the one hand, and creation, on the other, is in the Bible itself. As we have already seen, a number of biblical texts present God's defeat of the sea and/or sea monster as part and parcel of God's creative work. Psalm 74:13–15 presents God as defeating the sea, dragons, and Leviathan:

> You broke the sea by your might;
>> you shattered the heads of the dragons in the waters.
> You crushed the heads of Leviathan;
>> you gave him as food for the creatures of the sea.
> You split open spring and wadi;
>> you dried up ever-flowing rivers.

The battle won, God then goes on in vv. 16–17 to establish creation:

> Yours is the day, yours also the night;
>> you established luminary and sun.
> You have fixed all the boundaries of the earth;
>> summer and winter—you made them.

Psalm 89:9–10 [10–11] contains a similar description of God's fight against sea and dragon:

> You rule the raging of the sea;
>> when its waves rise, you still them.
> You crushed Rahab like a carcass;
>> you scattered your enemies with your mighty arm.

And in vv. 11–12 [12–13], this is again followed by praise for God's creating the world:

> The heavens are yours; the earth also is yours;
>> the world and all that is in it—you have founded them.
> The north and the south—you created them;
>> Tabor and Hermon sing forth your name.

Job 26:12–13 depicts God as defeating the sea, Rahab, and the serpent:

> By his power he stilled the sea;
>> by his understanding he struck down Rahab.

> By his wind the heavens were made fair;
>> his hand pierced the fleeing serpent.

Again, this combat is set right in the midst of Job's description of God's creative activity in vv. 7–11:

> He stretches out Zaphon over emptiness,
>> and hangs the earth upon nothing.
> He binds up the waters in his thick clouds,
>> and the cloud is not split open by them.
> He covers the face of the full moon,
>> and spreads over it his cloud.
> He has described a circle on the face of the waters,
>> at the boundary between light and darkness.
> The pillars of heaven tremble;
>> they are astounded at his rebuke.

In Job 9, God is the one who "alone stretched out the heavens" (v. 8a) and the one who "made the Bear and Orion, the Pleiades and the constellations of the south" (v. 9). But he is also the one who "trampled the waves of the sea" (v. 8b) and the one of whom it is said, "Beneath him bowed the helpers of Rahab" (v. 13).

The strong connection in these passages between creation and combat with the sea suggests that Enuma Elish has supplied an element of backstory for the biblical authors that is simply not found in the extant Canaanite texts.[32] To be sure, the Canaanite traditions appear to form a backdrop for much of the Bible's description of God's battle against the sea. In some respects, it can be said that these Canaanite traditions supply the imagery and vocabulary of the biblical accounts.[33] It is only in the Mesopotamian traditions, however, that we see the defeat of the sea and the dragon linked specifically to the creation of the cosmos. It appears that to the early Canaanite traditions of divine combat, the Bible has added the later Mesopotamian traditions of combat followed by creation.

The Babylonian Story and the Bible: Kingship

A second and, I will argue, related area in which the Bible connects more readily with Babylonian rather than Canaanite traditions is in the Bible's depictions of God as king. As we have already seen, there may well be echoes of the Canaanite elevation of Baal to kingship after his defeat of

Yamm in the Bible's own descriptions of God's kingship. However, there are reasons to believe that the Babylonian traditions may have been even more influential in this regard. At issue is the nature of the kingship conferred upon Baal and Marduk.

The pronouncement of Baal's kingship is, without question, a key element in the Canaanite Baal Cycle. The goddess Asherah, for example, says of Baal:

> Our king is mighty Baal.
>> (He is) our ruler, and there is none above him.
>
> $(KTU\ 1.4\ IV,\ 43-44)$

The extravagance of this proclamation is tempered, though, by the fact that Baal's kingship is neither exclusive nor absolute. The craftsman god Kothar-wa-Hasis is depicted as seated on a throne ruling Memphis and Kaphtor (Crete).[34] Similarly, the god Athtar is said to exercise kingship over a limited realm, which he maintains despite his inability to achieve supreme rulership.[35] And Baal's opponent Mot, the god of death, has his own realm over which he exercises kingship.[36]

Most important as a limiting factor in Baal's exercise of kingship is the kingship attributed to the chief god El.[37] It is clear throughout the Baal Cycle that El retains ultimate authority over the pantheon and reigns as its true king. It is El who has the power to hand Baal over to Yamm ($KTU\ 1.2\ I,\ 36$), and it is El who authorizes the construction of Yamm's palace ($KTU\ 1.2\ III,\ 7$). When El elevates Yamm, the god Athtar is warned not to challenge him, lest El depose him from his throne and demote him from kingship ($KTU\ 1.2\ III,\ 17$). The same warning is issued to Mot later in the story when he prolongs his attacks against Baal ($KTU\ 1.6\ VI,\ 28-29$). Most importantly, even when Baal defeats Yamm, it is still to El that he must appeal for a palace of his own, and he is forced to enlist the aid of Anat and Athirat to help plead his case. Baal's continued subordination to El is evident as he is said to cry out "to Bull El, his father, to El, the king who established him" ($KTU\ 1.3\ V, 35-36;\ 1.4\ I,\ 5$). As she appeals to El on Baal's behalf, Athirat will use identical language to affirm El's continued rule over Baal ($KTU\ 1.4\ IV,\ 47-48$).

The kingship to which Marduk ascends in Enuma Elish is of an entirely different character than that of Baal. Marduk's destiny is signaled from the moment of his birth, recounted in Tablet I, as the author devotes more than twenty lines to a description of his superlative features. His lineage traces its way back through the greatest of the ancestor gods (at least by Enuma Elish's reckoning): Ea, son of Anu, son of Anshar. Marduk is "mighty from the beginning," "perfect," "remarkable in divinity," and "superior in comparison to the gods" (I.81–104). His elevation to kingship is then charted over a long span of text centering on his defeat of Tiamat and his subsequent creation of the world. When he first appears before Anshar to secure his blessing for the battle with Tiamat, Marduk demands as his reward for victory kingship over the gods: "Convene an assembly, and proclaim for me an exalted destiny." Lest there be any doubt about his ruling as some sort of co-regent or subordinate king, he insists, "Let me, with my utterance, decree destinies *instead of you*" (II.155–162). It is precisely this that the most ancient deities agree to do for Marduk (III.138).[38] Even before Marduk engages Tiamat in battle, the gods assemble to confer kingship on him:

> They set a princely dais for him;
>> he took his place before his fathers for kingship.
>
> (IV.1–2)

They go on to say:

> You are Marduk, our avenger;
>> we have given you kingship over all and everything.
>
> (IV.13–14)

When Marduk does defeat Tiamat, his kingship is confirmed by the gods.[39] The ancient gods embrace him and declare his title to be "Victorious King" (V.79), then the younger gods bow down before him and proclaim, "Behold the king" (V.88). The ancient gods announce, "Previously Marduk was our beloved son, now he is your king; heed his command!" (V.110). The supreme nature of Marduk's kingship is underscored by the fact that he establishes the realms of creation, dictates which god will rule over each one, and decrees where their temples will be (Tablets V–VI). Finally, in the recitation of the fifty names of Marduk (Tablets VI–VII), it is evident that the powers formerly held by other deities have now begun to coalesce in the person of the one deity Marduk.

The kingship of Marduk is one that is absolute. He rules over all the gods, even the ancestral deities, and over all creation. Baal's kingship, on the other hand, is provisional. His realm is limited to the highlands that receive his rains, and his exercise of authority is limited to those areas that El allots to him. It is likely that a number of factors led to the distinction between the kinds of kingship enjoyed by Marduk and Baal. The depiction of Baal as god of the thunderstorm may have been so strong as to impede the development of a Baal theology that could transcend this meteorological connection. Given the seasonal nature of the rain in the Levant, a deity permanently tied to the thunderstorm would of necessity have been prevented from exercising absolute control over the pantheon. After all, as the meteorological component of the Baal Cycle indicates, when the storm (Baal) moves east into the desert (connected with Mot), he dies.[40] While Marduk is also cast as a storm god, the connection between Marduk and the storm is much more tenuous. Marduk's storms are merely weapons or forces that he deploys in his conquests; they are not rains bound to a particular season. As a result, Marduk's role in the Babylonian pantheon could be more easily expanded.

An additional factor that contributed to the distinction between Baal and Marduk was simply the nature of the developing pantheons in Ugarit and Babylon. The Canaanite pantheon as it existed at Ugarit was still very much formed along the lines of a royal family, with El as the king and *pater familias*; his wife, Asherah, as the queen mother; and his various children and their associates vying for position at court. El's permissive manner toward Yamm, Baal, Anat, and Mot looks like nothing if not the shrewd machinations of a king balancing the competing claims of ambitious members of the peerage. Baal's exercise of kingship fits the mold of a crown prince, eager to rule but still subject to the dictates of the king. The nature of the pantheon depicted in Enuma Elish is quite different from that found at Ugarit. Here, familial relations are only important as they chart the lineage of Marduk. When the gods who precede Marduk turn over kingship to him, family ties recede into the background. Marduk's rule is absolute, and no further jockeying for position is permitted. Viewed from another angle, it can rightly be said that the extraordinary elevation of Marduk in Enuma Elish is a step in the direction of monotheism. The fifty names accorded to Marduk at the end of Enuma Elish include several names of deities whose identities and attributes are simply absorbed by Marduk. Marduk is not yet a monotheistic deity in Enuma Elish, but the coalescing of other deities in the person of Marduk and the growing distance between the character of Marduk and that of the gods he rules are steps in that direction. The result of this is that Marduk quite naturally enjoys a form of kingship that far outstrips that held by Baal.

Lastly, the absolute nature of Marduk's kingship is also linked to his role as a creator deity. Early in Enuma Elish, Ea addresses his father, Anshar, the god who to this point had acted as the de facto king of the gods, praising Anshar's creative power:

My father, unfathomable, who decrees destiny,
> who has the power to create and to destroy,
Anshar, unfathomable, who decrees destiny,
> who has the power to create and to destroy.
>> (II.61–64)

Later, as the ancestral deities prepare to confer kingship on Marduk, they hold out one pivotal test:

In their midst, they set up a certain constellation.
> To Marduk, their firstborn, they spoke,
"Your destiny, O Lord, shall be foremost of all the gods;
> destruction and creation—command and let it take place.
At your command, let the constellation disappear;
> at your command again, let the constellation reappear."
>> (IV.19–24)

Although the gods have already begun the process of making Marduk king, before his kingship can be affirmed he must exercise the power of creation by destroying and then re-creating a constellation. In the lines that follow, Marduk passes this crucial test:

He commanded and the constellation disappeared;
> he commanded again, and the constellation came into
>> being again.
When the gods, his fathers, saw his command,
> they rejoiced and hailed, "Marduk is the king!"
>> (IV.25–28)

It is Marduk's ability to create that affirms the worthiness of his claim to kingship. Marduk demonstrates this worthiness again as he defeats Tiamat and then creates the world from her carcass. Not to be missed, though, is the fact that Marduk is only heralded as king once he has performed the task of creation, *not* when he has bested Tiamat. Only after his creative work is accomplished do the gods proclaim him "Victorious King" and announce, "Behold the king!" (V.79, 88). Other deities, both in Mesopotamia and in Canaan, were lauded for defeating powerful enemies like the sea.[41] It is the combination of this victory *with the exercise of the power of creation*, however, that distinguished Marduk as the ultimate king over the gods.

The texts in which the Bible's depiction of God as king is connected with his victory over sea and dragon tell us that the biblical authors were influenced by the kingship traditions prominent among Israel's ancient neighbors. The influence of the Canaanite tradition of Baal's ascension to the throne after his defeat of Yamm and Lītān is evident in the language and imagery of the biblical texts, especially as these texts refer to the Sea (Yamm), Leviathan (Lītān), and *tannîn* (*tunnan*). The Canaanite traditions alone, though, cannot account for the style of kingship the biblical authors attribute to Israel's God. Here, there is a strong case to be made that the Babylonian traditions embodied in Enuma Elish have influenced the Bible as well. The Bible accords an absolute kingship to YHWH comparable to that held by Marduk. Most importantly, the Bible regularly links YHWH's kingship to his rule over the sea *and* to his creative work. In Psalm 74:12, the psalmist cries out, "God my king is *from of old*," apparently echoing the same primordial setting envisioned by Enuma Elish. The psalmist then goes on in vv. 16–17 to praise God for his work in creation. Psalm 89 strikes a similar tone. Though it does not use the title "king," it praises God for his incomparability, his unmatched rule over all the hosts of heaven (vv. 5–8 [6–9]). Then, the psalmist goes on to praise God for his work in creation (cf. vv. 11–12 [12–13]). Yet another psalm, Psalm 93, begins by exclaiming:

> YHWH is king, he is robed with majesty;
>> YHWH is robed, he has girded himself with strength.
> The world is established;
>> it shall never be moved.
> Your throne is established *from of old*;
>> you are *everlasting*.
>
> (Ps 93:1–2)

This language is particularly significant as the psalm goes on, in vv. 3–4, to link together divine kingship, God's rule over the sea, and creation:

> The floods have lifted up, O YHWH,
>> the floods have lifted up their voice;
>> the floods lift up their roaring.
> Mightier than the voice of mighty waters,
>> mightier than the waves of the sea,
>> YHWH on high is mighty!

We see a similar connection in Psalm 95:3–5, as the psalmist addresses God as king, praises him for his creative work, and affirms his control of the sea:

> For YHWH is a great God,
>> and a great king above all gods.
> In his hand are the depths of the earth;
>> the heights of the mountains are also his.
> The sea is his, for he made it,
>> and his hands formed the dry land.

Psalm 96:10 contains a similar link between creation and kingship:[42]

> Say among the nations,
>> "YHWH is king!
> The world is firmly established;
>> it shall never be moved."

Psalm 24 begins with creation and ends with kingship:

> The earth is YHWH's and all its fullness,
>> the world, and those who dwell in it;
> for he has founded it on the seas,
>> and established it on the rivers.
>
> (vv. 1–2)

> Lift up your heads, O gates!
>> And be lifted up, O ancient doors!
>> —that the king of glory may come in.
> Who is this king of glory?
>> YHWH, mighty and valiant,
>> YHWH, valiant in battle.
> Lift up your heads, O gates!
>> And be lifted up, O ancient doors!
>> —that the king of glory may come in.
> Who is this king of glory?
>> YHWH of hosts.
> He is the king of glory!
>
> (vv. 7–10)

The Bible repeatedly connects celebrations of God's kingship with celebrations of his role as creator. Of particular importance is the fact that the kingship envisioned here is not the sort of limited kingship enjoyed by Baal. When YHWH is cast as the creator-king, his kingship is on par with that of Marduk. As we will see below, there is an important reason for this parallel.

The Babylonian Story and the Bible: Additional Echoes

The primary ties between the biblical creation traditions we have considered and Enuma Elish are the connections between creation and the defeat of the sea/dragon and between creation and kingship. It is interesting to consider, however, whether there may be additional, less prominent echoes of Enuma Elish in our texts as well. In Enuma Elish, it is first and foremost with his *winds* that Marduk subdues Tiamat (IV.43–48); in the midst of a passage describing God's defeat of the sea, Rahab, and serpent, Job insists, "*By his wind* the heavens were made fair" (Job 26:12–13). As terrifying as Tiamat in Enuma Elish are the dreadful monsters she spawns to aid her (I.133–143; II.19–30; III.23–34, 82–92); it is noteworthy that when Job despairs of confronting God, he laments, "God will not turn back his anger; *the helpers of Rahab bowed beneath him.* How then can I answer him, choosing my words with him?" (Job 9:13–14). So terrifying is Tiamat in Enuma Elish that the gods quail at the sight of her; in its description of Leviathan, the book of Job observes, "*Even the gods were overwhelmed* at the sight of him," and "When he rises up, *the gods are afraid*; at the crashing, they retreat" (Job 41:9, 25 [1, 17]).

Of particular note among these "additional echoes" of Enuma Elish in the biblical creation accounts is the emphasis both give to the ordering of the celestial bodies. As noted above, the initial test of Marduk's creative powers is the destruction and re-creation of a constellation (IV.19–28). When Tiamat is finally slain, Marduk's first creative acts revolve around creating the heavens (IV.137–146) and arranging the sun, moon, and stars that inhabit them (V.1–46). In the biblical passages that echo God's combat against the sea, God's creative work in the heavens is also emphasized. Psalm 74:16 proclaims: "Yours is the day, yours also the night; you established luminary and sun." In Job 9, a passage that speaks of God's confronting both the sea (v. 8) and Rahab (v. 13), God is also praised as:

> He who commands the sun, and it does not rise;
>   who seals up the stars;

who alone stretches out the heavens
>   and tramples the heights of the sea;
who makes the Bear and Orion,
>   the Pleiades and the chambers of the south.

(vv. 7–9)

In the divine speeches that form the closing chapters of Job, God draws Job's attention to the dragon Leviathan and boasts of his control of the unruly sea. He also demands of Job:

Can you bind the chains of the Pleiades,
>   or loose the cords of Orion?
Can you lead forth the Mazzaroth in their season,
>   or can you guide the Bear with its children?
Do you know the ordinances of the heavens?
>   Can you establish their rule on the earth?

(Job 38:31–33)

We have previously seen that Job 26 describes God's striking Rahab and piercing the fleeing serpent. Importantly, this same passage also speaks of God's handiwork in the heavens (vv. 7–11):

He stretches out Zaphon over the void,
>   and hangs the earth upon nothing.
He binds up the waters in his thick clouds,
>   and the cloud is not split open by them.
He covers the face of the full moon
>   and spreads his cloud over it.
He has described a circle on the face of the waters,
>   at the boundary between light and darkness.
The pillars of heaven tremble
>   and are astounded at his rebuke.

Alone, elements such as the wind of God, the helpers of Rahab, divine terror in the face of Leviathan, and the attention given to the creation of the celestial bodies would not be enough to posit a connection between the Bible and Enuma Elish. Alongside the more important echoes noted above, however, they may well serve as supporting evidence, bolstering the case for a connection between these two traditions.

Summary

In a topic as complicated as Canaanite and Babylonian mythology, it is easy to get lost in a forest of strange deities, odd deeds, and obscure decrees. If we step back for a moment, though, there is an important "big picture" that should not be missed. As we look at some of the poetic materials in the Bible—Psalms, Job, the Prophets—we find a collection of unusual texts in which God battles not only the sea (which would be odd enough) but also dragons called Leviathan, Rahab, and *tannîn*. Just as peculiar is the fact that these episodes of divine combat are regularly associated with God's creation of the world. A careful reader must surely ask just what in the world these odd texts could be describing.

The answer to this question lies in our recognizing that there is a backstory to this imagery. This backstory is not found in the Bible itself, but rather in the traditions of Israel's Canaanite and Mesopotamian neighbors. Among the Canaanites, Baal was said to have fought the sea god Yamm, a god who was linked to the dragons Lītān and Tunnan. It was Baal's defeat of Yamm and the dragon(s) that led to his being declared king of the gods. Among the Babylonians, it was Marduk who fought against the sea goddess Tiamat, a deity who was herself connected with dragons. Marduk not only defeated Tiamat, he also went on to use her carcass to create the world. In return, Marduk received a status as king that far outstripped the limited kingship enjoyed by Baal. Marduk was made an absolute ruler, not merely a crown prince.

The connection between the Bible and these Canaanite and Babylonian traditions is readily apparent. The Scriptures repeatedly echo the images of divine combat preserved in these extrabiblical texts. Like Baal and Marduk, God fights against and defeats both sea and dragon; and as is the case for both of these deities, God's kingship is confirmed through his martial victories. But if the Bible borrows the *vocabulary* of the Canaanite texts—Hebrew *yām*, *liwyātān* (Leviathan), and *tannîn* as cognates of the Ugaritic terms Yamm, Lītān, and Tunnan—it borrows the *imagery of God as creator-king* from Babylon. Like Marduk, God's kingship is tied both to his victory over the sea *and to his work in creating the world*. And like Marduk, God's kingship is declared to be *absolute* and not provisional. That the Bible draws upon these traditions—traditions, I stipulate, not necessarily texts—of Israel's neighbors seems beyond dispute. The lingering question, though, is why the Bible would do so. What was it that led the biblical authors to echo to such an extensive degree these strange Canaanite and Babylonian notions?

CHAPTER 5

Why These Traditions?

In the New Testament book of Acts, a book full of fascinating twists and turns, the account of Paul's speech before the Areopagus in chapter 17 is particularly interesting. As Luke recounts the story,[1] Paul finds himself in Acts 17:15 stranded in the Greek city of Athens, waiting for his traveling companions to rejoin him. Never one just to sit idly by, Paul becomes a regular feature both in the local synagogue, where he argues with his fellow Jews, and in the *agora*, the Athenian marketplace, where he argues with gentiles. Paul's persistent prodding eventually brings him to the attention of the Athenian philosophers. When some of the philosophers ask, "What does this babbler[2] want to say?" and others reply, "He seems to be a proclaimer of foreign divinities," they finally bring Paul before the Areopagus to give an account of his teaching.[3] The way in which Paul responds to the Epicureans and Stoics who question him may offer some insight into the matter of why Babylonian and Canaanite traditions appear so frequently in the pages of the Hebrew Bible.

Speaking in the Language of One's Neighbors

Luke tells us that as Paul had walked around the streets of Athens, he was distressed to see the many idols that filled the city (v. 16). Criticism of these idols forms the heart of Paul's challenge to the members of the Areopagus.[4] He begins in vv. 22–23:

> Men of Athens, I observe how very religious you are in every way. For as I passed through the city and looked carefully at the objects of your

worship, I found an altar on which was inscribed, "To an unknown god." What therefore you worship as unknown, this I proclaim to you.

From this introduction, Paul proceeds to use the ideas of the Epicureans and Stoics, the very groups who had challenged him in Athens, to defend the beliefs of Christianity.[5]

When Paul argues in v. 24 that "the God who made the world and everything in it, being Lord of heaven and earth, does not live in shrines made by human hands," he is echoing the arguments made by Greek philosophers like Heraclitus (ca. 540–480 BCE), who maintained:

> You ignorant men, don't you know that god is not wrought by hands, and has not from the beginning had a pedestal, and does not have a single enclosure? Rather the whole world is his temple, decorated with animals, plants, and stars.[6]

When Paul goes on to say in v. 25, "Nor is he served by human hands, as though he needed anything, since he himself gives to all life and breath and all things," he is speaking in the same language that the Stoic Seneca (4 BCE–65 CE) used:

> But let us forbid lamps to be lighted on the Sabbath, since the gods do not need light, neither do men take pleasure in soot. Let us forbid men to offer morning salutation and to throng the doors of temples; mortal ambitions are attracted by such ceremonies, but God is worshipped by those who truly know Him. Let us forbid bringing towels and flesh-scrapers to Jupiter, and proffering mirrors to Juno; for God seeks no servants. Of course not; he himself does service to mankind, everywhere and to all he is at hand to help.
>
> (Seneca, *Ep.* 95.47 [Gummere, LCL])

Even more explicit is v. 28, as Paul alerts his audience to the fact that he is quoting one of their own philosophers: "For 'in him we live and move and have our being'; as even some of your own poets have said, 'For we too are his offspring.'" The grammar of the verse is sufficiently ambiguous as to make it unclear whether Paul intends to quote two poets or one. If the first half of the verse, "In him we live and move and have our being," is intended as a quotation, the Greek text from which it derives appears not to have survived. The sentiments it expresses, though, accord well with Stoic thought. Epictetus (ca. 55–135 CE), for example, maintains:[7]

But if our souls are so bound up with God and joined together with Him, as being parts and portions of His being, does not God perceive their every motion as being a motion of that which is His own and of one body with Himself?

(Epictetus, *Diatr.* 1.14.6 [Oldfather, LCL])

The second half of the verse, "For we too are his offspring," is a direct quote from the poet Aratus (*Phaen.* 5), who lived ca. 315–240 BCE and who was actually a student of Zeno, the philosopher to whom Stoicism traces its origins. These same ideas are expressed by another Stoic, Cleanthes, who lived ca. 330–232 BCE:

Zeus, lord of nature, who governs the universe according to law, all hail! It is fitting to praise you, for we are indeed all your offspring, and we alone, of all that lives and moves here on earth, are endowed with speech.[8]

(Cleanthes, *Hymn to Zeus* 1–8 [*SVF* 1.537])

Paul's interaction with the Athenian philosophers is a study in contrasts from the way he is said to have dealt with his fellow Jews in the synagogue. In Acts 17:2, Luke tells us that Paul went to the synagogue in Thessalonica, as was his custom, and there "he argued with them *from the Scriptures.*" This was his practice again in Berea, where—as vv. 10–11 tell us—he *examined the Scriptures* with his fellow Jews in the synagogue. This was doubtless his approach in Athens as well as he argued with his fellow Jews in the synagogue (v. 17). Yet, when Paul debates with the gentile philosophers of the Areopagus, neither Luke nor Paul ever explicitly mentions the Scriptures. Core beliefs from the Hebrew Scriptures permeate Paul's message to the Athenians, but when Paul speaks to the these gentile philosophers, his language is that of Athens not Jerusalem.[9]

When Paul spoke to the philosophers of the Areopagus, he addressed them in a style and a language that they would understand; he spoke in the language of his neighbors. To return now to our discussion of the Hebrew Bible, it seems likely that some of the Canaanite and Babylonian language found there was meant to serve a similar purpose. Unlike the audience of Paul's sermon in Acts, the audiences of the various passages we have considered in Psalms, Job, and the Prophets likely would not have consisted of the actual nations whose traditions were being used. They would, however, have included Israelites who had been influenced by these traditions. Because the Canaanites and Israelites emerged from the same geographical and cultural matrix, Canaanite influence on Israel's religion was long lived and extensive.[10] As waves of Assyrian and Babylonian imperial conquest washed over Israel and Judah beginning in the eighth century BCE, Mesopotamian influence grew increasingly important as well.[11] This influence was naturally at its peak as the upper classes of Judah were exiled to Babylon during the sixth century. Importantly, nearly all of the creation texts we have considered thus far appear to have been composed during this period of extensive Mesopotamian influence. An Israelite author discussing creation in this period might well have felt the need to speak in the language of Israel's neighbors to be properly understood.

Though not concerned with creation, one example of speaking in the language of one's neighbors is found in the book of Hosea. As he prophesies against the Northern Kingdom, Israel, Hosea regularly makes use of language associated with Baal. In the last episode of the Baal Cycle, the god Baal, fresh from his victory over Yamm and newly ensconced in his palace on Mount Zaphon, overplays his hand by demanding obeisance from Mot, the god of death.[12] Mot rebuffs Baal's demand and threatens Baal in turn. Now it is Baal whose safety is in danger. Through an elaborate ruse, Baal manages to escape Mot's attacks, but he is forced to hide in the one place Mot would never think to look for him: the netherworld itself. The other gods, unaware that Baal has gone into hiding, think he has instead been devoured by Mot. El and Anat weep for Baal, mourning his death by wearing sackcloth and ashes and gashing themselves with pieces of flint. With the death, or at least the disappearance, of Baal, rainfall ceases, and attempts at irrigation are insufficient to prevent the land from withering and dying as well. It is only when the goddess Anat attacks Mot and demands the return of Baal that the storm god's fructifying rains finally return.

Hosea alludes to this imagery from the Baal Cycle repeatedly as he condemns the people of Israel for worshiping this Canaanite deity. In Hosea 6:1–3, for example, the prophet declares:

> Come, let us return to YHWH;
>> for it is he who has torn, but he will heal us;
>> he has struck down, but he will bind us up.
> *He will bring us back to life* on the second day;
>> on the third day *he will raise us up*
>> *that we may live* before him.
> Let us know, let us press on to know YHWH;
>> like the dawn, his appearing is sure;

he will come to us *like the showers*,
   like the spring rains that water the earth.

The language of reviving and resurrecting in v. 2 is surely not chosen at random. The prophet's "he will bring us back to life" and "he will raise us up that we may live" echo the language of Baal's revival and reappearance in the Baal Cycle. This echo is reinforced by Hosea's reference in v. 3 to the return of the spring rains: "He will come to us like the showers, like the spring rains that water the earth." It was the return of the seasonal rains that signaled for the Canaanites (and, unfortunately, for Baal-worshiping Israelites) Baal's return to life.

A similar example of using the language of the Canaanites is found in Hosea 13. Here, the prophet gives voice to YHWH's pronouncement of judgment upon the people of Israel. God insists that he was the one who brought the nation out of Egypt and led the people in the wilderness, yet they have forgotten him (vv. 4–6). Now, God promises not to bless but to punish (vv. 7–13). He asks rhetorically in v. 14:

Shall I ransom them from the hand of Sheol?
   Shall I redeem them from Death?
Where are your plagues, O Death?
   Where is your pestilence, O Sheol?
Compassion is hidden from my eyes.

The Hebrew word for *Death* in this passage, *môt*, is the same term now familiar to us from the Baal Cycle as *mot*, the Ugaritic word for "death," and, perhaps more importantly, as *Mot*, the Canaanite god of Death. Just as importantly, the term *sheol* is one of the Hebrew terms for the netherworld.[13] Together, Môt and Sheol provide such a strong echo of Baal's conflict with Death that it is difficult to know whether the prophet here intends merely to personify Death and the netherworld or whether he is, in fact, metaphorically summoning *the god Mot* to bring destruction.[14] The prophet need not actually believe in the existence of Mot to do so; he is merely using the language of Baal and his deathly enemy to highlight the judgment that is coming (v. 15):

Although he [Ephraim/Israel] flourishes among rushes,[15]
   the east wind shall come, the wind of YHWH,
      rising from the wilderness.

And his fountain shall dry up,
>   his spring shall be parched.
It shall plunder his storeroom
>   of every precious thing.

The effects of God's summoning Mot to judge Israel are identical to those that afflict the land in the Baal Cycle as Baal goes into the netherworld: drought devastates the land, drying up fountain and spring and stripping storerooms of their produce.

Some of the echoes of the Baal Cycle are so deeply embedded in Hosea's language that they are not apparent in translation.[16] This is particularly evident in the allusion found in Hosea 2:16 [18]. Here, the New International Version translates the text this way:

"In that day," declares the LORD,
>   "you will call me 'my husband';
>   you will no longer call me 'my master.' "

A surface reading of this text might point to a day when Israel would enjoy a more intimate relationship with God ("my husband") than she does now ("my master"). As we dig deeper into the text, however, we see this is not the point of the verse at all. God does not reject the term "master" here because it lacks intimacy; he rejects it because it is the Hebrew word *ba'al*. While we know the word *ba'al* primarily as the name of the famous Canaanite god, it is actually a common word that simply means *master, owner,* or *husband.* It only secondarily came to serve as the proper name Baal. But it is this secondary association that presents a problem. God's insistence here is that Israel's dalliance with Baal has been so offensive that he intends to banish the term *ba'al* from the nation's vocabulary altogether. God is Israel's husband, but he will not be addressed as *ba'al*, whether that term can mean husband or not. A different word—in this case, another Hebrew word for husband, *'îš*—will have to do.

The concentration of Baal-related language and themes in the book of Hosea is not difficult to explain. For those who dwelled on the rich and well-watered farmland in the north of Israel, there was an enduring temptation to worship the god Baal alongside or even in place of YHWH. Hosea intends to rebuke the people for breaking covenant with YHWH to worship Baal, and so he infuses his prophetic oracles with language drawn from the stories the Canaanites themselves told about their deity. He speaks in the language of Israel's neighbors to underscore the themes in his own message.

Co-Opting Traditions

Simply speaking in the language of one's neighbors, however, does not fully capture the reason for the Bible's incorporation of these foreign traditions. If we return to Paul's speech before the Areopagus, it is interesting to note that Paul quotes and paraphrases the ideas of the Epicurean and Stoic philosophers *for a particular effect,* namely, to marshal their ideas against his Athenian opponents.[17] A similar dynamic seems to be at work in the Bible's use of Canaanite traditions related to Baal and Babylonian traditions related to Marduk. There is undoubtedly an element of speaking in the language of one's neighbors involved in our texts. More important than this, however, is the way these texts *co-opt* the Baal and Marduk imagery, taking over this imagery to make the case that it is the God of Israel who bears the characteristics and accomplishes the deeds they have attributed to Baal and Marduk.

Elijah and the Prophets of Baal

One passage in which we see this dynamic vividly at work is 1 Kings 17–18, the account of Elijah's contest with the prophets of Baal.[18] The persistent temptation to worship Baal that plagued the Northern Kingdom, Israel, was due in part to the fact that the northern reaches of Israel bordered the southern reaches of Phoenicia, the territory where the worship of Baal figured most prominently. Because the Phoenician Canaanites and the northern Israelites shared the same geography and climate, their cultures and religions tended to overlap greatly as well. Although the picture of Israel presented in movies and television shows is often one of barren sand dunes and desolate cities of stone, the coastal and northern areas of Israel are actually quite fertile and productive. Difficult as it may be to believe, northern Israel receives more than twice as much rain on average each year as do locales like London, Paris, and Berlin. Economically, the result of this abundant rain was a heavy reliance on agriculture; northern Israel was blanketed with farms producing grain for bread, grapes for wine, olive trees for oil, and sheep and cattle. Religiously, Israel's rains produced a strong temptation to venerate the deity best known for bringing rain, Baal, god of the thunderstorm.

As discussed above, the book of Hosea vividly illustrates the consequences of this temptation. Hosea uses marital imagery to describe the relationship between God and Israel, characterizing the nation's turn toward Baal as tantamount to spiritual adultery. The prophet charges:

For their mother has played the whore;
    she who conceived them has acted shamefully.
For she said, "I will go after my lovers,
    the ones who give me my bread and my water,
    my wool and my flax, my oil and my drink."

(Hos 2:5)

Hosea catalogs the agricultural blessings Israel has enjoyed, but he argues the nation has abandoned the true source of those blessings. Speaking for YHWH, he insists:

She did not acknowledge that I was the one who gave her
    the grain, the wine, and the oil.
I lavished upon her silver
    and gold that they used for Baal!

(Hos 2:8)

The prophet goes on to threaten the punishment that will surely come if the nation continues to worship Baal:

Therefore I will take back
    my grain in its time,
    and my wine in its season;
and I will snatch away my wool and my flax,
    which were to cover her nakedness.
. . .
I will devastate her vines and her fig trees,
    of which she said,
"These are my fee
    that my lovers have given me."
I will turn them into a forest,
    and the wild animals shall devour them.
I will punish her for the festival days of the Baals,
    when she offered incense to them
and decked herself with her ring and her jewelry
    and went after her lovers
    and forgot me, declares YHWH.

(Hos 2:9, 12–13 [11, 14–15])

If the nation persists in giving Baal credit for the blessings YHWH has provided, the prophet warns, YHWH will strip those blessings away.

There is an element of co-opting tradition in Hosea's insistence that it was YHWH, not Baal, who provided the rains that gave Israel her fertility.[19] It is the prophet Elijah, however, who co-opts the Baal traditions in much more dramatic fashion. The story of Elijah is directly tied to that of Israel's most infamous king and queen, Ahab and Jezebel. The closing verses of 1 Kings 16 tell us that Jezebel was the daughter of King Ethbaal of Sidon, one of the prominent city-states in Phoenicia. As one might expect for a Phoenician princess, Jezebel was a devotee of Baal.[20] The strength of her devotion to Baal and the power of her influence over the Israelite nation was apparently felt immediately. The author of 1 Kings notes:

> And as if it had been a small thing for him to walk in the sins of Jeroboam son of Nebat, Ahab took as his wife Jezebel daughter of Ethbaal, king of the Sidonians, and went and served Baal and worshiped him. He set up an altar for Baal in the temple of Baal that he built in Samaria. Ahab also made a sacred pole. Ahab did more to provoke YHWH, the God of Israel, to anger than had all the kings of Israel who were before him.
>
> (1 Kgs 16:31–33)

As books like Hosea indicate, there was a long-standing tendency in Israel for people to worship both Baal and YHWH. The persecution of the prophets of YHWH alluded to in passages like 1 Kings 18:4 ("When Jezebel was killing off the prophets of YHWH . . .") tells us that Jezebel was no longer interested in maintaining this liturgical détente. Her mission was to promote the worship of Baal and, if possible, stamp out the worship of his rival, YHWH, altogether.

It was Jezebel's malign intentions that prompted the man who would become her chief antagonist to take the stage. In the very next paragraph after Jezebel's entrance, we meet for the first time the prophet Elijah. With a name that meant "My God is YHWH," Elijah was bound to stir up trouble for Jezebel. Living up to his name, the very first words recorded from the prophet's mouth were these: "As YHWH the God of Israel lives, before whom I stand, there shall be neither dew nor rain these years, except by my word" (1 Kgs 17:1). Elijah's pronouncement was a direct challenge to Jezebel's god. Baal was venerated as the god of the thunderstorm, the deity who sent his life-giving rains to the coasts of Phoenicia and Israel. Elijah swore by YHWH himself that he would put that reputation to the test. The initial results of Elijah's assault on Baal were decidedly in favor of YHWH, not Baal. In a land that was accustomed to getting plentiful rain each year, a three-year drought ensued. Baal, it would appear, had grown impotent in the face of this lone Israelite prophet. The drought alone would not suffice, though, to put the final nail in the coffin of Baal's supposed power. As the land languished under the withering effects of the drought, 1 Kings 18:1 tells us, YHWH finally informed Elijah that he would once again send rain on Israel. Wanting there to be no doubt about just who was providing those long-awaited rains, Elijah proposed to King Ahab that a contest be held. YHWH would challenge Baal to see just who was God after all.

The contest would be a simple one. With Elijah representing YHWH and the prophets of Baal representing their god, YHWH and Baal would be called upon to send fire upon an altar their representatives had constructed. As we read the text closely, it is evident that Elijah's famous contest with the prophets of Baal was designed to make things as easy as possible for Baal. Baal was the god who lived high up in the clouds; the contest would be held high on a mountain. Baal's clouds were at home over the Mediterranean; Mount Carmel is less than ten miles from the Mediterranean coast. Baal was the god famous for his thunder and lightning; the contest would require him merely to send one bolt of lightning to strike his altar. The task demanded of Baal could hardly have been better suited to his divine attributes. Now, with four hundred and fifty prophets on his side, the time had come for Baal to show his superior power. But after a full day of chanting and dancing and special rites (like gashing themselves, just as El and Anat had done) to call forth Baal's power, there was nothing. The so-called god of the thunderstorm could not manage to produce a single bolt of lightning.

If the contest had been designed to be an easy one for Baal, Elijah wanted to ensure that it was equally as difficult for YHWH. He dug a trench around YHWH's altar and ordered that barrels of water be poured over it to drench it. Three times he ordered them to repeat the process, until the wood and the animal were soaked, the water ran down from the altar, and even the trench around the altar was full. Then, he offered a simple prayer:

> O YHWH, God of Abraham, Isaac, and Israel, this day let it be known that you are God in Israel, that I am your servant, and that I have done all these things according to your word. Answer me, O YHWH! Answer

me, so that this people may know that you, O YHWH, are God, and that you have turned back their hearts!

(1 Kgs 18:36–37)

The response from YHWH was instantaneous. Fire—undoubtedly lightning, given the point of the story—struck from heaven, causing the sacrifice, the wood, the water, and even the dirt and stones of the altar to be consumed. YHWH had done what Baal could not. Only then was it time for the rains to return to Israel. Elijah sent his servant to scan the horizon, and after he had looked for some time, the servant finally saw off in the distance a cloud "the size of a man's hand." As the cloud approached, it was clear that this was the cloud that would bring rain once again. After the events of the past three years, though, who could possibly believe that this was a rain cloud sent from Baal? Through the drought and then the contest with Baal's prophets, YHWH had demonstrated that if any god should be considered god of the thunderstorm, it was YHWH and not Baal. To demonstrate this, YHWH co-opted the traditions associated with Baal and laid claim to them.

Baal Imagery in the Psalms

As more information on the Canaanite mythologies associated with Baal have come to light at Ugarit and other sites, we have been able to get a better view of just how often the biblical authors appropriated language originally intended for Baal to describe the God of Israel. A prominent motif in the Canaanites' description of Baal is that of the divine warrior who strides into battle or rides the clouds, convulsing nature in his wake, bellowing his thunderous voice, and shooting his thunderbolts from the skies. In one text from the Baal Cycle, for example, we read:

> A window was opened in the house,
> > an opening in the midst of the palace.
> Baal opened up a rift in the clouds,
> > Baal gave forth his holy voice,
> > Baal repeated the issue of his lips.
> His holy voice covered the land;
> > at the sound of his voice, the mountains trembled,
> > the high places of the earth tottered.

The enemies of Baal clung to the trees of the forest,
   the haters of Haddu clung to the sides of the mountains.

(*KTU* 1.4 VII, 25–37)

In another Canaanite text, it is said of Baal:

Baal was seated like an immovable mountain,
   Haddu . . . like the ocean,
in the midst of his mountain, the divine Sapan,
   on the mountain of victory.
Seven lightnings he had,
   eight storehouses of thunder,
   a tree trunk of lightning he [   ].

Indeed, the most common epithet of Baal is *rākibu ʿurpāti*, "rider of the clouds" (cf. *KTU* 1.2 IV, 8, 29; 1.3 II, 40; III, 38; IV, 3, 6, 27; 1.4 III, 11, 18; V, 60; 1.5 II, 7).

Biblical authors often take up this Baal imagery and use it to describe YHWH's own actions. One psalm that makes prodigious use of this imagery is Psalm 68. As the psalmist implores God to rise up and protect the nation from its enemies, he urges in v. 4 [5]:

Sing to God, extol his name;
   lift up a song to *him who rides upon the clouds.*

The epithet applied to the God of Israel here (*rkb bʿrbt*) is identical to that found at Ugarit to describe Baal (*rkb ʿrpt*).[21] As the psalmist continues in vv. 7–10 [8–11], he recalls God's past works of deliverance in language highly reminiscent of that of the Canaanites:

O God, when you went out before your people,
   when you marched through the desert, (Selah)
the earth quaked; even the heavens poured down rain
   at the presence of God, the One of Sinai,
   at the presence of God, the God of Israel.
Rain freely you showered abroad, O God;
   you restored your heritage when it was weary;
your flock found a dwelling in it; in your goodness,
   you provided for the needy, O God.

As with the god Baal, here all of creation is said to respond to the march of the God of Israel. The earth quakes, the heavens pour down rain, and God's people reap the benefits of his showers.

The psalmist goes on in vv. 14–18 [15–19] to describe God's ascension to his mountainous palace in language reminiscent of Baal's enthronement on Mount Zaphon:

> When the Almighty scattered kings there,
> > snow fell on Zalmon.
> O mountain of God, mountain of Bashan;
> > O many-peaked mountain, mountain of Bashan!
> Why do you look with envy, O many-peaked mountain,
> > at the mount that God desired for his dwelling?
> > Indeed, YHWH will reside there forever.
> The chariots of God are twice ten thousand,
> > thousands of thousands;
> > the Lord is among them at Sinai in his holy place.
> You ascended to the heights, taking captives captive
> > and receiving gifts from people,
> even from those who rebel
> > against YHWH God's abiding there.[22]

As the psalmist reaches the conclusion of his song of praise in vv. 32–35 [33–36], he again evokes imagery that is most commonly associated with Baal:

> O kingdoms of the earth, sing to God!
> > Sing praise to the Lord! (Selah)
> *To the rider in the heavens, the ancient heavens;*
> > *listen, he sends out his voice, his mighty voice.*
> Ascribe strength to God,
> > whose majesty is over Israel
> > and whose strength is in the skies.
> *Awesome is God in his sanctuary,*
> > the God of Israel;
> > he is the one who gives strength and power to his people.

Once again, the God of Israel is cast as the "rider in the heavens, the ancient heavens," the one who is "awesome in his sanctuary," and whose "mighty voice" receives special attention.[23]

One particularly bold example of co-opting Canaanite tradition is found in Psalm 29. Scholars have long observed several oddities in the psalm, including, most notably, the repeated attention the psalmist draws to "the voice of YHWH." Seven times the psalm refers to God's mighty voice, and it is clear from the psalmist's description that he actually has in mind the sound of thunder. In v. 3, for example, the psalmist actually sets the two in parallel: "The *voice of YHWH* is over the waters; / the God of glory *thunders*." God's voice is said to be powerful and majestic (v. 4). It breaks cedars (v. 5). It sets personified Lebanon and Sirion running like frightened livestock (v. 6). It is accompanied by flashes of lightning (v. 7). It shakes the wilderness (v. 8) and blasts trees (v. 9). All of these are descriptive of peals of thunder. Added to the psalm's emphasis on the voice of YHWH is the connection the psalmist makes between the voice of YHWH and its location *over the waters*. At the beginning of v. 3, the psalmist proclaims, "The voice of YHWH is *over the waters*," and at the end, he describes YHWH as being "*over mighty waters*." In v. 10, YHWH is said to sit "enthroned *over the flood*." Finally, it is important to note how odd the geography of the text is for an *Israelite* psalm. The psalm appears to be set in Phoenicia, as it says God's voice "breaks the *cedars*" (v. 5). The problem, of course, is that cedars are exceedingly rare in Israel; it is in the land of Israel's northern neighbor, Phoenicia/Lebanon, that this species thrives.[24] The psalm goes on to make the connection with Lebanon certain as it clarifies, "YHWH breaks the cedars *of Lebanon*." YHWH's voice is said to make Lebanon skip like a calf and to make Sirion—another name for Mount Hermon, which stands at the northern boundary between Israel and Lebanon—skip like a wild ox (v. 6).

What are we to make of these odd features? It seems likely that they stem from the fact that Psalm 29 was not originally composed for YHWH at all. It was instead a hymn to Baal, and the ancient Israelites laid claim to it,[25] co-opting it and putting it into service as a hymn praising the God of Israel. While this may seem odd at first glance, it is really no more than a hymnic version of what Elijah did through his battle with the prophets of Baal. To demonstrate that YHWH was God and not Baal, Elijah attributed to the God of Israel the characteristics that were normally given to Baal. He co-opted Baal imagery to show that the God of Israel, not Baal, was responsible for rain and lightning. Here in psalmic form, an Israelite poet has done the same thing.[26]

Marduk Imagery

The biblical authors also co-opted traditions concerning Marduk. The second part of the book of Isaiah, chs. 40–55, is written to address the concerns of God's people near the end of the Babylonian Exile. In the year 605 BCE, the Babylonian King Nebuchadnezzar had imposed his will on Judah and forced King Jehoiakim to transfer his allegiance from Egypt to Babylon (2 Kgs 24:1). Jehoiakim never fully embraced this shift, though, and when the opportunity for rebellion against Babylon presented itself, he took it. The result of this rebellion was that the Babylonian army marched on Israel, Jehoiakim died (likely at the hands of an assassin), and Nebuchadnezzar exiled the upper echelons of Israelite society to Babylon (2 Kgs 24:14). This forced exile would last for decades, until finally the Persian King Cyrus defeated Babylon in 539 BCE and permitted the exiles to return home the following year.

The circumstances of Cyrus' defeat of Babylon form a key point of controversy for the second part of Isaiah. The last king of the Neo-Babylonian Empire, Nabonidus (556–539 BCE), was extraordinarily unpopular. And no wonder! Although the patron deity of Babylon, and thus of the Babylonian empire, had been the god Marduk for more than a millennium, Nabonidus dethroned Marduk and installed the moon god Sîn in his place at the head of the pantheon.[27] He established a temple for Sîn in the city of Harran, insisted that Sîn be worshiped in Babylon, and even prevented the celebration of Babylon's annual Akītu festival that was meant to commemorate Marduk's victory over Tiamat. Nabonidus then decided to retreat to the desert oasis of Tema, where he spent a decade attending to his health (and perhaps worshiping Sîn—worship of the moon god was especially prominent in the desert). In his place, Nabonidus left in charge Belshazzar, the ill-fated regent known from the book of Daniel as the ruler who saw the writing on the wall announcing the end of Babylon's empire (cf. Dan 5).

The reign of Nabonidus (and his regent, Belshazzar) came to an end when Cyrus defeated the city of Babylon. It appears that he was able to do so essentially without having to fire a shot. Why? Because the priests of Marduk, furious as they were with Nabonidus' having demoted their patron god, opened the gates and invited Cyrus to march right in. The famous Cyrus Cylinder records:

Upon hearing their cries, the lord of the gods [Marduk] became furiously angry, and he left their borders; and the gods who lived among

them forsook their dwellings, angry that he had brought them into
Babylon. Marduk turned towards all the habitations that were abandoned and all the people of Sumer and Akkad who had become corpses;
he was reconciled and had mercy upon them. He surveyed and looked
throughout all the lands, searching for a righteous king whom he would
support. He called out his name: Cyrus, king of Anshan; he pronounced
his name to be king over all the world. . . . He ordered him to march
to his city Babylon. He set him on the road to Babylon and like a com-
panion and friend, he went at his side. His vast army, whose number,
like the water of the river, cannot be known, marched at his side fully
armed. He made him enter his city Babylon without fighting or battle;
he saved Babylon from hardship.[28]

Cyrus claimed that he had taken the city so effortlessly because Marduk
had appointed him to do so. Marduk, he insists, had "surveyed and looked
throughout all the lands, searching for a righteous king whom he would support." That king was Cyrus, the one concerning whom the Cyrus Cylinder
says, "He called out his name: Cyrus," and, "He pronounced his name to be
king over all the world."

The second part of Isaiah responds directly and forcefully to this notion.[29] In the opening verses of Isaiah 45, the prophet insists:

> Thus says YHWH to his anointed one, to Cyrus,
>   whose right hand I have grasped
> to subdue nations before him,
>   and to ungird the loins of kings,
> to open doors before him
>   and gates that shall not be closed.
> I am the one who will go before you
>   to level the mountains.
> I will break the doors of bronze,
>   and the bars of iron I will cut through.

(Isa 45:1–2)

In these verses, YHWH insists that he, not Marduk or some other claimant, is the one who has paved the way for Cyrus to secure his victories. This
point is emphasized again in v. 3:

> I will give you the treasures of darkness
>   and hidden riches,

so that you may know that it is I, YHWH,
> the God of Israel, who calls your name.

The prophet goes on to argue that the purpose for which YHWH has raised up Cyrus as his anointed one is not the one supposed by the priests of Marduk. In v. 4, YHWH insists:

For the sake of my servant Jacob,
> and Israel my chosen one,
I call you by your name.
> I proclaim your title, though you do not know me.

Then, as if to put the final nail in the coffin of Marduk's claims to greatness, YHWH declares:

I am YHWH, and there is no other.
> Besides me, there is no god.
I arm you, though you do not know me,
> so that they may know, from the rising of the sun to its setting,
> that there is none besides me.
I am YHWH, and there is no other.

(Isa 45:5–6)

This important passage in Isaiah marks another example of co-opting foreign tradition. These voices are pointed in their insistence that it is YHWH, the God of Israel, who enabled Cyrus to defeat Babylon; it was not Marduk. And it was for the purpose of sending his people home from Babylon that YHWH did so; it had nothing to do with the restoration of Marduk to his supposed throne. Here, Isaiah has taken claims attributed to Marduk and co-opted them to refer to the God of Israel instead.

Actual Belief

As the previous examples indicate, in some cases, it seems likely that psalmists and prophets in ancient Israel took advantage of Canaanite and Babylonian imagery to speak in the language of their neighbors, whether to those neighbors themselves or, more likely, to fellow Israelites who had been influenced by that language. In other cases, the biblical authors appear to have used this imagery as a way of co-opting the traditions of their neighbors, insisting that if a particular divine power were exercised, it would be the God of Israel, not some foreign deity, who would do so. We must also consider the possibility that in some cases, though, biblical writers linked creation with God's fight against sea and dragon simply because this was their view of how creation occurred. One text in which this seems especially evident is Psalm 74.

In our previous discussions of Psalm 74, we saw that the psalm blends God's combat with the sea, dragons, and Leviathan (vv. 12–15) with his work of creation (vv. 16–17). What is particularly interesting is the role this passage plays in the rhetoric of the psalm as a whole.[30] Psalm 74 was composed by a poet frustrated with the enduring indignities suffered by Jerusalem during the time of the exile. The psalmist laments, "O God, why do you cast us off forever?" (v. 1), as he continues to be confronted with the ruinous state of the city. In vv. 2–3, he implores God to turn his attention to the city:

> Remember your congregation, which you acquired long ago,
>> which you redeemed as the tribe of your heritage,
>> Mount Zion itself, where you came to dwell.
> Lift your steps to the enduring ruins,
>> to all the outrages the enemy has wrought in the sanctuary.

Though Jerusalem was God's city, it now lies in ruins, seemingly forgotten by the God who once claimed it as his dwelling place. To this plea for remembrance, the psalmist then adds in vv. 4–9 an attempt to rouse God's anger, to stir him to action by reminding him of what enemies did to his sanctuary:

> Your foes have roared in the midst of your meeting place;
>> they set up their own banners there.
> At the upper entrance they hacked
>> the wooden trellis with axes.[31]
> And then, its carved work
>> they smashed with hatchets and hammers.
> They set your sanctuary on fire;
>> they defiled the dwelling place of your name in the dust.[32]
> They said to themselves, "Let us destroy them altogether."
>> They burned all the meeting places of God in the land.
> We do not see our banners;
>> there is no longer any prophet,
>> and there is no one among us who knows how long.

The psalmist pleads with God, "How long, O God, is the foe to taunt? Is the enemy to revile your name forever?" (v. 10). He then concludes this section of his argument with a particularly biting question: "Why do you hold back your hand? Why do you keep your hand in your bosom?" (v. 11). In modern parlance, the psalmist asks, "God, why are you just standing there with your hands in your pockets? Take them out and do something!"

It is at this point, though, that the psalmist's rhetorical tack veers in an entirely different direction. Having worked for eleven verses to elicit God's pity toward his people and to provoke God to anger toward his enemies, the psalmist now attempts to give God a word of encouragement. He seeks, as it were, to give God a pep talk:

> Yet God my King is from of old,
>> working salvation in the midst of the earth.
> You broke the sea by your might;
>> you shattered the heads of the dragons in the waters.
> You crushed the heads of Leviathan;
>> you gave him as food for the creatures of the sea.
> You split open spring and wadi;
>> you dried up ever-flowing rivers.
> Yours is the day, yours also the night;
>> you established luminary and sun.
> You have fixed all the boundaries of the earth;
>> summer and winter—you made them.
>
> (Ps 74:12–17)

The essence of the psalmist's encouragement is simple enough: God, you defeated the sea, the dragon, and the Leviathan; you created heaven and earth; you can defeat a foe as insignificant as Babylon! What should not be overlooked in this pep talk is the degree to which it hinges on the psalmist's belief that God *actually did the things that are mentioned*. It would be a miserable pep talk indeed that attempted to remind God of past victories and accomplishments that had never really happened. The psalmist would not encourage God to remember his victory over sea and dragon at creation if he did not believe God had, in fact, achieved that victory.

The suggestion that the author of Psalm 74 regarded the creation battle in a straightforward way is supported by parallels with other psalms that harken back to God's past deeds. In Psalm 22, for example, the psalmist urges God to intervene in the midst of his suffering: "Do not be far from me, for trouble is near, and there is no one to help!" (v. 11 [12]). He bases his confidence in God's ability to rescue him *now* on the deliverance God had provided for the psalmist's ancestors *in the past*. He reminds God:

> In you our ancestors trusted;
>> they trusted, and you delivered them.
> To you they cried, and they escaped;
>> in you they trusted and were not put to shame.
>
>> (vv. 4–5 [5–6])

Psalm 44 follows a similar pattern. In the opening verses of the psalm, the psalmist praises God for the extraordinary deliverance he provided for the nation in the past:

> O God, we have heard with our ears;
>> our ancestors have told us
> what deeds you performed in their days,
>> in the days of old.
> You with your own hand drove out the nations,
>> but them you planted;
> you afflicted the peoples,
>> but them you set free.
> For not by their own sword did they take the land,
>> nor did their own arm save them,
> but your right hand and your arm,
>> and the light of your face,
>> for you delighted in them.
>
>> (vv. 1–3 [2–4])

For the psalmist, though, *these past acts of deliverance* only throw into sharp relief the fact that God is not delivering his people *now*. He cries out:

> Yet you have rejected us and humiliated us,
>> and you have not gone out with our armies.
> You made us turn back from the foe,
>> and those who hate us have plundered us.
> You have made us like sheep for slaughter,
>> and you have scattered us among the nations.
> You have sold your people for a pittance;
>> you asked no great price for them.

You have made us the taunt of our neighbors,
    the derision and mockery of those around us.
You have made us a byword among the nations,
    a shaking of the head among the peoples.

(vv. 9–14 [10–15])

As in Psalm 22, the rhetoric of Psalm 44 hinges on the psalmist's belief that
God *had* delivered the psalmist's ancestors in the past and thus *could* deliver
the psalmist (and his people) in the present. Psalm 74 falls into this same
category of lament, as the psalmist reminds God of his former mighty works
at creation and urges him to display the same power today.

We might say the same of various other passages as well. In Psalm 89,
for example, the psalmist laments that God has apparently abandoned his
covenant with David and his royal descendants:

You have spurned and rejected him;
    you have become enraged with your anointed.
You have repudiated the covenant with your servant;
    you have defiled his crown in the dust.
You have breached all his walls;
    you have made ruins of his strongholds.
All who pass by plunder him;
    he has become the reproach of his neighbors.
You have exalted the right hand of his foes;
    you have made all his enemies rejoice.
You have turned back the edge of his sword,
    and have not supported him in battle.
You have brought his splendor to an end,
    and hurled his throne to the ground.
You have cut short the days of his youth;
    you have covered him with shame. (Selah)

(vv. 38–45 [39–46])

As the psalmist challenges God to restore his "steadfast love of old"
(v. 49 [50]) and give the present Davidic king victory over his foes, he does
so based on two convictions. First, he argues that God has an obligation to
defeat the nation's enemies because he has sworn an oath to remain faithful
to David's line:

I have made a covenant with my chosen one;
    I have sworn to David, my servant:
"I will establish your seed forever
    and build your throne for all generations." (Selah)

(vv. 3–4 [4–5])

Second, the psalmist argues that God has the ability to defeat the nation's enemies because he is the God who defeated sea and dragon as he created the world:

O YHWH God of hosts,
    who is as mighty as you, YHWH?
    Your faithfulness surrounds you.
You rule the raging of the sea;
    when its waves rise, you still them.
You crushed Rahab like a carcass;
    you scattered your enemies with your mighty arm.
The heavens are yours; the earth also is yours;
    the world and all that is in it—you have founded them.
The north and the south—you created them;
    Tabor and Hermon sing forth your name.
You have a mighty arm;
    strong is your hand, high your right hand.

(vv. 8–13 [9–14])

Here the psalmist appears to make no distinction between his confidence in God's having established a covenant with David and his confidence in God's having defeated Rahab and the sea. It seems likely that this martial version of creation was simply the version of creation that the psalmist accepted.

Conclusion

The poetic rehearsals of creation found in the Bible—whether in Psalms, Job, or the Prophets—often deploy the language of combat as they describe God's work in creation. They cast the God of Israel in the role of a deity who establishes his kingship by defeating sea and dragon, Leviathan and Rahab, and by creating the world in the wake of his victory. As the biblical poets present God in this fashion, they draw on a rich treasury of similar combat and creation imagery found in the literature of their ancient Near Eastern neighbors. It seems likely that at times the biblical authors borrow this Canaanite and Babylonian imagery merely to speak in a language their neighbors, or more likely their fellow Israelites who have been influenced by these neighbors, will understand. In other cases, the Bible's poets move beyond borrowing to instead co-opt traditions; they take over the traditions of their neighbors to make the case that if any deity were to defeat the forces of chaos, to rule the sea and its waves, to bring the nourishing rains of the thunderstorm, it would be Israel's God and not the deities of the surrounding nations. In still other cases, it seems likely that the biblical authors did not need to co-opt particular traditions from their neighbors, since they already shared a similar outlook on the manner in which creation came to be. For them, the defeat of the sea and the dragon was simply part of God's work of creation, and they appealed to this victorious act in the past as the basis for God's ability to deliver in the present.

The use of this sort of creation imagery in Psalms, Job, and the Prophets is fascinating, even if it seems somewhat unexpected. But at some level, these poetic descriptions of creation remain just that: *poetic* descriptions of creation. With its heavy concentration of literary figures—metaphor, metonymy, simile, hyperbole, personification, and the like—poetry may blur the line between what happened *historically* and what is described *artistically*. Surely, the better place to look to fully understand the Bible's creation traditions would be the foundational story of creation, Genesis 1. It is to this account that we turn in the following chapter.

CHAPTER 6

Genesis 1

In the waning days of 1968, the crew of NASA's Apollo 8 mission became the first humans to leave earth's orbit and travel to the moon. Though their spacecraft was not equipped to land on the lunar surface, astronauts Frank Borman, Jim Lovell, and William Anders orbited the moon ten times, performing tests and collecting data that would be vital for future lunar missions. It was on this mission that the crew emerged from the far side of the moon on one of their lunar orbits and managed to capture the stunning image that came to be known as *Earthrise*, a photograph of the distant earth rising over the lunar horizon. Later on that same day, on Christmas Eve, the crew beamed back to earth one of the most famous broadcasts in human history. William Anders began with the words, "For all the people on earth, the crew of Apollo 8 has a message we would like to send you." He then proceeded to read the first four verses of Genesis 1:

> In the beginning God created the heaven and the earth. And the earth was without form, and void; and darkness was upon the face of the deep. And the Spirit of God moved upon the face of the waters. And God said, Let there be light: and there was light. And God saw the light, that it was good: and God divided the light from the darkness.

Jim Lovell followed with verses 5–8:

> And God called the light Day, and the darkness he called Night. And the evening and the morning were the first day. And God said, Let there be a firmament in the midst of the waters, and let it divide the waters from the waters. And God made the firmament, and divided the waters

which were under the firmament from the waters which were above the firmament: and it was so. And God called the firmament Heaven. And the evening and the morning were the second day.

Finally, mission commander Frank Borman concluded with verses 9–10:

And God said, Let the waters under the heaven be gathered together unto one place, and let the dry land appear: and it was so. And God called the dry land Earth; and the gathering together of the waters called he Seas: and God saw that it was good.[1]

He then added, "And from the crew of Apollo 8, we close with good night, good luck, a Merry Christmas, and God bless all of you, all of you on the good Earth."

The verses Anders, Lovell, and Borman read on that Christmas Eve now more than fifty years ago are among the best-known words in the Bible. With their familiar cadence of "and God said," "and God saw that it was good," "and there was evening and there was morning," these words and the rest of Genesis 1 have become deeply embedded in the literary canons of the Western world. Their majestic description of God's creative work has served as a touchstone for theological reflection in both Judaism and Christianity. As we read the words of this key biblical text, it seems obvious that we are far removed from the poetic descriptions of creation found in works like Job and the Psalms. Gone is the language of battle and the various descriptions of sea monsters, dragons, Leviathans, and Rahabs. In Genesis 1, surely, we find a text unencumbered by these ancient Near Eastern motifs. And yet . . . while Genesis 1 is a very different sort of text than the poetic passages we have considered thus far, a close reading of its language reveals substantial parallels even between this text and the Canaanite and Babylonian creation traditions.

Primordial Waters

Although the first three verses of Genesis 1 constitute one of the most familiar passages in all of Scripture, our very familiarity with the text can lead us to overlook a key link between this passage and the Babylonian creation story. Importantly, when we go back to the beginning of creation in both Genesis 1 and Enuma Elish, the waters *are already there*.

Evident in the Structure of Genesis 1

The primordial nature of the waters in Genesis 1 is particularly evident when we consider the structure that marks the various days of creation. The description of each day follows a similar pattern:

- *"And God said."* Each day of creation and each of God's creative acts in the account is introduced by the Hebrew expression *wayyō'mer 'ĕlōhîm*, "And God said." This expression is found once each on Days 1, 2, 4, and 5 (cf. vv. 3, 6, 14, 20) and twice each on what I will argue below are the pivotal Days 3 and 6 (cf. vv. 9 and 11, 24 and 26).

- *Divine edict in the third person.* With only one exception, the introductory "and God said" is followed by an edict in the third person: "Let there be light" (v. 3), "Let there be a dome" (v. 6), "Let the waters be gathered" (v. 9), "Let the earth sprout vegetation" (v. 11), "Let there be lights" (v. 14), "Let the waters swarm with swarms of living creatures" (v. 20), and "Let the earth bring forth living creatures" (v. 24). The lone exception to this pattern is the cohortative expression found, significantly, in the creation of humanity in v. 26 as God says, "Let us make humankind in our image."

- *Supplementary description.* After the initial, spoken edict of creation, a fuller description of God's creative handiwork follows. On the first day of creation, for example, God is said not only to speak light into existence but also to separate light from darkness and to give names to each. On the fourth day, the text not only records God's having said, "Let there be lights," but it goes on to specify that God made a greater light to rule the day and a lesser light to rule the night, that he made the stars, too, and that he set the lights in the heavens. A similar pattern is evident on the other days of creation as well.

- *"And God saw that it was good."* For all but one day of the creation week, Day Two, the text includes a description of God's positive assessment of his creative work: "And God saw that it was good." In the majority of cases, this familiar phrase occurs at the end of a particular act of creation, supplying a conclusion to match the introductory "And God said" that opens each description (vv. 10, 11, 18, 25, 31; compare vv. 4, 21).

- *"And there was evening and there was morning."* Finally, each day of creation concludes with the refrain "And there was evening and there was morning, the *nth* day" (cf. vv. 5, 8, 13, 19, 23, 31).

The effect of Genesis 1's repetitive style is to give the narrative an almost poetic cadence, with the orderliness of the text's structure underscoring the orderliness of God's creation. As we return to vv. 1–3, we see that the consistency of the text's structure also sheds light on what should be regarded as God's first work of creation in the chapter. *Each and every one of God's creative acts in Genesis 1 begins with the words "And God said."* The issue, of course, is that we first encounter this language in v. 3, not vv. 1–2. The first act of creation that Genesis 1 narrates is God's command "Let there be light." But if this is the case—and the tight structure of the chapter insists that it must be—what are we to make of v. 2? *This is the text's description of the world as it was when God began his work of creation.* In the words of Genesis 1, when creation commenced, "The earth was unformed and unfilled, and darkness was over the face of the deep, and the wind of God was hovering over the waters." Although our own ears may be trained to listen for a description of creation that begins with *nothing* and goes on to narrate the emergence of *something* (i.e., "creation *ex nihilo*"), this is not the tack followed by Genesis 1.[2] On the contrary, at the beginning of creation in Genesis 1, the chaotic, primordial waters are already there.

Evident in the Story of the Flood

It is not only Genesis 1 that evinces this understanding of the beginning of creation. Even in the New Testament, we find a passage like 2 Peter 3:5–6, which declares, "Heavens existed long ago, and an earth was formed *out of water* and *by means of water*, by the word of God, by means of which the world that then was was flooded by water and destroyed." The reference to the flood in these verses is also suggestive. The biblical story of the flood in Genesis 6–8 begins with a divine act of "de-creation." Before God re-creates the world after the flood, he first has to undo his original act of creation. But what form does this reversal of creation take? God does not remove the creation from existence; instead, he sends it back to its *original watery state.* Importantly, there are also echoes of Genesis 1 in God's re-creation of the world in the aftermath of the flood: just as in the creation account, the scene in Genesis 8 begins with the chaotic waters covering the earth, and *a wind from God* blows to restrain the waters and permit the dry land to appear.

Evident in the Manner of Creation

When God creates in Genesis 1, he does so by speaking. He says, "Let there be," for the light of Day One and for the lights of Day Four. He says,

"Let there be a dome," on Day Two; and, "Let the dry land appear," and "Let the earth put forth vegetation," on Day Three. He says, "Let the waters bring forth," for the fish of Day Five; and, "Let the earth bring forth," for the animals of Day 6. What the text never records God saying, however, is "Let the waters be." Genesis 1 does not narrate God's creation of the primordial waters of Genesis 1:2, because they are already there when his creative work begins. Indeed, a proper understanding of Genesis 1's notion of creation suggests that the text *could not* narrate the creation of these chaotic waters.[3] For the author of Genesis 1, *creation* is bound up with notions of order, life, and wholeness. As we will see in more detail below, the waters of v. 2 represent the opposite of all of these things. To *create chaos* would be an oxymoron on par with Romeo's "heavy lightness," "serious vanity," and "misshapen chaos of well-seeming forms" (*Romeo and Juliet*, 1.1.174–179). Interestingly, the latter chapters of Isaiah appear to recognize this notion. In Isaiah 45:18, the prophet insists that God did not create the world as *chaos*, using the same Hebrew word for chaos, *tōhû*, that is found in Genesis 1:2:

> For thus says YHWH, who created the heavens (He is God!), who formed the earth and made it (He established it; he did not create it as chaos [*tōhû*]; he formed it to be inhabited!): I am YHWH, and there is no other.

The prophet may even be responding to a misreading of Genesis 1 itself that had suggested God *did* initially create the world as chaos.

If v. 3 of Genesis 1 narrates God's first act of creation and v. 2 describes the chaotic state that preceded his creative work, what then is the function of v. 1? Although the verse has often been understood as describing the first act of creation, the structure of God's creative acts in the rest of the chapter and the incompatibility of the chaotic waters with God's creative work indicates that this must not be case. Verse 1 is not a description of the initial act of creation but rather a summary of God's creative activity in the whole of the creation week. In other words, it is a synopsis and title for the entirety of God's creation. As scholars have long noted, it may even be the case that v. 1 should be understood as a dependent clause introducing the state of affairs that existed at the beginning of creation in v. 2.[4] In this case, the text would be more properly understood along the lines of "In the beginning when God created the heavens and the earth, the earth was . . ." (NRSV) or "When God began to create heaven and earth—the earth being . . ." (NJPS). The complexities of the grammar of the first few words of v. 1 are such that a definitive answer to this question will likely never be reached. Whether the verse should be understood as a complete sentence by itself or as a dependent clause has little effect, however, on the verse's overall function: it is a summary of all that is to follow, not a description of the first act of creation.[5]

With this understanding of the structure of vv. 1–3 in place, the parallels between our text and the Babylonian creation story are readily apparent. Conceptually, both creation accounts begin with primordial waters. If either the Babylonians or Israelites ever considered the question of where the waters themselves came from, they did not do so in Genesis 1 or Enuma Elish. As E. A. Speiser and others have noted, this conceptual parallel is also matched by a literary parallel.[6] The first eight lines of Enuma Elish describe the watery state that preceded creation; only in line 9 does the text turn to the emergence of creation itself. Genesis 1 follows the same structure, as it first describes the waters that preceded creation, in v. 2, before turning to the actual work of creation, in v. 3.

Enuma Elish	*Genesis 1*
When on high no name was given to heaven, nor below was the netherworld called by name, Primeval Apsu was their progenitor, and Matrix-Tiamat was she who bore them all. They were mingling their waters together. No canebrake was intertwined, nor thicket matted close. When no gods at all had been brought forth, none called by names, no destinies ordained—	Now the earth was unformed and unfilled, and darkness covered the face of the deep, and the wind of God was hovering over the face of the waters.
Then were the gods formed within these two . . .	And God said, "Let there be light."

Verses 2–3 of the Genesis account, like the opening lines of the Babylonian epic, narrate a story that begins with what is not yet formed and then moves on to the first act of creation. Only v. 1 of the Genesis account falls outside of this parallel literary structure, a point of some significance for our discussion below.

The Deep

As we look more closely at the nature of the primordial waters of v. 2, we find another important echo of the Babylonian account of creation. It is found in the term English versions of the Bible translate as "the deep." To understand the significance of this echo, we must first turn aside for a moment to the matter of language families. Most individual languages belong to larger *families* of languages that are closely related to one another. The so-called Romance languages, for example, include Spanish, Portuguese, French, Italian, Romanian, and a host of lesser-known local languages, such as Catalan, Sicilian, and even Walloon. Because the Romance languages derive from a common linguistic ancestor, they share a great deal in the way of grammar and vocabulary. In Latin, for example, the word for "bread" is *panem*. This is echoed in the Spanish *pan*, Portuguese *pão*, French *pain*, Italian *pane*, Romanian *pâine*, and Catalan *pa*. To use another example, the Latin word *homo*, "man," is echoed in the Spanish *hombre*, Portuguese *homem*, French *homme*, Italian *uomo*, Romanian *om*, and Catalan *home*.

As a general rule, the correspondences between languages in a language family follow regular patterns. Thus, for example, English and German, which belong to the Germanic language family, show a fairly predictable pattern of correspondences with one another. The consonant cluster preserved in German as *ch* developed along different lines in English to become our odd *gh*. As a result, the German *acht* becomes *eight* in English, *Nacht* becomes *night*, and *Tochter* becomes *daughter*. This latter example includes another predictable correspondence, as the initial German "t" is shifted to "d" in English words. Thus, German *Tief* becomes *deep*, *trinken* becomes *drink*, *Tag* becomes *day*, and so forth.

Hebrew is itself part of a language family, the Semitic language family, which includes Phoenician, Ugaritic, Aramaic, Akkadian (i.e., Babylonian and Assyrian), Arabic, Amharic, and a number of other languages, both living and extinct. The Semitic languages show the same sorts of similarity in vocabulary that other language families do. Thus, the word for *father* shows up in Akkadian as *abu*, in Hebrew as *ʾāḇ*, in Aramaic as *ʾabbā*, and in Arabic as *ʾab*. The word for *soul* (which is really the word for *throat* in the Semitic languages) is expressed as *napištu* in Akkadian, *nepēš* in Hebrew, *napšā* in Aramaic, and *nafs* in Arabic. Also like other language families, the Semitic languages have regular patterns of sound correspondences. For example, an accented long *ā* vowel in most of the Semitic languages becomes a long *ō* vowel in the Canaanite dialects (including Hebrew). As a result, the word for *peace* in a language like Arabic, *salām*, becomes *šalōm* in Hebrew, and the word for *three* in Akkadian, *šalāš*, and in Aramaic, *təlāṭ*, becomes *šālōš* in Hebrew. A similar kind of shift is evident as a letter like *heh* in Hebrew is preserved in Akkadian as the letter *aleph* (represented by the symbol ʾ).

This leads, for example, to the word for *flame* being preserved in Hebrew as *lahaḇ* but in Akkadian as *laʾbu*.

So why is all of this important for our study of Genesis 1? The answer lies in a particular word found in v. 2, *təhōm*, the word usually translated as *deep* in the clause "And darkness was upon the face of the *deep*." When we chart the sound correspondences within the Semitic family of languages, we see that the Hebrew word *təhōm* is equivalent to the Akkadian (Babylonian) word *tiʾāmat*.[7] The Hebrew *təhōm* is not an actual loanword from Akkadian; both *təhōm* and *tiʾāmat* derive from an earlier Semitic word, *tihām(at)*. In its present context describing the chaotic waters that God will order and control in creation, however, the use of the word *təhōm* in Genesis 1:2 represents a powerful echo of the Babylonian creation tradition.[8]

Sea Monsters

As we have seen, Genesis 1 begins with the same primordial waters found in Enuma Elish and contains a subtle echo of the Babylonian story in its use of *təhōm* to describe the deep. What would seem to be missing, though, is any reference to the dragon-like monsters that are so prominent in Enuma Elish and even in our "odd" biblical creation texts. As we read further in Genesis 1, however, we find that these figures do make an appearance even in this text. In v. 21, the text tells us, "And God created the great sea monsters." The term used here for sea monster is *tannînîm*, the plural of the term *tannîn* discussed in detail above. There is no question that the *tannînîm* play a different role in this passage than they do in texts such as Psalm 74:13 and Isaiah 27:1 and 51:9. Most importantly, God is not portrayed as battling against these monsters in Genesis 1, an element that dominates our other creation texts.[9] It is interesting to note, though, how one of the earliest interpreters of Genesis 1, the psalmist who penned Psalm 104, understood the *tannînîm*.[10] As the psalmist retraces the days of Genesis 1's creation account, offering his own poetic description of God's handiwork, he muses over the works of Day Five:

> Yonder is the sea, great and wide;
>> creeping things without number are there,
>> living things, small and great.
> There go the ships,
>> and Leviathan that you made to sport with.

(Ps 104:25–26)

Although the psalmist writes in poetry rather than prose, it is interesting to note the connection he draws between the Leviathan and Genesis 1's *tannînîm*. This early commentary of sorts on Genesis 1 highlights the way the text would have been understood by its first readers. It also strongly suggests that the great sea monsters in v. 21 mark another connection with the Babylonian creation account, where sea monsters, in the form of both Tiamat and her helpers, feature so prominently. Of particular interest in Genesis 1, though, is why these monsters arrive only on Day Five of creation and not at the beginning (or even before the beginning) of creation, as they do in other biblical texts. For the moment, though, the reason for the tardy arrival of these monsters will have to be put on hold.

Wind

The echoes of Enuma Elish in Genesis 1's primordial waters, *təhōm*, and *tannînîm* may point toward an additional connection in v. 2: *the divine wind*. While most translations render the last clause of Genesis 1:2 along the lines of "And *the Spirit of God* was hovering over the face of the waters," a number of translations move in a different direction, suggesting it was "a wind from God," "a mighty wind," or " a divine wind" that the text portrays as sweeping across the waters.[11] The Hebrew noun *rûaḥ* that heads the construction *rûaḥ ʾĕlōhîm* is capable of conveying either meaning.

In the Hebrew Bible, *rûaḥ* is most often used to refer to the *spirit* of God (cf. Judg 3:10; 1 Sam 10:6; 1 Kgs 18:12; Ps 139:7) or of a person (cf. Gen 41:8; 45:27; Isa 19:3; Job 6:4), but it is also frequently used for *breath* (whether human—cf. Job 9:18; 19:17; Isa 42:5; 2 Chr 9:4; or divine—cf. Exod 15:18; Job 4:9; Ps 135:17) or a transitory *breeze* (cf. Job 7:7; Ps 78:39; Jer 5:13). Importantly, on more than a hundred occasions, *rûaḥ* refers to *wind*. Thus, for example, 2 Kings 3:17 records the word of assurance from Elisha, "You shall see neither wind [*rûaḥ*] nor rain, but the wadi shall be filled with water, so that you shall drink—you, your cattle, and your animals." At the end of the contest between Elijah and the prophets of Baal, the drought ends with the description, "The heavens grew black with clouds and wind [*rûaḥ*]; there was a heavy rain" (1 Kgs 18:45). Proverbs 25:14 describes the one who "boasts of a gift never given" as "like clouds and wind [*rûaḥ*] without rain."

On numerous occasions, the wind that the word *rûaḥ* describes is one that expresses God's great power. Thus, in the book of Jonah, we read, "And YHWH hurled a great wind [*rûaḥ*] upon the sea, and such a great tempest came upon the sea that the ship threatened to break up" (Jonah 1:4). The power of God's wind is especially evident in his creative acts. The prophet Amos, for example, declares:

> For behold, the one who forms the mountains, creates
> the wind [*rûaḥ*],
> tells his thoughts to mortals,
> makes the daybreak darkness,
> and treads on the heights of the earth—
> YHWH, the God of hosts, is his name!
>
> (Amos 4:13)

God's creative power is evident again in Psalm 135:5–7 as the psalmist announces:

> For I know that YHWH is great;
> and our Lord is greater than all gods.
> All that YHWH pleases he does,
> in heaven and on earth,
> in the seas and all deeps.
> He makes the clouds rise from the end of the earth;
> he makes lightnings for the rain
> and brings out the wind [*rûaḥ*] from his storehouses.

Jeremiah expresses similar sentiments as he contrasts YHWH the creator with other gods who cannot lay claim to creation:

> Let the gods who did not make the heavens and the earth perish from
> the earth and from under these heavens.[12]
> He is the one who made the earth by his power,
> who established the world by his wisdom,
> and by his understanding stretched out the heavens.
> When he gives forth his voice, there is a tumult of waters in
> the heavens,
> and he makes clouds rise from the ends of the earth.
> He makes lightnings for the rain,
> and he brings out the wind [*rûaḥ*] from his storehouses.
>
> (Jer 10:11–13)

Several lines of evidence suggest that the *rûaḥ* in Genesis 1:2 should also be understood as a manifestation of the divine wind. In the first place, it is interesting to note that the creation hymn discussed above, Psalm 104, twice uses *rûaḥ* to describe winds marshaled in God's service in the early stages of creation:

> He lays the beams of his chambers on the waters;
>> he makes the clouds his chariot;
>> he rides upon the wings of the wind [*rûaḥ*].
> He makes the winds [*rûḥôṭ*, pl.] his messengers,
>> fire and flame his ministers.
>
> (Ps 104:3–4)

These verses raise the strong possibility that the author of this psalm, at least, understood the *rûaḥ* of Genesis 1 as God's powerful wind.

Secondly, as noted above, it is particularly noteworthy that at the end of the flood story, Genesis 8:1 uses *rûaḥ* to describe a wind from God that subdues the waters of the deluge:

> And God remembered Noah and all the wild animals and all the domestic animals that were with him in the ark. And God made a wind [*rûaḥ*] blow over the earth, and the waters subsided. The fountains of the deep and the windows of the heavens were shut, the rain from the heavens was restrained, and the waters steadily receded from the earth.
>
> (Gen 8:1–3)

Through the flood, the world is "de-created"—that is, returned to its watery and chaotic state. Then, as in Genesis 1, it is the *rûaḥ* from God that exhibits God's power and control over the waters and sets the stage for the world's (re-) creation. The fact that the *rûaḥ* in Genesis 8:1 clearly refers to a *wind* from God argues strongly for a similar understanding of the term in Genesis 1:2.[13]

The third piece of evidence suggesting a reference to God's wind in Genesis 1:2 is, of course, the fact that divine winds feature so prominently in the stories from outside of Israel of gods' controlling the chaotic seas. In the case of Baal, this is seen especially in his epithet *Cloud Rider*, which depicts the clouds as the chariot on which he rides the winds. Even more closely parallel to Genesis 1 is Enuma Elish's description of the winds Marduk prepared for his combat with Tiamat:

He stationed the four winds so that no part of her might escape:
South Wind, North Wind, East Wind, West Wind.
He fastened at his side the net, a present from his father, Anu.
He formed Evil Wind, Storm, Dust Storm,
Four-fold Wind, Seven-fold Wind, Severe Wind, Irresistible Wind.
He sent out the winds he had made, seven of them.
They followed behind him to stir up the insides of Tiamat.

(IV.42–48)

The text then goes on to describe Marduk's deployment of the winds:

Bēl [the Lord] spread out his net and encircled her.
The Evil Wind stationed behind him he let loose in her face.
Tiamat opened her mouth to swallow it.
He sent in the Evil Wind so she could not close her lips.
Fierce winds bloated her belly.
Her insides were stopped up as she opened her mouth wide.

(IV.95–100)

We have already seen an echo of Marduk's winds in one of our "odd" creation texts, Job 26:

By his power he stilled the sea;
  by his understanding he struck down Rahab.
By his wind [*rûaḥ*] the heavens were made fair;
  his hand pierced the fleeing serpent.

(Job 26:12–13)

There is likely another echo in Isaiah 27. As we have seen previously, v. 1 of this chapter describes an eschatological victory of YHWH over the Leviathan. In v. 8, however, the prophet adds that the destruction of God's enemies is accomplished through his "fierce wind [*rûaḥ*]."

It would certainly not be surprising to find another, similar echo of Marduk's winds in Genesis 1:2. As in Enuma Elish, the wind in v. 2 conveys the notion of divine power, a point underscored by the addition of the divine epithet *'ĕlōhîm* (God) to the *rûaḥ*. On a number of occasions in the Hebrew Scriptures, the word *'ĕlōhîm* serves the grammatical function of emphasizing the greatness or power of a person or object. In Jonah 3:3, for example, the greatness of the city of Nineveh is highlighted as the text describes it as, literally, "a great city to Elohim." As many translations recognize, the real import of the phrase is that Nineveh is "an exceedingly large city."[14] In Job 1:16, a servant reports that the "fire of God" (*ʾēš ʾĕlōhîm*) fell from heaven and consumed Job's cattle and servants. The true import of this expression is likely not that a fire *from God* wreaked such havoc on Job's possessions but that a *mighty* fire did so. Similarly, in 1 Samuel 14:15, the indication that a "panic of God" (*ḥerdat ʾĕlōhîm*) took place is almost certainly meant to convey the idea not that God was thrown into a panic but that a *mighty* panic had beset the camp.[15] It seems likely that that the expression *rûaḥ ʾĕlōhîm* in Genesis 1:2 is intended to refer to a "mighty wind." Even if the phrase is better understood simply as "wind of God," however, the point of connection with the winds of Baal and Marduk would still be very much in evidence.

Creation as Separation

As echoes of the Canaanite and Babylonian creation accounts accumulate in Genesis 1, evidence for connections in less prominent features of the text grows as well. One example of such a potential connection lies in the fact that in Genesis 1 God is said to create through the act of *splitting or separating*: on five different occasions, the text describes God's creative labors as acts of separating (Hebrew *hibdîl*) one thing from another (cf. vv. 4, 6, 7, 14, and 18). On Day One, the text tells us, "God *separated* the light from the darkness" (v. 4). This separation is reinforced on Day Four as God sets lights in the heavens "to *separate* the day from the night" (v. 14) and later "to *separate* the light from the darkness" (v. 18).[16]

Most significant of all, though, is the echo of Enuma Elish in Genesis 1's account of God's separating the waters below from the waters above on Day Two (vv. 6–7). In the closing lines of Enuma Elish Tablet IV, we read:

> Bēl [the Lord] rested, examining her carcass,
> so as to divide the monster and create clever things.
> He *split* her in two like a fish for drying.
> Half of her he set up and stretched out as the heavens.
> He pulled tight the skin and stationed guards.
> He commanded them not to let her waters escape.
>
> (IV.135–140)

Marduk's act of splitting Tiamat in two and spreading out her hide as a cover that forms the heavens and holds back the waters above is remarkably similar to the description of God's work on Day Two of creation:[17]

> And God said, "Let there be a firmament[18] in the midst of the waters, and let it separate the waters from the waters." And God made the firmament and separated the waters that were under the firmament from the waters that were above the firmament. And it was so. God called the firmament "heaven." And there was evening and there was morning, a second day.
>
> (Gen 1:6–8)

While a fuller discussion of the dynamics of vv. 6–8 must be put on hold for a moment, it is important to note the parallel between Enuma Elish and Genesis 1 in their descriptions of separating the waters to form the heavens.[19]

Ordering the Heavens

An additional similarity between the description of creation in Genesis 1 and the text of Enuma Elish is found in the language used for God's assigning calendrical tasks to the sun and moon. Enuma Elish describes Marduk's ordering of the skies as follows:

> In her [Tiamat's] belly, he placed the heights.
> He made the moon shine forth, entrusted the night to it.
> He appointed him as the jewel of the night to determine the days.
> Every month without ceasing he marked him with a crown.
>
> (V.11–14)

Similar language appears to be used of the sun in lines 25 and following, though the tablet is too badly broken at this point to give a full translation. The extant portion of the text does go on to specify the manner in which the moon and sun are to organize days and months and years (cf. lines 15–24, 35–46). This is echoed in Genesis 1's language of God's appointing "the greater light to rule the day and the lesser light to rule the night" (v. 16) and in his command that they serve "for signs and for seasons and for days and for years" (v. 14).

The Temple

Though other connections between Enuma Elish and Genesis 1 could be mentioned, it will suffice to conclude with just one more example, namely, the manner in which both stories conclude. Once Marduk has completed the creation of the world (as narrated in Tablet V of Enuma Elish), he moves on (in Tablet VI.1–38) to create human beings, saying, "Let them bear the burden of the gods so the gods may rest" (VI.6). It remains then for Marduk to take up residence in his temple, Esagila, where he will exercise rule as king. The parallel with the Genesis creation account is striking. Having set the world in order, God finally creates humans on Day Six, giving them the task of subduing the earth and having dominion over it. Then, on Day Seven, he rests from his creative labors. As John Walton has rightly argued, the description of God's resting on the seventh day is integrally linked to his taking up residence in his temple, in this case the cosmos itself.[20] Note, for example, the language of Psalm 132:

> Let us go to *his dwelling place*;
>   let us worship at *his footstool.*
> Arise, O YHWH, to *your resting place,*
>   you and your mighty ark!
>
> (vv. 7–8)

> For YHWH has chosen Zion;
>   he has desired it *for his seat.*
> "This is my *resting place* forever;
>   here will I sit, for I have desired it."
>
> (vv. 13–14)

As the Genesis account culminates in God's assigning to humanity the job of continuing his creative work and in God's taking up residence in the temple where he will rule as king, it echoes the quite similar structure of the Babylonian account.[21]

Conclusion

On its surface, Genesis 1 appears to have little in common with either the Babylonian creation tradition or the odd creation traditions preserved in the Bible's poetic texts. As we dig deeper into the text, however, we find that Genesis 1 contains a number of significant echoes of these traditions. Like Enuma Elish, Genesis 1 begins with primordial waters already in place. These waters are described in Genesis 1:2 with the pregnant term *təhōm*, the cognate and echo of Enuma Elish's *Tiamat*. The sea monsters are present in Genesis 1, though their appearance is delayed until v. 21. The divine wind appears in v. 2, demonstrating God's power over the chaotic waters in a fashion quite similar to Marduk's own use of the winds against the sea. God creates in Genesis 1 in a manner reminiscent of Marduk's creative work, as God separates first light from dark, then water from water, and finally water from land. Both God in Genesis 1 and Marduk in Enuma Elish assign to moon and sun the task of ordering the days, months, and years of the calendar. Finally, both stories culminate with the creation of human beings, the description of the work assigned to them, and the narration of the deities' taking up residence as king in their divine temples. To be sure, there are important differences in the way the ancient Near Eastern creation traditions appear in Genesis 1 as compared to the various "odd" creation traditions we saw above in Job, Psalms, and the Prophets. Genesis 1 is not as overt in its use of the Canaanite and Mesopotamian imagery as are these poetic passages. Yet, even in Genesis 1, the Bible's foundational account of creation, there are powerful echoes of the Mesopotamian story. The lingering question is *why those echoes are here.*

CHAPTER 7

Your Gods Are Too Small

A close reading of the Bible's poetic texts reveals a number of passages that borrow imagery from the Canaanite and Mesopotamian creation accounts. Various texts in Psalms, Job, and the Prophets share with the creation accounts of their ancient neighbors the description of a divine battle with the sea or sea monster that establishes the deity's power and lays the foundation for his creative work. In the preceding chapter, though, we saw that these motifs are not limited to just the Bible's poetry. The Bible's first and most famous creation account—Genesis 1—is also marked by Babylonian creation imagery. In the case of a poetic text, perhaps we might pass off this sort of imagery as just a bit of exuberant artistry on the part of the poet, an elaborate figure of speech not meant to be understood as historical fact. But in a text as important as Genesis 1, a creation account written in prose, not poetry, mere figure of speech does not seem to be a sufficient explanation for the text's Babylonian echoes. Why then are these echoes here?

The Genre of Genesis 1

Most of us have experienced the embarrassing moment of being introduced to someone with an unusual name and trying, failingly, to squeeze the sounds of that name into one we already know. My wife's name, Michaela, is one that we have encountered only a handful of times in the circles in which we travel. Rarer still is the pronunciation of Michaela's name; she pronounces it with a "sh" sound in the middle, *mi-shay-lah*, rather than a harder "k" sound. We have yet to meet anyone at all who pronounces the name this way. The results can be fairly comical when people first try to pronounce her name: Michelle? Miss Shayla? Mahalia? It can certainly be a wonderful tool for screening out telemarketers from callers who actually know us. Stepping back, though, why is it that people try to fit the sounds of Michaela's name into a name they already know? It is because we humans are pattern makers. To maneuver through a complex world of sights, sounds, smells, and tastes, we organize the things our senses perceive into groups we are better able to manage. As children, we learn to group things by color and by shape. As we grow older, we distinguish numbers and letters, consonants and vowels, nouns and verbs. Eventually, we move on to patterns as complicated as the periodic table, the taxonomy of flora and fauna, library catalogs, and a thousand other ways of organizing our world.

Hand in hand with our talent for *making* patterns is our skill at *discerning* patterns. We hear the seemingly random sounds of words we do not know, and yet we can usually pick out the language to which those sounds belong. We recognize the letters of our alphabet across innumerable oddly shaped fonts. We spot the subtle symmetry of shape that helps distinguish an arrowhead from the dozens of rocks lying around it. Through the simplest arrangements of a line or two, we can identify countless landmarks—the Eiffel Tower, Big Ben, the Empire State Building, the Sydney Opera House, the Golden Gate Bridge. So good are we at recognizing these forms that we often see patterns that are not really there. Our brains turn the random shapes of clouds into elephants or turtles or school buses. We see faces in the craters of the moon, in an oddly shaped melon or tomato, or in the inkblots of a Rorschach test. We turn the stars into constellations and parts of states into "panhandles." Our minds automatically and subconsciously impose patterns we know on features that connect with part of that pattern, and we "fill in the blanks" for what is missing.

What is true of clouds, stars, and an artist's lines is equally true when it comes to reading texts. Our minds set us up with pattern expectations that often cause us to gloss over certain aspects of a text because we know in advance what the text is *supposed* to say. This is especially true in Genesis 1. Because we know how the universe is structured, we tend to read this first creation account in a way that coincides with our prior knowledge. As we read the text, we impose the pattern of *the world we know* onto the shape of *the world Genesis 1 describes*. Nowhere is this more evident than in the chapter's description of the waters of creation.

Heavenly Waters

Genesis 1:6–8 offers this description of the second day of God's creative work:

> And God said, "Let there be a *rāqîaʿ* in the midst of the waters, and let it separate waters from waters." And God made the *rāqîaʿ* and separated the waters that were under the *rāqîaʿ* from the waters that were above the *rāqîaʿ*. And it was so. God called the *rāqîaʿ* "heaven." And there was evening and there was morning, a second day.

The picture of creation painted by the author here merits especially close attention. For the moment, I have left untranslated the Hebrew term *rāqîaʿ* that occurs so often in these verses. We can return to what the *rāqîaʿ* is in a moment; for now, it is enough to observe what the *rāqîaʿ* does. Verse 6 tells us that the *rāqîaʿ* separates "waters from waters," clarifying in v. 7 that it separates those waters that are "under the *rāqîaʿ*" from the waters that are "above the *rāqîaʿ*." Already, a challenge emerges: These verses describe in simple and straightforward fashion a world in which there is not only the lower ocean we know as the sea but also an upper ocean, an additional body of water stretched out over our heads. Our tendency to impose upon the text patterns we already know, in this case the structure of the world we know from our science classes, might lead us to explain away this upper ocean as nothing more than clouds or some sort of canopy of water vapor.[1] This is manifestly *not* what the text describes, however. The text here is at pains to mark a parallel between the two bodies of water. The waters below are matched by the waters above.

But if the author describes an ocean of water overhead, how did he imagine that it remained there? The answer is the *rāqîaʿ*. While some translations render *rāqîaʿ* as *expanse* (ESV, NJPS) or *vault* (NIV), these terms fall short of the structure Genesis 1 describes. Closer to the term's meaning is the King James Version's rendering *firmament*, which rightly captures the fact that the biblical authors envisioned the *rāqîaʿ* as a solid ("firm") structure stretched out above the earth to form a heavenly dome. The solidity of the *rāqîaʿ* is underscored by the usage of the verb *rāqaʿ*, from which the noun *rāqîaʿ* is derived. Most often, *rāqaʿ* refers to the process of hammering out metals, whether to make an object like a bowl or to overlay a surface with gold, silver, or bronze. Thus, Exodus 39:3 refers to gold leaf that is *hammered out* and cut into decorative threads. Numbers 16:38–39 [17:3–4] orders that the censers carried by

Korah and his companions be *hammered* into plates for overlaying the altar. Isaiah 40:19 describes a craftsman's work of *hammering out* gold to overlay the wood of an idol. Jeremiah 10:9 refers to silver imported from Tarshish that has been *hammered* into plates.[2] The verb *rāqaᶜ* is also used in connection with creation. Isaiah 42:5 describes the earth as *stretched out*. Psalm 136:6 similarly describes the earth as *stretched out* upon the waters. In Job 37:18, God asks Job if he can match God's ability to "*spread out* the skies, hard like a molten mirror." This last usage is particularly interesting, as it compares the spreading out of the heavens to the fashioning of a hard, metal structure.

The nominal forms derived from the verb *rāqaᶜ* similarly attest to the biblical understanding of the *rāqîaᶜ* as a solid structure spread out to form the heavens. In Ezekiel 1, the prophet recounts an elaborate vision he experienced in which strange "living creatures" fly back and forth across the earth:

> And the shape over the heads of the living creatures was a dome [*rāqîaᶜ*], with the appearance of awe-inspiring ice/crystal, stretched out above their heads. Under the dome [*rāqîaᶜ*] their wings were stretched out, one toward another; and each had two wings covering its body. And when they moved, I heard the sound of their wings like the sound of mighty waters, like the sound of the Almighty, the sound of a crowd like the sound of an army. When they stood still, they let down their wings. And there came a voice from above the dome [*rāqîaᶜ*] over their heads. When they stood still, they let down their wings. And above the dome [*rāqîaᶜ*] that was above their heads was something like a throne, like sapphire-stone in appearance; and above the likeness of a throne was the likeness of something like a human form in appearance.
>
> (Ezek 1:22–26)

The prophet's description fits well with the notion of some sort of heavenly dome overhead but not at all with an immaterial vault or expanse. For the living creatures to be depicted as beneath the *rāqîaᶜ* and the divine throne above it, it must be a bounded structure, not merely empty space. This is doubly true since the *rāqîaᶜ* is said by the prophet to shine like crystal, a description that again fits with a solid dome, not merely the sky.

The notion of a solid dome accords perfectly with the author's descrip tion of creation in Genesis 1. The solidity of the *rāqîaᶜ* in this text is evident from its function in supporting the waters above, separating them from the waters below (Gen 1:6–8). As Genesis 1:6 explains, "Let it [the *rāqîaᶜ*] separate the waters from the waters." That the *rāqîaᶜ* is not merely the sky or an expanse is also clear from the fact that the birds are portrayed as flying "*across the face of* the dome [*rāqîaʿ*] of the heavens" (Gen 1:20). From the perspective of the author, the *rāqîaʿ* lies behind (i.e., above) the birds as they fly.[3]

That the earth was covered by a heavenly dome supporting a supra-terrestrial ocean was the implicit view of the cosmos shared both by the biblical authors and by the Bible's earliest interpreters.[4] It is this view that helps make sense of the Hebrew Bible's polyvalent term *šāmayim*, "heaven." In some cases, *šāmayim* refers merely to the skies, the place where birds fly and clouds gather to bring forth rain.[5] *Šāmayim* is also used, though, to refer to the heavenly dome, the *rāqîaʿ* that holds up the waters above the heavens. Thus, in Genesis 1:8, God names the *rāqîaʿ* "*šāmayim*," and in vv. 15, 17, and 20, the dome is called "the dome of the *šāmayim*." Finally, in still other cases, *šāmayim* describes the heavenly abode of God himself, an abode that is pictured as resting on top of the heavenly waters.[6]

A host of biblical and extrabiblical texts align with this ancient conception of the world's structure. In Psalm 148:4, for example, we read, "Praise him you highest heavens, and you waters above the heavens." Note that, like the author of Genesis 1, the psalmist envisions waters that lie above the heavens. A similar view is found in Psalm 104, the lengthy psalm that, as we have seen, rehearses in poetic form the prose account of creation in Genesis 1. Echoing God's creation of light on the first day of creation, the psalmist praises God as one who is "wrapped in light as with a garment" (v. 2a). This is followed by the psalmist's recollection of God's creating the dome that holds up the heavenly waters on Day Two: "You stretch out the heavens like a tent. *You set the beams of your chambers upon the waters*" (vv. 2b–3a). The language of Psalm 29:10 is quite similar: "YHWH sits *enthroned over the flood*; YHWH sits enthroned as king forever."[7] This structure may also help to make sense of the mysterious experience the apostle Paul describes in 2 Corinthians:

> I know a man in Christ who fourteen years ago—whether in the body or out of the body I do not know, God knows—was caught up to the third heaven. And I know that such a man—whether in the body or out of the body I do not know, God knows—was caught up into Paradise and heard inexpressible words that no mortal is permitted to utter.
>
> (2 Cor 12:2–4)

Paul's reference to "the third heaven," the heaven that is God's heavenly dwelling, fits perfectly with the structure of the cosmos outlined in the passages we have considered.[8]

Similar understandings of the structure of the cosmos are found in postbiblical books as well. In the apocryphal book known as 2 Esdras,[9] for example, the writer describes creation in a manner similar to that found in the preceding passages:

> [The Lord] said, "Let the earth be made," and it was made, and "Let the heaven be made," and it was made. At his word the stars were fixed in their places, and he knows the number of the stars. He searches the abyss and its treasures; he has measured the sea and its contents; he has confined the sea in the midst of the waters; and by his word he has suspended the earth over the water. *He has spread out the heaven like a dome and made it secure upon the waters.*
>
> (2 Esd 16:55–59 NRSV)

The writer's description of the sea as being "confined in the midst of the waters" and the earth as being "suspended over the waters" is reminiscent of the various biblical passages that posit the existence of subterranean waters on which the earth rests (cf. Exod 20:4; Job 26:5; Pss 24:1–2; 136:6). Importantly, though, the writer also pictures God's spreading out the heavens *like a dome* (*quasi cameram*) that he secures on the waters.

For the pseudepigraphic book 3 Baruch, the dome appears in connection with the Tower of Babel. As the story would have it, an angel leads Baruch on a journey in which he sees a series of heavenly mysteries. In one of these visions, Baruch is shown the punishments visited upon the instigators of the Tower of Babel's construction. There, his angelic guide explains to him that the purpose of the Tower's great height was so the people could pierce the dome of heaven and determine the material of which it was made: "And taking an auger, they sought to pierce the heaven, saying: 'Let us see whether the heaven is made of clay, or of brass, or of iron' " (3 Bar. 3:7). That the heavenly dome was solid was taken for granted; it remained only to determine what material the dome was made of. The material composition of the dome is taken up by the historian Josephus as well. In his retelling of the story of creation in *Antiquities of the Jews*, Josephus specifies that on the second day, God set the heaven above the universe, separating it from the rest of creation with a structure he describes as *krustallon*, a Greek word referring to either ice or crystal (*Ant.* 1.1.30). The ambiguity of Josephus' term here actually preserves a similar ambiguity found in Ezekiel's description of the dome. The Hebrew term *qeraḥ*, which the prophet uses in reference to the dome, is also used to refer to ice (cf. Ps 147:17; Job 6:16; 37:10; 38:29).[10]

Speculation about the nature of the heavenly dome continued well beyond the biblical period. In the Babylonian Talmud (completed ca. 500 CE), for example, the rabbinic scholars of the period offer an extended argument concerning the thickness of the *rāqîaʿ* (see b. Pesaḥ. 94a). As part of this discussion, they conclude that the reason one can see light before one sees the sun rise in the morning and after it has set in the evening is because it is during those periods that the sun is passing through the *rāqîaʿ*. The rabbis apparently thought that the translucent (crystalline?) dome would permit light to be seen even when the sun was not yet (or no longer) visible.

Heavenly Lights

If we step back from Genesis 1 and the texts that interpret it, the overall picture that emerges is quite clear. For the biblical texts and the traditions that followed in their wake, the world was thought to be bounded by two bodies of water, a lower sea that was believed to lie under the earth and an upper sea that was suspended overhead. *The problem, of course, is that this bears little relation to the world as we know it to exist scientifically.* And yet, we have still not fully plumbed the depths of the problem presented in Genesis 1. Not only does the text describe a world in which an upper ocean is thought to stretch out over our heads, but we also find the following in its description of the fourth day of creation:

> And God said, "Let there be lights *in the dome of the heavens* to separate between the day and the night; and let them be for signs and for seasons and for days and years; and let them be lights *in the dome of the heavens* to give light upon the earth." And it was so. And God made the two great lights, the greater light to govern the day and the lesser light to govern the night—and the stars. And God set them *in the dome of the heavens* to give light upon the earth, to rule over the day and over the night, and to separate between the light and the darkness. And God saw that it was good. And there was evening and there was morning, the fourth day.
>
> (Gen 1:14–19)

A careful reader will note that the text says, in v. 14, that the "lights" are set *in the dome of the heavens* to separate between day and night. Likewise, the next verse, v. 15, states that the lights are placed *in the dome of the heavens* to give light upon the earth. Verse 17 specifies that the greater light and the lesser light and the stars are placed *in the dome of the heavens* to give light on the earth. Thus, not only does Genesis 1 describe a world in which an upper ocean of water is suspended above creation, it also describes the sun, moon, and stars as being located *underneath* this watery body. In this respect, the prose account in Genesis 1 accords perfectly with the poetic description found in a text like Psalm 148:

> Praise him, sun and moon;
> > praise him, all you shining stars!
> Praise him, you heaven of heavens,
> > *and you waters that are above the heavens!*
>
> > > > (Ps 148:3–4)

Like Genesis 1, the psalmist envisions a cosmos in which there are heavenly waters above the sun, moon, and stars.

It is not hard to understand why Genesis 1 would describe the world in this fashion. To the naked eye, this is precisely what the world looks like. The sun may be ninety-three million miles from earth and the edge of our atmosphere only fifty to sixty miles high, but this is not what the world looks like to a naked and untrained eye.[11] From the time we were first asked to draw pictures in kindergarten, we have known intuitively that we should draw a yellow sun with a blue *background*. We do this because whatever their relative distances from us, the sun *appears* to be on this side of the blue sky. The same is true of the moon, which, when visible in the daytime, seems to appear on this side of the blue sky behind. Even in the case of stars, there is reason for thinking they are on this side of the blue. Several of the planets, which were thought to be "wandering stars" in antiquity, are visible from time to time during daylight hours. This is especially true of Venus and, to a lesser degree, of Jupiter and Mars. Even in the case of genuine stars, on an almost nightly basis stars begin to appear at dusk while the sky retains its deep and beautiful dark blue color. When these stars and planets begin to shine, they do so on what appears to be this side of the blue curtain behind.

That the sun, moon, and stars would be thought to inhabit a bowl overhead is also easy to understand. Like the sun and moon, those stars that are not circumpolar appear to rise in the sky from the east, travel overhead in an arc, and set in the west. Even the constellations and asterisms into which we organize patterns of stars point toward the bowl-shaped illusion created by the sky.[12] Steeped as we are in modern science, we know that the stars are fantastically far away and that some stars are far more distant from us than others. And yet, when we spot a constellation, we tend to think of the stars in it as existing in a flat or slightly curved plane. When we think of the stars of the constellation Orion, for example, it is easy to imagine that we might take an exceptionally speedy spaceship and travel to a point where we could look at the stars of the constellation from its side, seeing them all line up together. The problem is that the stars of Orion would permit no such thing. The star that marks the hunter's left shoulder, Bellatrix, is 243 light-years away from earth; but the star that marks his left knee, Rigel, is 777 light-years away. In other words, after reaching Bellatrix, one would have to keep traveling 186,282 miles per second for 534 years—3.1 quadrillion miles—to get as far away from the earth as Rigel is. That is certainly not how the stars appear to our naked eye, however. They appear as if they are fixed in a bowl over our heads, a dome as it were, in which the stars of constellations and asterisms appear to reside side by side.

The picture of the physical world described by Genesis 1 is one that fits well with what might have been divined about the universe from the perspective of an ancient Israelite. Again, however, the problem is that *it does not fit at all* with what we know today to be scientifically true of the universe. There is no ocean of water stretched out over our heads. There is no *rāqîaʿ*—crystal, metal, porcelain, or otherwise—holding that ocean up. And by no means are the sun, moon, and stars fixed in a dome and set under the heavenly waters. Put simply, if Genesis 1 purports to be a scientific text, it is a scientific text whose science is wildly wrong. But this is key: Genesis 1 does not purport to be a scientific text; it is a text of an altogether different sort. Importantly, it is the very echoes of the Babylonian creation tradition that point us toward just what sort of text it intends to be.

Theological Polemic

In the last several decades, biblical scholars have given increasing attention to the literary phenomenon of *allusion*. Allusion occurs when an author borrows elements from another text—vocabulary, imagery, structure, etc.— and deploys those elements in his or her own text. As Robert Alter observes:

> Allusion occurs when a writer, recognizing the general necessity of making a literary work by building on the foundations of antecedent literature, deliberately exploits this predicament in explicitly activating an earlier text as part of the new system of meaning and aesthetic value of his own text.[13]

The reasons that lie behind one author's "activation" of another text vary widely. New Testament authors frequently allude to passages from the Hebrew Scriptures to demonstrate that events in the life of Jesus were anticipated by the prophets or to reinforce their particular theological arguments. One author in the Hebrew Bible might allude to another biblical author to draw out the meaning of the earlier text. Thus, for example, Psalm 78 alludes to a wide swath of Israel's early historical texts to draw conclusions about God's selection of Jerusalem as his city and David as his king. An author can also allude to a text in order to interpret or explain it. Again in Psalm 78, the psalmist alludes to the version of the plague narratives he had inherited in order to explain some of the underlying features of that earlier text.[14]

Allusions and echoes can also be deployed for more polemical purposes.[15] As Israel's psalmists praised the majesty of God, they paused to wonder how the God of creation could condescend to pay attention to lowly human beings. Psalm 8:3–4 [4–5] muses:

> When I look at your heavens, the work of your fingers,
>   the moon and the stars that you have established,
> *what are humans [māh ʾĕnôš] that you remember them,*
>   *and mortals [ûben-ʾādām] that you pay attention to them?*

Psalm 144:3–4 strikes the same tone as it wonders:

> O YHWH, *what are mortals [māh ʾādām] that you regard them,*
>   *humans [ben-ʾĕnôš] that you think of them?*
> *A human [ʾādām] is like a breath [lahebel];*
>   *their days are like a passing shadow.*

As Job laments the terrible trials that have overwhelmed him, however, he subtly echoes these passages but in a way that reverses their original intent. Job cries out:

> I loathe my life; I would not live forever.
>   Let me alone, for my days are a *breath [hebel].*
> *What are humans [māh ʾĕnôš], that you make so much of them,*
>   *and that you set your heart on them?*
>
> (Job 7:16–17)

The psalmists marveled at the graciousness of God's attention to and care for humans; Job uses the same language to voice his wish that God would turn his attention elsewhere.

A different sort of polemic through allusion is found in the story of the golden calf in Exodus 32. While the general outline of the story is quite familiar, a close reading of vv. 4–5 reveals two oddities in the text. First, although Aaron makes only one golden calf for the Israelites, the people declare, "*These* are your gods, O Israel, who brought you up out of the land of Egypt" (v. 4, 8). Second, although Aaron had fashioned an idol for the people, he insists on proclaiming, "Tomorrow shall be a festival *to YHWH*" (v. 5). Key to resolving these oddities in the text is a recognition that the golden calf story not only condemns Aaron, it also alludes to and polemicizes against Jeroboam's installation of golden calves at shrines in Dan and Bethel. Note the language used in 1 Kings as the author describes Jeroboam's shrines:

> So the king took counsel and made *two calves of gold*. And he said to the people, "You have been going up to Jerusalem long enough. *Here are your gods, O Israel, who brought you up out of the land of Egypt*."[16]
>
> (1 Kgs 12:28)

Through its subtle off-note—"these" rather than "this"—the golden calf story *activates* the story of Jeroboam's calves and alerts the reader to its two-pronged polemic. In both cases, the condemnation is swift for the people's attempt to worship the right God (YHWH) in the wrong way.

The echoes of Enuma Elish in Genesis 1 serve the same purpose as those in Exodus 32. Unlike Psalm 74 or 89, Genesis 1 does not recapitulate the Babylonian story in any meaningful way; it does not cast God as victor over sea and dragon. Instead, it uses its *echoes* of Enuma Elish to activate the Babylonian creation tradition in the minds of its readers and, as we will see below, to alert them to the polemic it will launch against this tradition.[17] In the same way that Exodus 32's language serves to put Jeroboam on notice, Genesis 1's language says, as it were, "Babylon, I'm talking about you."[18]

"In the beginning, God . . ."

The contrasts between Genesis 1 and Enuma Elish begin in the very first verse of the biblical account: "In the beginning, God created the heavens and the earth." As we noted above in ch. 6, Genesis 1:2–3 lines up well with the Babylonian account. Verse 2's description of the watery chaos that precedes creation aligns with lines 1–8 of Enuma Elish, which describe the same watery, primordial state. Then, in v. 3, just as in line 9 of Enuma Elish, the first moves of creation are described. The line that finds no parallel in the Babylonian tradition is v. 1, the biblical author's attribution of all the work of creation to just one God. Altogether absent from Genesis 1 is Enuma Elish's description of primeval Apsu and Tiamat and its theogony of their descendant gods, Lahmu and Lahamu, Anshar and Kishar, Anu and Ea, and eventually Marduk himself. As Hermann Gunkel observes, "There is nothing in the cosmogonies of other peoples that can compare with the first sentence of the Bible."[19] Claus Westermann goes further:

> The creation of the world by God is expressed in one sentence as in the praise of God. And because this sentence is prefixed to the actual account of creation, it acquires monumental importance which distinguishes it from other creation stories.[20]

The author of Genesis 1 begins echoing Enuma Elish in v. 2, but by prefacing this verse with v. 1, he has made a powerful statement: The God of Genesis 1 stands alone, *independent of* and *precedent to* creation.

Tiamat Defanged

One of the most powerful echoes of the Babylonian creation tradition in Genesis 1 is v. 2's use of *təhōm*, the Hebrew cognate of the Akkadian word for Tiamat, to describe the primordial deep. As we discussed above, although others have rightly pointed out that *təhōm* is not a loanword from Akkadian, it is hardly necessary that *təhōm* fit the linguistic requirements of a loanword for it to serve as an *echo* of the Babylonian account. Allusions often operate on the level of sound play and similarity as they activate coordinate texts. On an admittedly pedestrian level, we might think of a line like, "I'm not a smart dog, but I know what road kill is." On its face, this might not seem to be an allusion at all. When delivered in the right cadence, however, and in a movie in which Tom Hanks plays a starring role (or at least provides a starring voice), this line from Slinky Dog in *Toy Story 2* forms an obvious echo of Forrest Gump's protest to Jenny, "I'm not a smart man, but I know what love is." More sophisticated are the allusions to the book of Job in Archibald MacLeish's play *J.B.* In another context, there would be little to suggest that characters named J.B., Mr. Zuss, and Nickles have anything to do with Job. As the play wrestles with the same issues as the biblical story, however, it takes only a modicum of readerly imagination to grasp that J.B. is Job, Mr. Zuss is a stand-in for Zeus, head of the gods, and Nickles draws on "Old Nick," a folk name for the devil. For there to be an echo of the Babylonian story in Genesis 1, it is no more necessary for *təhōm* to derive linguistically from Tiamat than it is for Zuss to be an English cognate of the Greek word for Zeus.[21]

But if there is an echo of Tiamat in v. 2's description of the watery deeps, why is it there? It is surely meant to highlight the fact that though the deeps/Tiamat may be present in Genesis 1, they are entirely passive in the face of the creator. In Enuma Elish, Tiamat is an opponent so fearsome that even the most powerful gods despair of challenging her. Anshar, the last of the primordial gods, is distraught when he hears that Tiamat has determined to attack the gods:

> Anshar heard; the matter was deeply disturbing.
> "Woe!" he cried aloud and bit his lip.
> His insides were angry, his heart was restless.
>
> (II.49–51)

The god Ea, who defeated Apsu earlier in the epic, is similarly terrified when he thinks of confronting Tiamat:

> Ea went to discover Tiamat's strategy.
> He stopped, numb with fear, then turned back.
>
> (II.81–82)

> Speaking to Anshar, he says:
> My father, Tiamat's deeds are beyond me.
> I sought out her course, but my spell could not withstand it.
> Her strength is mighty; she is full of dread.
> She is altogether mighty; none can advance against her.
>
> (II.85–88)

Identical language is used to describe the fear of the great god Anu when he tries to confront Tiamat (II.105–111). Even Marduk is said to waver when he first encounters her:

> Bēl [Marduk] drew near to examine the inside of Tiamat;
> he was probing the strategies of Qingu, her spouse.
> As he looked, his thoughts became confused.
> His plans were in disarray, his actions disturbed.

And the gods his allies, those who went at his side,
when they saw the foremost warrior, their sight failed them.

(IV.65–70)

Contrast these descriptions of the terror Tiamat instills in the Babylonian gods with the passivity of the deeps in Genesis 1:2. The təhōm and waters of v. 2 do nothing at all; they lie there inactive before the God who will bring order to them.[22]

It may be that the author of Genesis 1 intends to add insult to injury as he describes the mighty divine wind that sweeps over the waters. Although the waters merely lie there passively before God, God still sends his divine wind to highlight his absolute power over them. On the other hand, it may be that we are to understand the passivity of the təhōm to be the *result* of the divine wind's exercise of power over the waters. Perhaps the waters would resist if they could, but they cannot because they are subject to the divine wind's control. Although the waters may be primordial, they are not beyond God's power. A similar situation obtains with respect to the dragon-like monsters that form Tiamat's retinue. The dragons are still there in Genesis 1, but they have been reduced to just one more part of the created order as the "great sea monsters" of v. 21—monsters that Psalm 104, the first commentary on Genesis 1, suggests God made simply to sport with (v. 26).[23] There are echoes of Tiamat in Genesis 1, but Tiamat has been defanged.

An Effortless Creation

As noticeably absent from Genesis 1's creation story as the carnage of Marduk and Tiamat's battle is the graphic and even macabre fashion in which Marduk butchers his foe's carcass to create the world. In Enuma Elish, Marduk examines Tiamat's body (IV.135), splits her like a fish for drying (IV.137), and stretches out her hide (IV.139). He gathers her foams to form clouds (V.47–49) and her spittle to make rain (V.50–51). He pours the waters out of her head to fill the deeps (V.53–54) and gouges out her eyes to let their fluid form the Tigris and Euphrates (V. 55). He blocks up her nostrils (V.56), heaps up her breasts to form mountains (V.57), and bores wells into her body to form springs (V.58). He weaves her tail into a bond called the durmāḫu to tie heaven, earth, and the apsû (the freshwater remains of the foe Ea defeated) together (V.59), then he uses her crotch as a prop to hoist heaven into position (V.60–62). Later Marduk severs the arteries of Qingu and uses his blood to form humankind (VI.5–34).

All of this messy work is conspicuously absent from Genesis 1. Indeed, one of the most noteworthy aspects of this first creation account is the sheer effortlessness that characterizes God's creative activity. Though I am guilty myself of using expressions that describe God's "creative *works*" or "creative *labors*," there is little in this first chapter of Scripture that registers as labor at all. In Genesis 1, God merely speaks, and the elements of creation fly to obey his will. The cumbersome translation, "Let there be," that English demands actually masks the much softer *yǝhî* found in the Hebrew (vv. 3, 6, 14).[24] God's creative decree is almost a whisper, and yet its effects are profound. By contrast, on only one occasion does Marduk create by speaking, in Tablet IV.19–26, as he commands the annihilation of a constellation set before him by the gods and then commands its re-creation. This singular creative decree only highlights the difference between the creative powers of Marduk and those of the God of Israel. Marduk truly labors to create; the God of Genesis 1 creates *effortlessly*.[25]

"Let there be light"

The first act of creation in Genesis 1 is found in vv. 3–5:

And God said, "Let there be light," and there was light. And God saw that the light was good, and God separated the light from the darkness. And God called the light Day, and the darkness he called Night. And there was evening and there was morning, a first day.

The words that narrate this first day of creation are among the most familiar in all of Scripture. The command "Let there be light" graces the seals of universities from Los Angeles to Liverpool and has served as the title for any number of books, stories, songs, plays, and works of art.[26] Our very familiarity with the verse's language, however, can obscure some of the difficulties these lines present. First, when the text tells us, "And there was light," where are we to imagine the light had come from? From a scientific perspective, we know that light is not a free-floating and independent phenomenon but rather the visible part of a much larger spectrum of electromagnetic energy given off by excited atoms. Light begins at a source, those atoms excited by an excess of energy, and streaks away from that source in a burst of electromagnetic radiation. The ancient Israelites could not be expected to know about atoms and radiation, but they certainly knew light invariably came from a light-giving source. Why doesn't Genesis 1 mention that source?

This leads to a second question: How can light be separated from darkness? In our own experience, we might think of separating light from darkness by putting up a physical barrier to prevent the one (light) from invading the other (darkness). Verse 4, though, appears to treat both light and dark as if they were physical substances that could be segregated into self-contained spaces. This runs afoul of what we know about light and especially what we know about darkness, which is nothing more than the absence of light.

Third, in what sense can light be accurately described as "day" and darkness as "night"? While it may be true that we call the period of time when we see the sun's light *day* and the period of time when we do not *night*, the phenomenon of light itself is entirely indifferent to such titles. The celestial bodies that fill the heavens churn out vast amounts of light, but that light could hardly be called "day." Even in the case of our sun, day and night have nothing at all to do with the amount of light the sun gives off; the sun's output of light is relentlessly constant. Day and night have to do rather with our ability to see or not see that light.

Fourth, and lastly, what can the text mean when it says, "And there was evening, and there was morning, a first day," when there is as yet no sun to rise or to set, to give light or to withhold it? What is evening absent the withdrawal of the sun's light, and what is morning absent its return the next day?

From a scientific perspective, these problems are insurmountable. They exhibit an understanding of the properties of light and the relationship between light and darkness and day and night that runs afoul of what we know about the physical world. This would be a terrible problem *if indeed Genesis 1 were intended to be read as a scientific text*. But the description of light and darkness in these verses has nothing at all to do with science. These verses signal a theological polemic and must be judged on *those terms*, not scientific terms. The nature of the polemic intended by the creation and ordering of light on Day One is particularly evident when account is taken of what is *not* said to be created on this day. On the first day, God is said to create light, but there is no mention at all of any *light-bearers*. This creation of light without sun may well be a direct challenge to the connection Enuma Elish draws between Marduk and the sun when Marduk first appears in the epic.[27] When Marduk first arrives on the scene, the gods hail him as "the Son, the Sun-god, the Sun-god of the gods."[28] Genesis 1 accords no such pride of place to "the Sun-god of the gods"; instead, it portrays God as creating light alone on the first day and relegates the sun, moon, and stars to the fourth day of creation. The text says, as it were, *God can create light, and he needs no help from the gods to do so.*[29]

This diminution of the roles of the sun, moon, and stars in Genesis 1 is thrown into sharp relief when one compares their place in the Mesopotamian pantheon. In Mesopotamia, the stars were thought to be gods, so much so that in Sumerian script the pictographic symbol for *god* was a star.[30] Marduk was associated with Jupiter, the warrior god Ninurta with Saturn, the god of the netherworld Nergal with Mars, the goddess Ishtar with Venus, and the scribal god Nabû with Mercury. Added to this group were the gods of the sun and moon, Utu and Nanna in Sumerian, Shamash and Sîn in Akkadian. As god of the sun, Shamash was connected with justice, since he saw all that occurred on earth as he traveled overhead. It is Shamash who was depicted as giving kingship to Hammurapi when Hammurapi presented him with a worthy code of laws, and this same god was thought to have protected Gilgamesh on his long quest for immortality. As god of the moon, Sîn was connected with herding cattle and with fishing, as his crescent shape resembled the curved horns of cattle and the curved shape of Mesopotamian fishing boats. Though less bright than Shamash, Sîn ranked somewhat higher in the pantheon than the sun god. He was considered to be the son of Enlil and was often cast as the father of Shamash and of Ishtar, his sister.

It is noteworthy that in Enuma Elish, the installation of the gods in their celestial abodes is one of Marduk's first creative acts. He splits and stretches out Tiamat's carcass to form a dome overhead (IV.136–142) and then immediately sets to ordering the stars into constellations and giving instructions to the moon and sun concerning their roles. As he does so, the divine aspect of the sun, moon, and stars is strongly emphasized. Tablet V begins: "He fashioned the stations for the great gods; he established constellations for the stars that correspond to them" (V.1–2). This is followed by an elaborate description of the moon's being given the "jewel of the night" (V.13) and by Marduk's personal instructions on how the moon is to shine to mark weeks and days. The sun is addressed in similar fashion, though regrettably the text of the Babylonian story is too broken at this point for his instructions to be fully fleshed out. Enough of the text remains, however, to perceive Marduk's continued reliance on the sun and moon to provide justice for the land (V.24–25). Importantly, it is only after Marduk has ordered the heavens and entrusted the execution of justice to the sun and moon that he uses the rest of Tiamat's body to create the land and its features (V.46–66).

By starting with the creation of light detached from the heavenly lights and by delaying the creation of those lights until the second half of the creation week, Genesis 1 dramatically undermines the importance of Marduk

("Sun-god of the gods") and these other celestial entities. Further, even when the text does finally get to the creation of sun and moon, these two are not dignified with names. They are referred to as "the two big lights," "the bigger light," and "the smaller light" but never as "sun" or "moon" (v. 16). When "the bigger light" and "the smaller light" are created, they are assigned calendrical duties: they serve "for signs and seasons and days and years" (v. 14), and their dominions are limited to daytime, for the bigger light, and to nighttime, for the smaller light and stars (v. 15). Not to be missed, of course, is the fact that the greater and lesser lights are *actually created by God* in Genesis 1. In Enuma Elish, Marduk only assigns stations to Shamash and Sîn; he does not create them.

We might say that the sun and moon are demythologized in Genesis 1, but it seems nearer the mark to say they are dethroned. They have been re-moved from their perches as gods and treated as mere tools in the creator's hands. Nowhere is this dethronement more evident than in the last words of v. 16: "and the stars." With just two Hebrew words, *wə'eṯ hakkôḵāḇîm,* the author of Genesis 1 casually dismisses the vast ocean of stars visible overhead. For the Babylonians, the stars represented the greatest and most powerful of their deities, and yet it is as if the author of the biblical account has said (to put it colloquially), "Stars . . . whatever."

As science has furthered our understanding of the universe, it has be-come increasingly difficult to fathom either the number or size of the stars fixed over our heads. In terms of size, the sun seems an impressive body when compared to a planet like our own. Scientists estimate that it would take nearly a million earths to fill the sun, a fact that may not be that sur-prising since the sun accounts for almost 99.8 percent of the mass of our solar system. Earth and its sister planets Venus and Mars, tiny Mercury and Pluto, and even the great gas giants Jupiter, Saturn, Uranus, and Neptune fight over a mere two-tenths of 1 percent of the remaining mass in the solar system.[31] As one textbook has cheekily described the solar system, it is "the sun plus some debris."[32] Our sun is only a modest-sized star, though, when compared to other stellar objects. The brightest star in the northern hemi-sphere, Arcturus, is more than twenty-five times larger than our sun. Rigel, one of the stars in the constellation Orion, is nearly eighty times larger. But these are mere trifles compared to the largest stars discovered so far. Antares is 680 times, and Betelgeuse nearly 900 times, the size of the sun. The very largest stars, known only by scientific names like VY Canis Majoris and UY Scuti, are estimated to range from 1,400 to 1,700 times the size of the sun.[33] So large are these stars that if they were placed where our sun is, their outer edges would fall somewhere between the orbits of Jupiter and Saturn. Or, to think of the size comparison in another way, if you could hitch a ride on a 747 traveling at its maximum speed of 570 miles per hour, you could make your way around the sun in just under 200 days. The same ride around UY Scuti would take more than *920 years*.[34] Yet, Genesis 1 dismisses all of these great stars with language that treats them as an afterthought: "*and the stars.*"

As mind-boggling as the size of the stars is the sheer number of them. Our own galaxy, the Milky Way, is estimated to have at least 100 billion stars in it (and many estimates range much higher than this).[35] Within this mass of stars are found essentially all of the celestial objects visible to the naked eye. All the asteroids, comets, planets, stars, asterisms, constellations, and nebulae we see—these are all found within our own galaxy. Indeed, the only objects from outside of our galaxy that are visible to our eyes are four smudges of light representing four galaxies, the Andromeda Galaxy, the Triangulum Galaxy, the Large Magellanic Cloud, and the Small Magellanic Cloud. So faint are these objects that while a handful of philosophers had posited the existence of "island universes" outside of our galaxy beginning in the eighteenth century, as late as 1920 the preeminent astronomers of the day were still debating whether anything at all existed outside of our Milky Way.[36] A century later, and how the situation has changed! We now know that the 100 billion *stars* of our galaxy sit alongside at least 100 billion and possibly up to 2 trillion *separate galaxies*.[37] Even at the low end of these estimates, that works out to 10,000,000,000,000,000,000,000 stars—10 sextillion! And yet, again, Genesis 1 brushes aside all of these innumerable heavenly bodies as hardly worth mentioning. A single phrase, "and the stars," suffices to note their creation.

Of course, it might be objected that the authors of the Bible, bound as they were by the scientific limitations of their day, had no way of knowing just how many stars there are or how big those stars can be. In one sense, it is undoubtedly true that the biblical authors knew less about the starry sky than we know today. But in another sense, they also knew much more. Surrounded as most of us are by light-polluting homes, neighborhoods, and cities, the sky we see is almost entirely mute. A few bright stars stand out, perhaps enough for us to make out a few decent constellations, but most stars are simply too faint to outshine the streetlights and headlights and well-lit buildings that surround us. On those rare occasions, though, when we find ourselves out in a very dark place, on a camping trip or out in the country, we may get a taste of what the sky looked like to our ancestors long ago. We look up, and the sky is alive with so many stars that one seems to blend into the next. Constellations almost disappear because their key stars are lost in an ocean of other celestial lights competing for attention. The sky the biblical authors saw was so full of stars that they despaired of being able to count them. "Look toward heaven and count the stars, if you are able to count them; so shall your descendants be," said God to Abraham in Genesis 15:5. The biblical authors compared the number of stars in the sky to the number of grains of sand on the seashore (Gen 22:17; 32:12). Yet when they described God's creation of this vast sea of stars, they did so dismissively, with a simple "and the stars," in order to put these great objects—and from the Babylonian perspective, these great gods—in their place.

Your God Is Too Small

Various lines of evidence suggest that Genesis 1 was composed either shortly before or during the exilic period.[38] This was a time when the surviving kingdom of Judah felt terrific pressure from Babylonia and its imperial ambitions. As the Neo-Assyrian Empire collapsed in 609 BCE, Babylon became the region's hegemon, and in the decade stretching from 598 to 587, it subjugated and ultimately destroyed Judah, its capital Jerusalem, and its great temple (cf. 2 Kgs 25). In the face of such catastrophes, it would be hard not to wonder whether the god of the Babylonians, Marduk, had not proven superior to Israel's own God. Had not the Assyrians asked the same question of the nation just a century before?

> Do not listen to Hezekiah, for he is misleading you by saying, "YHWH will deliver us." Has any of the gods of the nations ever delivered its land from the hand of the king of Assyria? Where are the gods of Hamath and Arpad? Where are the gods of Sepharvaim, Hena, and Ivvah? Have they delivered Samaria from my hand? Who among all the gods of these countries have delivered their countries from my hand, that YHWH should deliver Jerusalem out of my hand?
>
> (2 Kgs 18:32b–35)

Judah would face similar questions again in the waning years of the exile. As we saw above in ch. 5, the Neo-Babylonian Empire's last king, Nabonidus, had removed Marduk from what was believed to be his rightful place at the head of the pantheon and had installed his beloved moon god, Sîn, in his place. The Marduk priests were scandalized by this turn of events, and when the Persian king Cyrus marched on the city, the priests swung wide the gates to welcome him in. As we saw in the famous Cyrus Cylinder, the Babylonian priests believed Marduk had grown angry toward the people because of his dethronement, but now he had turned toward them with mercy once again. They believed it was Marduk, now roused to action, who had called upon Cyrus to defeat Nabonidus and to restore Marduk to his rightful place at the head of the pantheon.

When the latter chapters of the book of Isaiah respond to these events, they insist that it was not Marduk but rather YHWH who had raised up Cyrus, and that, furthermore, Cyrus had been tapped not to restore Marduk to his place but to set God's people free. Thus, in Isaiah 45, we read:

> Thus says YHWH to his anointed one, to Cyrus,
> > whose right hand I have grasped
> to subdue nations before him,
> > and to ungird the loins of kings,
> to open doors before him
> > and gates that shall not be closed.
> I am the one who will go before you
> > to level the mountains.
> I will break the doors of bronze,
> > and the bars of iron I will cut through.
> I will give you the treasures of darkness
> > and hidden riches,
> so that you may know that it is I, YHWH,
> > the God of Israel, who calls your name.
>
> > (Isa 45:1–3)

And again a few verses later:

> It was I who aroused him [Cyrus] in righteousness,
> > and I will make straight all his paths.
> He shall build my city,
> > and he will set my exiles free,
> not for price and not for payment,
> > says YHWH of hosts.
>
> > (Isa 45:13)

The language of Cyrus' victory over Babylon is unmistakable: "to open doors before him and gates that shall not be closed" (v. 1b); "I will break the doors of bronze, and the bars of iron I will cut through" (v. 2b). But, the prophet piles phrase upon phrase to insist that it was YHWH, not Marduk, who had called Cyrus: "Thus says YHWH to his anointed, to Cyrus, whose right hand I have grasped" (v. 1a); "so that you may know that it is I, YHWH, the God of Israel, who calls your name" (v. 3b); "I arm you, though you do not know me" (v. 5b).

As the prophet responds to the supposed divinity of Marduk, he describes the God of Israel in ways that are almost unprecedented in the Hebrew Scriptures. Over the course of Isaiah 45, he says concerning YHWH:

> I am YHWH, and there is no other;
>> besides me there is no god.
>>
>>> (v. 5a)

> There is none besides me;
>> I am YHWH, and there is no other.
>>
>>> (v. 6b)

> I am YHWH, and there is no other.
>>
>>> (v. 18b)

> Who told this long ago?
>> Who declared it of old?
> Was it not I, YHWH?
>> There is no other god besides me.
> A righteous God and a savior—
>> there is no one besides me.
>>
>>> (v. 21b)

Perhaps to emphasize God's awesome power in comparison to the lesser gods of the nations that surrounded Israel, the prophet in this latter part of Isaiah places a heavy emphasis on God's work in creation. Repeatedly, as the prophet establishes God's credentials for the declarations he will make, he turns to God's work as creator. He says, for example, in Isaiah 42:5:

> Thus says God, YHWH,
>> the one who created the heavens and stretched them out,
>> the one who spread out the earth and what comes from it,
> the one who gives breath to the people upon it
>> and spirit to those who walk in it . . .

And again in Isaiah 44:24:

> Thus says YHWH, your redeemer,
>> and the one who formed you in the womb:
> I am YHWH, the one who makes all things,
>> the one who alone stretched out the heavens,
>> the one who by myself spread out the earth . . .

The prophet emphasizes the incomparable power of God as creator. In Isaiah 40:12, he declares:

> Who has measured the waters in the hollow of his hand
>> and marked off the heavens with a span,
> held the dust of the earth in a measure,
>> and weighed the mountains with a scale and the hills with a
>> balance?

The prophet's words of praise here rank among the most exalted in all of the Bible. As God is depicted as measuring the great deeps in the hollow of his hand, measuring the universe with the span of his hand, and measuring the great mountains in a scale, the prophet underscores the creative power of Israel's God, declaring it to be unmatched by that of any god known to Israel's neighbors. It is no wonder that he draws the conclusion in v. 18: "To whom would you liken God or to what likeness would you compare him?"

In this part of Isaiah, creation forms the basis not only for contrasting YHWH and Marduk but also for contrasting YHWH and humanity. Creation is a constant feature, for example, in Isaiah 40:22–28:

> It is he [YHWH] who sits above the circle of the earth,
>> and its inhabitants are like grasshoppers.
> He is the one who spreads out the heavens like a veil
>> and stretches them out like a tent to live in.
> He is the one who brings princes to naught
>> and makes the judges of the earth as nothing.
> Scarcely are they planted, scarcely sown,
>> scarcely has their stem taken root in the earth,
> when he blows upon them, and they wither,
>> and the storm carries them off like stubble.
> To whom would you liken me,
>> or who is my equal? says the Holy One.

Lift up your eyes on high and see:
    Who created these?
He is the one who sends out their host by number,
    calling them all by name.
Because he is great in power and mighty in strength,
    not one is missing.
Why do you say, O Jacob,
    and speak, O Israel,
"My way is hidden from YHWH,
    and my claim is disregarded by my God"?
Have you not known? Have you not heard?
    YHWH is the everlasting God,
    the one who creates the ends of the earth.
He does not faint or grow weary;
    his understanding is unsearchable.

Even in the description of his enlisting Cyrus, God's creative power is emphasized. He says in Isaiah 45:5–7:

I am YHWH, and there is no other.
    Besides me, there is no god.
    I arm you, though you do not know me,
so that they may know, from the rising of the sun to its setting,
    that there is none besides me.
    I am YHWH, and there is no other.
I am the one who forms light and creates darkness,
    the one who makes peace and creates calamity.
    I, YHWH, am the one who does all these things.

And again in vv. 12–13:

It was I who made the earth,
    and I created humankind upon it.
I by my own hands stretched out the heavens,
    and I commanded all their host.
It was I who aroused him [Cyrus] in righteousness,
    and I will make straight all his paths.

And once again in v. 18:

For thus says YHWH,
the one who created the heavens
    (He is God!),
the one who formed the earth and made it
    (He established it;
he did not create it as chaos;
    he formed it to be inhabited!):
I am YHWH, and there is no other.

This second part of the book of Isaiah is at pains to emphasize that the God of Israel is mightier than the god(s) of Babylon. Central to this claim is the insistence that it was Israel's God who had created the heavens and the earth. A similar dynamic appears to be at work in Genesis 1. Although this text is found in a different part of the Bible, it springs from a similar circumstance.[39] In response to the Babylonians' claim that Marduk was ruler over all, both the second part of Isaiah and Genesis 1 counter that it is instead the God of Israel who reigns. Standing behind the Babylonian claim was Enuma Elish, the story of creation that the Babylonians reaffirmed to themselves in each year's ritual ceremonies.[40] Outpacing the claims of Enuma Elish, though, was the depiction of God as creator found in Genesis 1. This is what a real God looks like, claimed the Israelites; the gods you serve, Babylon, are unworthy of the name.

Conclusions

Looking at the text through the eyes of faith, it is evident that the biblical authors presaged more than they could have originally imagined. In saying that God is the God who created the stars, they made a claim of tremendous import. Little did they know, however, just how great a claim they were making. For those who still believe that God is the one who created the stars, the magnitude of the divine work is far greater than the biblical authors could ever have imagined. We get just a taste of the vastness of God's creative work in a photo like the famous Hubble Deep Field. In an attempt to get an estimate of the number of galaxies the universe might contain, scientists trained the instruments of the remarkable Hubble telescope on one particular patch of the sky repeatedly over the course of a decade.[41] They needed to find a particularly "empty" piece of the sky for their observations, one that would not be obscured by nearby stars or the dust of nebulae.

Finally, they settled on a spot in the constellation Fornax, just southwest of Orion. Among the conventions scientists use to measure area in the sky are what are called *square arcminutes*. There are approximately 148,510,660 of these square arcminutes overhead. To give some sense of perspective, the full moon, on average, takes up only 758 of these. The Hubble initially focused on just 11 and finally on only 4.7. As scientists compiled the images from the Hubble's more than 2 million seconds (21.7 days) of exposure time, they found that in just that tiny 4.7 square arcminutes of sky lay 7,121 different galaxies. In other words, behind just one 30-millionth of the sky, a patch roughly the size of a grain of sand held at arm's length, lie thousands upon thousands of galaxies, each of which is composed of hundreds of billions of stars. The author of Genesis 1 looked at the riot of stars in the night sky and dismissed them with just a word . . . *stars*. Yet even he could not have imagined the real depths of God's creative power. It is little wonder that so much of the world came to embrace the vision of God cast by works like Genesis 1 and the latter chapters of Isaiah and left behind a god so paltry as Marduk.

CHAPTER 8

Darkness and the Sea

In the previous chapter, we considered one of the two main purposes of Genesis 1, the author's polemic against the Babylonian gods. Through its subtle allusions to Enuma Elish, Genesis 1 alerts the reader that the Babylonian gods are at issue as he casts a vision of God's majesty that far outstrips their meager claims to divinity. This vision of God is one that would be echoed not only in later Jewish reflection on the nature of God but also in Christianity and even in Islam. Casting this vision of God, however, was only one of the *two* main purposes of this seminal passage.

Darkness

As an exercise in my classroom, I often ask students to list their top three phobias. The answers I get often defy the imagination: feet, staplers, balloons, scotch tape, frogs—these are just a handful of the odd, irrational fears students mention. The more "normal" fears, the ones with fancy names to go with them, pop up every time the question is asked: spiders (*arachnophobia*), snakes (*ophidiophobia*), clowns (*coulrophobia*), flying (*aviatophobia*), heights (*acrophobia*), needles (*aichmophobia*), blood (*hemophobia*), tight places (*claustrophobia*), and the like. One phobia my students often omit is *darkness* (*achluophobia*, by the way). The truth is, we are all afraid of the dark. When we walk through a park or across campus in the daytime and hear a rustling in the bushes, we muse over whether a bird or chipmunk is the more likely culprit. When we hear the same sound alone in the dark, visions of hockey mask–wearing villains flood our heads as we listen for the sound of chainsaws coming our way.

When my wife and I were newlyweds, our blessed union of one full-time student and one part-time youth pastor ensured that we would have far more love than money in our relationship. To stave off full-blown Dickensian woe, the two of us took on the task of cleaning our church each week. As we finished the main part of the church and moved on to the gym, it was my task to clean the men's room. On one particular night, I entered the men's room with a mop in one hand and a pail in the other, ready to face the somewhat miserable task before me. Unfortunately, I realized only too late that I had forgotten to turn on the light switch located on the wall outside the restroom. As the outer door closed behind me, I now found myself in the small foyer to the restroom with no light at all to guide me. With only one more door to go, I felt sure I could manage, even in the pitch black that now surrounded me. One push on the door with a shoulder, a nudge on the light switch with an elbow, and I would be home free. It was as I attempted the first of these tasks that I was met with the most blood-curdling and terrifying scream I have ever heard. From somewhere on my left as I entered the door, a venomous screech that lacked only the smell of sulfur to verify its hellish origins assaulted my ears. Every trope of every horror movie I had ever seen flooded into my brain as I waited, frozen, sure that pitchforks would soon march me straight to perdition. In the moment of reprieve the demonic horde seemed to allow me, I reached with my right elbow and turned on the light switch, ready to see the fell creature I knew must be perched nearby. But as the light came on, I saw nothing there—a fact, incidentally, that made the situation decidedly worse, not better. I stepped back, finally letting go of the door I had continued to clutch. Now bathed in the glow of the fluorescent lights above, I heard the same sound as before, only minus the accompanying terror. It was the door! That accursed door was hanging too low and had scraped across the floor, making an unpleasant squeal. At first, a harbinger of my death; later, only a squeaky door—what made the difference? Nothing but the dark. We are all afraid of the dark.

Darkness in Scripture

The biblical authors shared our fear of the dark. The prophets often associated darkness with God's judgment, whether against his own people or against those who oppressed them. Isaiah warns the nation of the coming punishment at the hands of Assyria:

They will roar over it on that day,
    like the roaring of the sea.
If one looks to the land,
    behold, only *darkness and distress*;
and *the light grows dark with clouds.*

                       (Isa 5:30)

They will look to the land, but behold, only *distress and darkness*, the *gloom* of anguish; and they will be thrust into *thick darkness.*

                       (Isa 8:22)

Joel warns that the Day of YHWH will be:

A day of *darkness* and *gloom,*
    a day of *clouds* and *thick darkness*!
Like *blackness* spread upon the mountains—
    a great and powerful people.
From eternity, there has been nothing like them,
    nor will there be after them in ages to come.

                       (Joel 2:2)

Here, one term for darkness is heaped upon another to underscore the dread that is to come.

Darkness is frequently connected in the Bible with the grave and the netherworld. The psalmist who penned the mournful Psalm 88 lamented:

Do you work wonders for the dead?
    Do the shades rise up to praise you? (Selah)
Is your steadfast love declared in the grave,
    or your faithfulness in Abaddon?
Are your wonders made known *in the darkness,*
    or your righteous deeds in the land of forgetfulness?

             (Ps 88:10–12 [11–13])

The suffering Job, who expects that his days will soon come to an end, echoes a similar refrain:

Are not my days few, so cease!
    Leave me alone, that I may find a little cheer

before I go—and I shall not return!—
    to the land of *darkness and deadly shadows*,
the land of *gloom like the darkness of deadly shadows and chaos*,
    where *even light shines like darkness*.

(Job 10:20–22; cf. 17:13–15)

Even God is said to associate death with darkness in the divine response that occupies the concluding chapters of the book:

Have the *gates of death* been revealed to you,
    or have you seen the *gates of deadly shadows*?

(Job 38:17)

Again and again, darkness is cast as a negative state in the Hebrew Scriptures, a state set in contrast to the light:

They are thrust *from light into darkness*,
    and driven out from the world.

(Job 18:18)

For *deadly shadow is morning* to all of them;
    for they are friends with *the terrors of deadly shadow*.

(Job 24:17)

For when I hoped for good, evil came;
    and *when I waited for light, darkness came*.

(Job 30:26)

Then I saw that there is more profit in wisdom than in folly,
    just as there is more profit *in light than in darkness*.

(Qoh 2:13)

Woe to you who say evil is good
        and good evil,
*who put darkness for light
        and light for darkness,*
who put bitter for sweet
        and sweet for bitter!

(Isa 5:20)

That the Israelites should have feared the dark and cast it in such a negative light is not surprising. We all fear what we cannot see and thus cannot control. As darkness hems us in, limiting our ability to see what might lurk just beyond our reach, it creates a world of unknowns that our minds populate with worst-case scenarios. One candle banishes a host of unseen worries from our minds.

The Sea

Were we to pose the question of phobias to an ancient Israelite, another answer that would certainly rank high on the list would be fear of the sea (that would be *thalassophobia*). The pages of Scripture are filled with descriptions of the sea's intimidating size and power. The psalmist proclaims, "Yonder is the sea, *great and wide*; creeping things without number are there, living things, small and great" (Ps 104:25). As he searches unsuccessfully for something to compare to the vastness of God, Job's so-called friend Zophar the Naamathite insists:

> Can you find out the depth of God?
> Can you find out the limit of the Almighty?
> It is higher than heaven—what can you do?
> Deeper than Sheol—what can you know?
> Its measure is longer than the earth
> and *broader than the sea*.
>
> (Job 11:7–9)

The power of the sea was most evident to the Israelites in the roar of its waves. At times the biblical writers exhort the waves to roar all the louder in praise of God:

> Let the heavens rejoice, and let the earth exult.
> *Let the sea roar* and all that fills it.
>
> (Ps 96:11)

> *Let the sea roar* and all that fills it,
> the world and those who live in it.
>
> (Ps 98:7)

Sing to YHWH a new song,
    his praise from the end of the earth!
Let the sea roar[1] and all that fills it,
    the coastlands and their inhabitants.

(Isa 42:10)

More often, though, the roar of the sea is compared to the terrifying sounds of approaching enemies.

The Sea and Enemies

Isaiah invokes the sea as he describes the coming onslaught of the Assyrian armies:

Their arrows are sharpened,
    and all their bows bent.
The hooves of their horses seem like flint,
    and their wheels are like the whirlwind.
Their roaring is like a lion;
    they roar like young lions.
They growl and seize their prey;
    they carry it off, and no one can rescue.
They will growl over it on that day,
    like the roaring of the sea.

(Isa 5:28–30a)

He describes the impending destruction of Damascus in the same way:

Woe! The thunder of many peoples—
    they thunder like the thundering of the sea!
The roar of nations—
    they roar like the roaring of mighty waters!

(Isa 17:12)

Jeremiah uses similar language to describe the invasion of the Babylonians:[2]

Behold, a people is coming from the land of the north;
    a great nation is stirring from the farthest parts of the earth.

They grasp bow and javelin;
> they are cruel and have no mercy;
> *their sound is like the roaring sea.*

> (Jer 6:22b–23a)

Again and again in Scripture, it is the unruly and chaotic element of the sea that is emphasized. The psalmist insists:

Therefore we will not fear when the earth shakes,
> when the mountains totter *in the heart of the sea;*
> *when its waters roar and foam,*
> when the mountains quake at its *tumult.*

> (Ps 46:2–3 [3–4])

Jeremiah compares the trepidation of Israel's enemies to the tumult of the sea: "They quake in fear; *like the troubled sea, they cannot be quiet*" (Jer 49:23). Later, he describes the destruction of Babylon, saying, "The sea has risen over Babylon; she has been covered by *its roaring waves*" (Jer 51:42). Isaiah adds, "But the wicked are *like the tossing sea that cannot keep still*; its waters toss up mire and mud" (Isa 57:20).

The Sea and Suffering

The chaotic nature of the sea lent itself to descriptions of the suffering and distress experienced by Israel's poets.[3] The psalmist who composed Psalm 69 cried out:

Save me, O God,
> for the *waters* have come up to my neck.
> I sink in the *mire of the depths,*
> and there is no firm ground.
> I have come into *depths of waters,*
> and the *flood* sweeps over me.

> (vv. 1–2 [2–3])

With your saving faithfulness, rescue me
> from the *mire* and do not let me sink.
> Let me be delivered from those who hate me
> and from the *depths of the waters.*

Do not let the *floods of waters* sweep over me;
> do not let the *depths* swallow me up;
> do not let the Pit close its mouth over me.

(vv. 13b–15 [14b–16])

Other psalmists use images of water to lament over God's apparent assaults on them:

Deep calls to deep
> at the thunder of your *cataracts*;
all your breakers and your waves
> have gone over me.

(Ps 42:7 [8])

Your wrath lies heavy upon me,
> and you oppress me with all *your breakers*.

(Ps 88:7 [8])

In 2 Samuel 22, King David praises God for delivering him from troubles he compares to dreadful waters:

The *breakers of death* encompassed me;
> the *torrents of perdition* terrified me.
The cords of Sheol entangled me;
> the snares of death confronted me.

(v. 5)

He sent from on high, and he took me;
> he drew me out of *mighty waters*.

(v. 17)

Not surprisingly, the song attributed to the prophet Jonah echoes with imagery of the sea:

You cast me into *the depths*,
> into *the heart of the seas*,
> and *the flood* surrounded me.
All *your breakers and your waves*
> passed over me.

Then I said, "I am driven out
    from your sight.
How shall I look again
    upon your holy temple?"
The waters encompassed me up to my neck;
    the deep surrounded me.
Weeds were wrapped around my head,
    at the roots of the mountains.

(Jonah 2:3–5 [4–6])

The sense of desperation that accompanies being overwhelmed by the powerful waters of sea and river made for an apt illustration of the emotions of suffering, panic, and distress among Israel's poets.

The Sea as God's Opponent

It is the unruly aspect of the sea that so often casts the sea as an opponent that God must control. Job declares God to be the one who "trampled *the heights of the sea*" (Job 9:8). He despairs of challenging God's might, saying, "By his power he stilled *the sea*" (Job 26:12). He insists that he is no threat to God, demanding, "Am I *the Sea* or the Dragon that you set a guard over me?" (Job 7:12). God later asks of Job:

Who shut in *the sea* with doors,
    when it burst out from the womb,
when I made the clouds its garment,
    and thick darkness its swaddling band?
When I established limits for it,
    and set bars and doors,
and said, "This far you may come and no farther;
    and here shall *your proud waves* stop"?

(Job 38:8–11)

The sage in Proverbs uses similar language to describe God's control of the sea. Personified Wisdom insists that she was there "when he [YHWH] assigned to *the sea* its limit, so that *the waters* might not transgress his command" (Prov 8:29). The psalmists often speak of the relationship between God and the sea in the same way:

He stills *the roaring of the seas,*
   the roaring of their waves,
   the tumult of the peoples.

(Ps 65:7 [8])

You broke *the sea* by your might;
   you shattered the heads of the dragons *in the waters.*

(Ps 74:13)

You rule *the raging of the sea;*
   when its waves rise, you still them.

(Ps 89:9 [10])

The prophets add their own descriptions of God's conflict with the sea:

Do you not fear me? says YHWH.
   Do you not tremble before me?
I who placed the sand as a boundary *for the sea,*
   an eternal limit it cannot pass.
Though the waves toss, they cannot prevail.
   Though they roar, they cannot pass over it.

(Jer 5:22)

You trampled *the sea* with your horses,
   churning *the mighty waters.*

(Hab 3:15)

The Sea and Sea Monsters

The chaotic nature of the sea is illustrated by the fact that Israel so often depicted it as the place where monsters and "creeping things" lived. A close reading of Genesis 1 reveals a distinction in the way creatures of land and sea are described. In the creation of land animals on Day Six, the author distinguishes three categories of creatures: *ḥayyāt hāʾāreṣ, bəhēmâ,* and *remeś hāʾădāmâ.* The expression used for the first of these categories, *ḥayyāt hāʾāreṣ,* translates literally as *animals of the land.* In context, however, it is clear that this phrase refers to non-domesticated animals (cf. 1 Sam 17:46; Ezek 29:5; Ps 79:2). *Bəhēmâ* often has in mind simply cattle, but as is

frequently the case elsewhere in the Bible, it refers in Genesis 1 to domesticated animals generally (cf. Gen 47:18; Lev 1:2; Deut 5:14). This leaves
the third category, *remeś hāʾădāmâ, creepers on the ground*. While these
animals are declared by God to be good, along with the domesticated and
non-domesticated animals (v. 25), they will also be singled out as particularly unclean in the system of Israel's food laws. Wild animals and even
domesticated animals that did not chew their cud and have split hooves
were considered ritually unclean (*ṭāmēʾ*) and were not to be eaten. Those
animals that were labeled as "swarming" (from the verb **šrṣ*) or "creeping
things" (from the verb **rmś*), however, were considered not just unclean
but *detestable* or *abominable*. Leviticus 11:41–44 insists:

> All swarming things [**šrṣ*] that swarm [**šrṣ*] upon the earth are detest-
> able; they shall not be eaten. Whatever moves on its belly, and whatever
> moves on all fours, or whatever has many feet, all the swarming things
> [**šrṣ*] that swarm [**šrṣ*] upon the earth, you shall not eat, for they are
> detestable. You shall not make yourselves detestable with any swarming
> thing [**šrṣ*] that swarms [**šrṣ*]; you shall not defile yourselves with them,
> and so become unclean. For I am YHWH your God. Sanctify yourselves
> therefore, and be holy, for I am holy. You shall not defile yourselves with
> any swarming thing [**šrṣ*] that creeps [**rmś*] on the earth.[4]

Interestingly, when Genesis 1:20–21 describes the creation of sea creatures
on Day Five, it does not distinguish between the clean and unclean creatures
in the sea in the same way that it distinguishes among the land animals. All
of the sea creatures are lumped into just two categories, sea monsters and
swarming creatures:

> And God said, "Let the waters swarm [**šrṣ*] with swarms [**šrṣ*] of living
> creatures, and let birds fly above the earth across the dome of the sky." So
> God created the great sea monsters [*tannînîm*] and every living creature
> that creeps [**rmś*], of every kind, with which the waters swarm [**šrṣ*],
> and every winged bird of every kind. And God saw that it was good.

While Genesis 1 states that the land was inhabited not only by creeping
things but also by domesticated and non-domesticated animals, the seas are
said to be filled only with sea monsters and swarming things that swarm
and creep.[5] Psalm 104:25–26 echoes this treatment of the sea creatures in its
own reflection on Genesis 1:

Yonder is the sea, great and wide,
    creeping things [*rmś] without number are there,
    living things, small and great.
There go the ships,
    and *Leviathan* that you made to sport with.

(Ps 104:25–26)

Like the writer in Genesis, the psalmist emphasizes the *creeping things* and Leviathan (an equivalent of the *tannîn*) that fill the sea.

The presence of the *tannînîm* in Genesis 1 and Leviathan in Psalm 104 is representative of a larger pattern in which the sea is seen as a place from which monsters emerge. We have already seen this in the strong connection the Bible's poetic passages draw between the sea, on the one hand, and the *tannînîm*, Leviathan, and Rahab, on the other. The great sea monsters, the *tannînîm*, are consistently connected with the sea (cf. Gen 1:21; Job 7:12; Pss 74:13; 148:7; Isa 27:1; 51:9; Ezek 32:2; 29:3). The second divine speech in the book of Job draws an extensive connection between the Leviathan and the sea: The tools employed in the futile attempt to capture the creature are the fish-hook, the harpoon, and fishing spears (Job 41:1, 7 [40:25, 31]). It spreads itself on the miry clay (v. 30 [22]), it churns the deeps of the sea (v. 31 [23]), and it leaves a foamy wake behind it as it traverses the deeps (v. 32 [24]).

As we have seen previously, our various "odd" creation texts draw a similar connection between these creatures and the sea as they reflect on God's great deeds in the past (cf. Pss 74:13–14; 89:9–10 [10–11]; Isa 51:9–10). The biblical authors make similar links between monsters and the sea as they consider the apocalyptic portents of the future. In the so-called "Little Apocalypse" found in Isaiah 24–27, the prophet declares:

On that day, YHWH with his hard and great and strong sword will punish Leviathan the fleeing serpent, Leviathan the twisting serpent, and *he will kill the dragon that is in the sea.*

(Isa 27:1)

The apocalyptic visions of the book of Daniel contain this same sort of language as they describe the emergence of terrible beasts, each representing the great kingdoms that have afflicted God's people, rising from the sea:

In the first year of Belshazzar king of Babylon, Daniel saw a dream and visions of his head while he was in bed. Then he wrote down the dream, telling the beginning of the matter. Daniel answered and said: "I was looking in my vision at night, and behold, the four winds of heaven *were stirring up the great sea, and four great beasts were coming up out of the sea*, each different from the other."

(Dan 7:1–3)

It is no surprise that these beasts would be depicted as rising from the sea, given its chaotic and destructive associations. Later, the New Testament book of Revelation casts a vision along these same lines as it describes beasts emerging from the sea:

And I saw a beast rising out of the sea, having ten horns and seven heads; and upon its horns were ten diadems, and upon its heads were blasphemous names. And the beast I saw was like a leopard, and its feet were like those of a bear, and its mouth was like the mouth of a lion. And the dragon [*drakōn*] gave it his power and his throne and great authority.

(Rev 13:1–2)

Fear of the Sea in Daily Life

The chaotic nature of the sea and the fear it inspired in ancient Israel manifest themselves in any number of ways in the pages of Scripture. Although the territories ruled by the kings of Israel included as much as 150 miles of coastline along the Mediterranean Sea and reached to the Gulf of Eilat in the south, the nation made only fleeting attempts at forming a navy. First Kings notes that Solomon built a fleet of ships at Ezion-geber, a coastal town along one of the northern spurs of the Red Sea (1 Kgs 9:26). Even here, though, assistance from Tyre was needed to help the Israelites operate the ships: "Hiram sent his servants with the fleet, sailors who were familiar with the sea, together with the servants of Solomon" (v. 27). Some years later, the Judean King Jehoshaphat attempted to emulate Solomon's fleet, but his efforts met with even less success:

Jehoshaphat made ships of the Tarshish style to go to Ophir for gold, but they did not go because the ships were wrecked at Ezion-geber. Then Ahaziah son of Ahab said to Jehoshaphat, "Let my servants go with your servants in the ships," but Jehoshaphat was not willing.[6]

(1 Kgs 22:48–49 [49–50])

While it is true that Israel's coastline lacked the kind of harbors other countries enjoyed, this alone does not explain their lack of a navy.[7] In the end, the Israelites were simply reticent to take to the sea, relying instead on others to conduct their maritime trade (cf. Ps 48:7 [8]; Isa 2:16; 23:1, 14; 60:9; Ezek 27:9, 25, 29).

It is fascinating to see this dynamic play out in the story of Jonah. While Jonah makes for a miserable prophet, it is not hard to understand his reticence to go to Nineveh. The Assyrian Empire, which claimed Nineveh for its capital, was among the most vicious empires in human history. The kings who ruled Assyria boasted lustily over the tortures they inflicted upon those who opposed them. Beheading and dismembering conquered enemies, stripping the skins off their victims while they were still alive, impaling their foes on stakes—these were but a few of the gruesome punishments the Assyrians meted out to their enemies and memorialized in text and monument.[8] Had Jonah intended merely to shirk his call to go to Nineveh, though, the most likely destination for his flight would have been Egypt. Egypt and Mesopotamia formed a sort of polarity in the Bible, akin to America's "New York to L.A." The biblical authors repeatedly set Mesopotamia and Egypt as opposite poles, such that a person fleeing the former would quite naturally head toward the latter.[9] Jonah does not follow the normal route for one fleeing Assyria, however. Rather than flee to Egypt, Jonah takes to the sea (in a ship crewed by non-Israelites, by the way). The opening verses of the book of Jonah make clear his reason for doing so:

> Now the word of YHWH came to Jonah son of Amittai, saying, "Arise and go to Nineveh, that great city, and cry out against it, for their wickedness has come up before me." But Jonah arose and fled to Tarshish *from the presence of YHWH.* He went down to Joppa and found a ship going to Tarshish, so he paid his fare and went on board, to go with them to Tarshish, *away from the presence of YHWH.*
>
> (Jonah 1:1–3)

As these verses make clear, Jonah was not fleeing Nineveh; he was fleeing God himself. Even this prophet of Israel imagined the sea to be a place where God could not get him. Jonah's belief that fleeing to the sea could remove him from the presence of God speaks volumes to the way the Israelites conceived of the sea. The chaotic seas were thought—mistakenly, as the book of Jonah endeavors to show—to be outside of God's control.

Lingering Fear of the Sea

If we fast-forward to the present day, there is a sense in which the Israelites' fear of the sea is evident in our own culture as well. The surging waves of the sea give the ocean a kind of vitality that makes it seem almost alive. The powerful storms that form over the ocean waters give the sea a sense of majesty and power. When those storms crash from sea to shore, though, that same majesty seems tinged with an element of malice. There is something unnerving about sailing to a place where land is no longer in sight. Though one may be only a few miles from shore, to look out on an unbroken horizon of ocean is to get a glimpse of just how vast the seas can be. The stories we continue to tell one another about the sea underscore the deep-seated fear it continues to instill in us. To read *Moby-Dick* or *The Old Man and the Sea* or to see a movie like *Jaws* is to pull back the curtain on a fear we all share, the fear that the sea is somehow a living entity and that its power can be concentrated in one of the great creatures that appear from nowhere to draw us down into the depths.

Darkness and the Sea in Genesis 1

The Scriptures attest to a profound fear of darkness and the sea in ancient Israel. Key for our discussion is the fact that these same elements, darkness and water, play such a prominent role in the Bible's creation texts. We have already seen that this is the case (at least for the sea) in those passages from Psalms, Job, and the Prophets that portray God as fighting against sea and dragon. Darkness and the sea are equally prominent in Genesis 1, however. Indeed, if demonstrating to the Babylonians that their god is too small is the first purpose of Genesis 1, it is the role darkness and the sea play in this creation text that defines the second main purpose of the narrative.

Creation in Genesis 1 begins with water and darkness. As the text tells us what the world was like when God began his creative work, it specifies: "Now the earth was unformed and unfilled, and darkness covered the face of the deep, and a wind from God swept over the face of the waters" (Gen 1:1–2). As important as the fact that the waters and the darkness are already there when God begins his creative work is the fact that Genesis 1 casts these elements in a negative light. As we saw previously, the acts of creation in Genesis 1 are marked by a recurring literary structure: (1) an introductory "And God said," (2) a divine edict in the third person (e.g., "Let there be . . ."),

(3) a supplementary description of what is created, and (4) a concluding "And
God saw that it was good." So consistent is this pattern that there are only
three exceptions to it in the entire chapter. Once, in the pinnacle event that
is the creation of human beings (vv. 26–30), the narrative uses a first-person
(cohortative) statement, "Let us create humankind in our image," rather than
the third-person edict (e.g., "Let the earth bring forth . . .") found elsewhere
in the chapter. The other two exceptions concern God's recognition of the
goodness of creation.

The first of these two exceptions is found in the description of God's
creative acts on Day One:

> And God said, "Let there be light," and there was light. And God saw
> that the light was good, and God separated the light from the darkness.
> And God called the light Day, and the darkness he called Night. And
> there was evening and there was morning, a first day.
>
> (Gen 1:3–5)

Were this day to follow the pattern of the other days of creation, God's pronouncement of the goodness of creation would *follow* his naming of day
and night and *immediately precede* the concluding formula "And there was
evening and there was morning." Here, however, the divine pronouncement
of goodness has been moved to an earlier point in the narrative structure.
The reason for this move is obvious: *It is only the light, not the darkness, that
God recognizes as good.* After the creation of the land (v. 10), plants (v. 12),
luminaries (v. 18), fish and birds (v. 21), and animals (v. 25), the text declares,
"And God saw that it was good" (*wayyar* *ĕlōhîm kî-ṭôḇ*). The narrator with-
holds this recognition from the darkness, however, saying only, "And God
saw that the light was good" (*wayyar* *ĕlōhîm* *ʾeṯ-hāʾôr kî-ṭôḇ*). In keeping
with Israel's assessment of darkness elsewhere in Scripture, *the author of
Genesis 1 does not regard darkness as good.*

The second such exception falls along similar lines. Uniquely among
the days of creation, Day Two—the day on which God is said to have used
the *rāqîaʿ* to separate the waters above from the waters below—receives no
pronouncement of goodness at all:

> And God said, "Let there be a dome in the midst of the waters, and let
> it separate waters from waters." And God made the dome and separated
> the waters that were under the dome from the waters that were above

the dome. And it was so. God called the dome "heaven." And there was evening and there was morning, a second day.

(Gen 1:6–8)

Following the pattern of the other acts of creation, we expect the narrator to say, "And God saw that it was good," after the naming of the heavens. That pronouncement is again not found, however, and for the same reason it was not included for the darkness of Day One: *the primordial waters that God separates on Day Two are not considered good.*[10]

It might be objected that God does eventually declare all of creation to be good—indeed, *very* good: "God saw all that he had made, and behold, it was very good. And there was evening and there was morning, the sixth day" (v. 31). A careful reader will note the problem with this objection, however. Verse 31 does not declare *everything* in the chapter to be good; it only declares *everything God had made* (*ʾet-kol-ʾăšer ʿāśâ*) to be good. As we have already seen, Genesis 1 does not narrate God's creation of the waters or the darkness. These are primordial elements that are there when God begins his creative labors.[11]

The primordial waters and darkness of Genesis 1 are neither good nor even benign; they are malevolent entities the control of which is God's first task in creation. On the first day of creation, God speaks forth light to push back against the darkness. He separates the light from the darkness, restraining the darkness and putting it under bounds. On the second day, he forms the *rāqîaʿ* to do the same with the waters. He separates water from water, assigning some to the ocean below and the rest to the ocean above. Finally, on the third day, he forces back the waters, gathering them into one place so the dry land can appear. In the entirety of the first half of the creation week, only one act, the creation of plants at the end of Day Three, is not directed toward restraining the waters and the darkness (cf. v. 11).

As we have seen already, later interpreters picked up on this element of God's restraining the waters at creation. In Job 38, God speaks of shutting in the sea with doors, setting limits for it, enclosing it with bars and doors, and commanding its proud waves to stop (vv. 8–11). Proverbs 8 recalls God's setting limits on the sea that the sea must not transgress (v. 29). Jeremiah describes God's placing the sand as a boundary for the sea, a limit it cannot pass and over which its waves may not prevail (5:22). Once again, in Psalm 104, the psalmist speaks of God's rebuking the waters so they return to the place he established for them and of his setting a boundary for them that would restrain them from covering the earth (vv. 6–9). Each of these passages holds in common the notion that God's creative labors involved exerting control over the chaotic waters of the sea.

At the End of the Creation Week

Scholars have long noted the careful symmetry that marks the structure of the first six days of Genesis 1's creation account. After noting that the world was initially *unformed and unfilled* (*tōhû wā-ḇōhû*), the text goes on to chart the manner in which God rectifies these two conditions. On the first three days, God remedies the *unformed* problem. He creates light and separates it from the darkness; he creates the *rāqîaʿ* and uses it to separate waters below from waters above; he makes the dry land appear and clothes it with plants and trees. At the end of the third day of creation, the world is no longer *unformed* but *formed*. On the next three days of the week, God addresses the *unfilled* problem. The light he fills with lights (sun, moon, and stars), the water and sky he fills with fish and birds, and the land he fills with animals and people.

tōhû / unformed		*bōhû* / unfilled	
Day One	Light	Lights	Day Four
Day Two	Water	Fish	Day Five
	Sky	Birds	
Day Three	Land	Animals	Day Six
	Plants	Humans	

The climactic nature of Day Three as the conclusion to the first half of God's creative work and Day Six as the conclusion to the second half is underscored by the fact that only on these two days are two discrete acts of creation narrated.[12] As part of Day Three, vv. 9–10 describe the separation of land and sea, complete with all four of the structural elements adduced above: (1) "And God said," (2) third-person edict ("Let the waters . . . ," "Let the dry land . . ."), (3) supplemental description ("God called the dry land . . ."), and (4) "And God saw that it was good." Verses 11–13 then describe a

second act of creation on Day Three, again with each of these four structural elements: (1) "And God said," (2) third-person edict ("Let the earth
put forth . . ."), (3) supplemental description ("The earth brought forth . . ."),
and (4) "And God saw that it was good." It is only once both of these acts of
creation have been described that the concluding formula "And there was
evening and there was morning, the third day" is added (v. 13), bringing the
first half of the week to a close.

Day Six follows a similar pattern as it also narrates two distinct acts of
creation. Verses 24–25 repeat our familiar four structural elements: (1) "And
God said," (2) third-person edict ("Let the earth bring forth . . ."), (3) supplemental description ("God made the wild animals . . ."), and (4) "And God
saw that it was good." Then, vv. 26–31 narrate the creation of humanity
following these same four elements, albeit with a certain intensification of
the language as the creation story reaches its climax: (1) "And God said,"
(2) "Let us make humankind in our image . . . ," (3) supplemental description ("And God created humankind in his image . . ."), and (4) "And God
saw everything that he had made, and indeed, it was very good." As with
Day Three, it is only once both of these acts of creation have been described
that the concluding formula is given: "And there was evening and there
was morning, the sixth day" (v. 31). This brings to a close the second half
of God's creative labors.

Controlled but Not Banished

As the description of the sixth day of creation draws to a close, the twin
problems of the world's being unformed and unfilled have been addressed.
The world has been formed (Days One, Two, and Three) and now filled
(Days Four, Five, and Six). And so, on the seventh day, God stops:

> Thus the heavens and the earth were finished, and all their host. And
> God finished on the seventh day his work that he had done, and he
> ceased on the seventh day from all his work that he had done. And God
> blessed the seventh day and hallowed it, because on it God ceased from
> all his work that God had created to do.
>
> (Gen 2:1–3)

The Hebrew verb *šābat*, which is twice applied to God in this passage, is
usually translated as "rested." With the text's addition of the preposition *min*,

however, it is better understood as "ceased."[13] With the parts of creation now set in place, God ceases his creative work.

Though this aspect of the Genesis creation story is familiar to most, our very familiarity with the story can cause us to miss a key element of how the story is presented. Creation begins with waters and darkness, those chaotic forces that represented to ancient Israel the very opposite of creation. Through God's creative works, he controls those same malevolent forces. But as Day Seven arrives, as God ceases his creative activity, *the waters and darkness are only controlled, not banished.* They are still there, lurking, waiting, ready to break out again and unleash their devastating effects on the world. They are always there, ready to break out again on us, God's creatures. This is the second purpose of Genesis 1's creation story: *to capture the tension in creation between a God who is in control and a world that we so often experience as out of control.*

When the Waters Return

We have all shared in this experience: Our lives are moving along so swimmingly, and then, out of the blue, everything falls apart around us. I remember vividly a certain weekend years ago when my wife began to complain about a bad headache. As someone who had suffered through frequent migraines since I was a teenager, I was sympathetic but not overly concerned. When Michaela's headache lingered and intensified, she asked me to take her to the hospital. This seemed like an overreaction to me. When you get a headache, I thought to myself, you just take some ibuprofen and lie in a dark room, and it will finally go away. Being the model husband I am, however, I dutifully loaded up my wife and our then two- and four-year-old sons into the car and headed to the emergency room. At first the doctors asked questions. Then they began to poke and to prod. Then they began to take blood. Finally, they asked the boys and me to leave as they performed a spinal tap. I will never forget the doctor's words when the results came back: "Your wife has meningitis." While I am a doctor, I am not a "real" doctor; yet even I knew the ominous connotations of the word *meningitis.* This was the disease, I knew, that was met by doctors' pouring antibiotics into a patient's system only to see the patient finally succumb to the infection. Standing there at the doorway of my wife's room, holding the hands of my two young sons while they fussed with the surgical masks we had to wear, one thought swirled through my head again and again: How will I make it without my wife? How will I ever make it without my wife?

Life had been moving along so well. Everything seemed to be just great. Then, out of nowhere, chaos erupted into our lives like floodwaters threatening to drown us.

Thanks be to God, my wife recovered from meningitis. It was a slow process involving weeks of daily trips to the hospital (graciously organized by my mom, who came to help) for doses of antibiotics so strong that they had to be delivered intravenously. It took time, but she recovered. Other families have experienced far more difficult moments of tragedy. As a teacher, I am blessed to meet dozens of new students each term. But as the roster of students who have passed through my classroom has grown over the years, so has the number of students whom I will never get the chance to see again. I think of one who died from a diabetic attack and another who died when he was struck by lightning. Two died on the battlefields of Iraq and Afghanistan. Three have died in car accidents. Two more have taken their own lives. And this is to say nothing of the mothers, fathers, brothers, sisters, sons, and daughters of my students who have been lost, some to disease, some to accident, some to suicide, all to the continuing sorrow of those who have been left behind.

In his masterful study of the Bible's creation traditions, Jon Levenson summarizes the dilemma we face in this way:

> The survival of the tamed agent of chaos, whether imagined as the Sea, Leviathan, or whatever, points to an essential and generally overlooked tension in the underlying theology of these passages. On the one hand, YHWH's unique power to defeat and subjugate his adversary and to establish order is unquestioned. On the other hand, those passages that concede the survival of the defeated enemy raise obliquely the possibility that his defeat may yet be reversed. They revive all the anxiety that goes with this horrific thought. It is true that so long as God continues to exercise his magisterial vigilance and his suzerain faithfulness, the reversal of the chaos is impossible. But the experience of this world sorely tries the affirmation of this ever vigilant, ever faithful God, and it was in these moments of trial that the unthinkable was thought.[14]

There are times when the goodness of creation reverberates with such power that our hearts are almost ready to burst. To pause at "Tunnel View" in Yosemite and choke back tears at the granite formations that encircle that astonishing valley, to find a place away from the lights of civilization and look up to see the ocean of stars that form the Milky Way, to see the riot of colors on the New England hills in fall—all of these are grand echoes of the goodness of God's creation. We see this grandeur on a much smaller scale as well. To hold a newborn child in your arms, to see snowflakes parachute from the sky and blanket the ground, to savor the taste of a freshly picked peach—even in these small things, we know that creation is good and that God is in control. But then there are those times when the world turns on us with such terrifying force that our hearts are almost ready to break. To see the devastation left after a tornado has torn apart your childhood home, to tour the smoldering wreckage that just a few months before was the World Trade Center, to sit with those scarred by the recent death of a child—these are those moments when the world seems so cruel and so very much out of control. Genesis 1 was written, in part at least, to confront this tension in creation. God is a good God, and his creation is a good creation. God has controlled the sea and the darkness, but he has only *controlled* these forces, not *banished* them entirely. The sea and the darkness are still there, threatening at any moment to overwhelm us.

CHAPTER 9

Tiqqun and *Tiqvah*

One of the defining features of our shared humanity is our insatiable curiosity. Even before we can walk or talk as children, we snoop and smell and taste and explore as far as our hands and knees will take us. When at last we learn to speak, the curiosity God has instilled in us prods us to ask what and why about almost everything we see. To spend a long car ride being endlessly interrogated by an inquisitive toddler is to get just a sample of what 2 Peter 3:8 describes as God's experience of time: "One day is like a thousand years." As we grow older, our sense of curiosity changes, but it never truly goes away. It is our relentless curiosity that drives us to understand the world around us, to wonder why things are the way they are, to want to know more about how the world works. Curiosity plays as great a role in theology as it does in other areas of life. The Teacher in Qoheleth (a.k.a. Ecclesiastes) tells us that God has placed "eternity in our hearts," instilling in us a sense of something greater than ourselves and creating in us a desire to know more about the ways of God (Qoh 3:11a). Qoheleth goes on to say, though, that the same "eternity in our hearts" that causes humans to explore the things of God often leads to frustration. God's people know he is at work, "yet they cannot find out what God has done from the beginning to the end" (v. 11b). It is natural to ask questions about God; it is not always easy to find answers to those questions.

It strikes me that the sort of "unanswerable" questions about the ways of God with which humans wrestle fall into two types, *how* and *why*. The *how* questions can be difficult: How can there be one God and yet the Father, Son, and Holy Spirit all be divine? How can God be sovereign and yet give humans the ability to make meaningful choices? How do faith and works fit together in salvation? How can Jesus be both divine and human at the same time? How can he be divine and yet learn or grow tired, thirsty, or hungry? How can Scripture be both God's Word and human words? These are tough questions, to be sure, but they pale in comparison to the *why* questions. Why did God allow evil to enter the world? Why does God let the righteous suffer? Why does God let the powerful overwhelm the weak? Why do storms overwhelm and famines strike and diseases attack? These are the truly tough questions.

For the *how* questions, the biblical authors generally just affirm both sides of their paradoxical elements and move on. They assert in one breath that God's will is utterly uncontestable and in the next that humans make real choices, without bothering to sort through all the details of these two contrary propositions. They affirm Jesus' divinity and yet highlight his humanity without making any comprehensive attempt to show how these two natures can coexist. In the words of Paul, they seem content to acknowledge, "Now we see in a mirror dimly, but then face to face. Now I know only in part; then I will know fully, even as I have been fully known" (1 Cor 13:12). Like perceiving infrared or ultraviolet rays, understanding the *how* questions of theology requires eyes that we do not yet possess. One day we will understand, but that day is not yet here.

The biblical authors do not move so quickly past the *why* questions. These are the questions they bring to God again and again and again. The great leader of Israel, Moses, repeatedly turns to God with the question, "Why?" When Pharaoh rejects Moses' call to free the Israelites and instead doubles their workload, Moses pleads, "O Lord, *why* have you mistreated this people? *Why* did you ever send me?" (Exod 5:22). When YHWH threatens to destroy the Israelites after they have turned to the golden calf, Moses asks imploringly:

> O YHWH, *why* does your wrath burn against your people, whom you brought out of the land of Egypt with great power and with a mighty hand? *Why* should the Egyptians say, "It was with evil intent that he brought them out to kill them in the mountains and to annihilate them from the face of the earth"? Turn from your burning anger, relent from this evil against your people.
>
> (Exod 32:11–12)

When the Israelites press Moses for meat rather than manna, Moses turns to God, asking, "*Why* have you treated your servant so badly? *Why* have I not found favor in your eyes, that you put the burden of all this people on me?" (Num 11:11).

Not surprisingly, *why* questions feature prominently in the book of Job. As he curses the day of his birth, Job asks, "*Why* did I not die at birth, come forth from the womb and expire?" (Job 3:11).[1] Wishing only that he could die and be freed from his suffering, he reflects, "*Why* is light given to one in misery, and life to the bitter in soul?" (3:20). Later, he challenges God, saying, "If I sin, what do I do to you, you who watch humanity? *Why* have you set me as your target? *Why* have I become a burden to you?" (7:20). He begs to know, "*Why* do you hide your face, and reckon me as your enemy?" (13:24). Burdened with undeserved suffering, Job repeatedly calls out to God with the question, "Why?"

It is in the Psalter's songs of lament that the demands of God's people to know why reach their crescendo:

Why, O YHWH, do you stand far off,
   hide yourself in times of trouble?

(Ps 10:1)

My God, my God, *why* have you forsaken me?
   Why are you so far from helping me, from the words of my
      groaning?

(Ps 22:1 [2])

I will say to God, my rock,
   "*Why* have you forgotten me?
Why must I walk about mournfully
   because of the oppression of the enemy?"

(Ps 42:9 [10])

For you are the God who is my refuge;
   why have you rejected me?
Why must I walk about mournfully
   because of the oppression of the enemy?

(Ps 43:2)

Wake up! *Why* do you sleep, O Lord?
   Rouse yourself! Do not reject us forever!
Why do you hide your face?
   Why do you forget our misery and oppression?

(Ps 44:23–24 [24–25])

> O God, *why* do you reject us forever?
>> *Why* does your anger smoke against the sheep of your pasture?
>>> (Ps 74:1)

> *Why*, O YHWH, do you reject me?
>> *Why* do you hide your face from me?
>>> (Ps 88:14 [15])

Jesus himself echoes these same words when he is on the cross. In the throes of his most desperate moments of suffering, he cries out to God, asking why, using the very words that open Psalm 22: "My God, my God, *why* have you forsaken me?" (Matt 27:46; Mark 15:34).

There is no more potent word in the Psalter that the insistent question, "Why?" With this word, the psalmists cry out against the unjust treatment and oppression they have been forced to endure. They cry out against the sense of divine abandonment that has compounded the weight of their suffering. In a very real sense, though, the psalmists' insistent *why*s are only superficially a request for information. Far more than demands for an *explanation from God*, the poets' *why*s are a demand for *intervention by God*. This is evident in the fact that quite often the psalmists who cry out, "Why?" already know the reason for their predicament. When Moses pleads with God in Exodus 32:11, "O YHWH, why does your wrath burn against your people, whom you brought out of the land of Egypt with great power and with a mighty hand?" he knows full well the reason behind God's wrath. As Moses knew already, God was angry because his people had begun to worship the golden calf. In a similar vein, the psalmist who lamented to God in Psalm 74:1 over the Babylonian exile, "O God, why do you reject us forever? Why does your anger smoke against the sheep of your pasture?" knew precisely why God had been angry with his people. A steady stream of prophets had warned Israel of the impending destruction and exile that must take place if the people refused to repent. What Moses and the psalmist were truly asking God was not *why he was angry* but rather *that he stop being angry*. They ask why, not to gain an explanation from God but rather to turn God from wrath toward mercy.[2]

Truthfully, there are many moments of suffering that are so great as to defy any attempt at explanation. With all due respect to other grandmothers out there, no grandmother could hope to compare to my own Grandmother Shepherd, the person to whom this book is dedicated. She was, for all intents and purposes, the perfect grandmother. Kind, generous, loving to a fault, she lived to care for others around her. Though I have been blessed to study the Bible in college and seminary and grad school, I know I will never really know my Bible the way she did. Scripture seemed to be the lifeblood that coursed through her veins, the very air that she breathed. I remember vividly, though, the first moment she displayed symptoms of the Alzheimer's disease that would eventually take her life. At my grandmother and grandfather's fiftieth wedding anniversary celebration, we gathered around so the two of them could open the gifts friends and family had brought. A few gifts in, Grandmother opened a package to find a lovely strand of braided garlic bulbs like those that might decorate the walls of a nice Italian restaurant. Upon seeing the gift, this kind person who would have borne any burden for the sake of politeness said to the gathered audience, "I don't want that; it'll just stink up my house." Many of us gasped; several wiped away tears. What we did not know, though, was that this was just the first salvo in the difficult battle that would lie ahead.

I remember the last day my grandmother went to church, the day when something in Grandmother's dress was scratching her, and this genteel southern lady took off her dress in the middle of the sanctuary to fix it. I remember running down the halls of our church to find my mom and say, "Grandmother needs you." I remember coming home from school every few months and seeing the precipitous declines in Grandmother's health that had taken place while I had been away, seeing her finally bedridden, then no longer able to care for her own bodily needs, then no longer having any idea who I was. Many times over the course of those years, I asked God the question, "Why?" In some sense, I guess I did want to know, but the truth is that no answer would really have sufficed. I cannot conceive of an explanation for the torture this dear woman experienced that would allow me to say, "Well, in that case, I'm fine with it." When I asked God why, what I was really asking was just that he would stop—that he would stop being so aloof, that he would stop my grandmother's suffering.

Answers to the question *why* elude us whether we have in mind suffering on the scale of a single woman dying from Alzheimer's or a single child stricken with cancer or suffering on the grand scale of a natural disaster or the Holocaust. The greatest *why* question of all is where all of this suffering comes from in the first place. Why is there chaos and evil in the world at all? For reasons we may never fully be able to fathom, the Bible does not give a comprehensive answer to this question. The apostle Paul argues that sin and death entered the world through Adam, but even he does not venture beyond the first man to explain the origin of the serpent in the story of the

Garden or of the chaotic waters in Genesis 1. The Bible's creation traditions, whether in Job, Psalms, or Genesis, begin with chaos already present. They narrate God's control of the chaos; they never try to explain where the chaos came from to begin with. But if the Bible gives us only a little insight into the ultimate origins of chaos, it gives us a great deal of instruction on how to live in a world where that chaos is present. This instruction revolves around two Hebrew concepts, *tiqqun* and *tiqvah*.

Tiqqun

The notion of *tiqqun* is one that I believe is best captured in the English word *heal*. It is a kind of healing that runs far deeper than just tending to the sick, however. It carries with it notions of *repairing, setting in order,* and *making straight*.[3] In the epilogue of the book of Qoheleth, for example, the narrator describes the Teacher who speaks in the book as one who "*set in order* many proverbs" (Qoh 12:9), using the verbal root from which the noun *tiqqun* derives. This verb is used in a different but related way by the Teacher himself as he wrestles with life's challenges:

What is crooked cannot *be made straight,*
     and what is lacking cannot be counted.

(Qoh 1:15)

Consider the work of God;
     for who can *make straight* what he has made crooked?

(Qoh 7:13)

While the Teacher's reflections here are, not surprisingly, quite pessimistic, it is clear that the underlying sense of the term used here is that of *making straight* something that is crooked. The prophet Ezekiel uses the term in this same way as he challenges the Israelites for their accusation that God's ways are not *straight*, meaning they are not *right* or *correct*: "You say, 'The way of the Lord is not *straight*.' Hear now, O house of Israel: Is my way not *straight*? Is it not your ways that are not *straight*?" (Ezek 18:25; cf. 18:29; 33:17, 20). The psalmist uses the same term to describe God's work of preserving creation: "When the earth totters, with all its inhabitants, it is I who *keep steady* its pillars" (Ps 75:3 [4]). Finally, we find a related use of the term in the Aramaic portion of the book of Daniel as Nebuchadnezzar recalls, "I was *reestablished* over my kingdom" (4:36 [33]).

The uses of the verb *tiqqēn* in the Bible to describe the process of setting in order what is in disorder, straightening what is crooked, and steadying what has grown unsteady paved the way for the term to take on a greater role in postbiblical Hebrew. This is especially true as the idea of *tiqqûn* was linked to the term *ʿôlām*, a word referring originally to *eternity* and eventually to the *world* or *universe*. In an early style of Jewish commentary on the book of Genesis called *midrash*, the notion of *tiqqun olam* refers to God's ordering of creation itself (Gen. Rab. 4:7). Thus, the division of the waters on the second day of creation is said to have been undertaken in order "to *establish* the world" (*lətiqqûnô šel ʿôlām*). The second paragraph of the ancient Hebrew prayer called the *Aleinu* uses the expression with greater ethical and religious overtones as it declares:

> Therefore we put our hope in you, YHWH our God,
> to see soon the glory of your might,
> to remove all idols from the earth so that all false gods will be cut off,
> *to repair the world* [*lətaqqēn ʿôlām*] by the kingship of the Almighty,
> so that all the people of flesh will call upon Your name.

Key to this section of the prayer is the notion that the world (and humanity) is not as it should be and so cries out to be healed or repaired. Over time, the idea of *tiqqun olam* would pass through the Mishnah, the Talmud, and even the canons of Jewish mysticism, before taking on a prominent role in the justice concerns of modern Judaism.

At the heart of the term *tiqqun* has always been the sense of fixing something that is broken, healing something that is wounded, or shoring up something that is unsteady. Although the word *tiqqun* itself does not appear in Genesis 1, the sentiments associated with it certainly do. This is especially true as God's creative works on the first three days of this account center around God's controlling and subduing the forces of water and darkness. God's creating light and separating that light from darkness on Day One, his separating the waters from the waters on Day Two, his separating waters from the land on Day Three—all of these acts fit into the category of *tiqqun olam*. Through these acts, God transforms the world from chaos to creation, *establishing* the world by *repairing* its chaotic state.

The task of pushing back the bounds of chaos does not end with God's work on Day Three, however. When God creates humankind on Day Six, he entrusts to them responsibility for extending his rule over creation:

And God said, "Let us make humankind in our image, according to our likeness, and *let them rule* over the fish of the sea and over the birds of the heavens and over the livestock and over all the earth and over every creeping thing that creeps upon the earth." So God created humankind in his image; in the image of God he created them; male and female he created them. And God blessed them, and God said to them, "Be fruitful and multiply and fill the earth and *subdue it and rule* over the fish of the sea and over the birds of the heavens and over every living thing that creeps upon the earth."

(Gen 1:26–28)

Note that God twice refers to humanity's position over creation. In v. 26, God declares his intention that humanity "rule over" creation, and in v. 28, he commands humanity to do so. Many translations render the Hebrew verb *rādâ* used in this passage with the somewhat passive meaning *have dominion*. An examination of the term in other contexts in the Hebrew Bible suggests a much more active meaning, however. *Rādâ* is the verb used in contexts where supervisors are said to be in charge of workers (1 Kgs 5:16 [30]; 9:23; 2 Chr 8:10) and where masters are commanded not to rule harshly over their slaves (Lev 25:43, 46, 53). It is a term often used to describe the rule of kings over their people and their subjugation of their enemies (1 Kgs 4:24 [5:4]; Pss 72:8; 110:2). It extends even to the description of nations who conquer other peoples and subdue them (Neh 9:28; Isa 14:2, 6; Ezek 29:15; Lev 26:17). Above all, the verb points toward an active exercise of control.

This sense of active control is underscored by another term found in Genesis 1, the verb *kābaš*, "to subdue." *Kābaš* is a term that almost always refers to subduing or subjugating a hostile opponent. It is the term used to describe the state of peace that will exist when Israel has *subdued* the land through the conquest (Num 32:22, 29; Josh 18:1). It describes King David's subjugation of other nations (2 Sam 8:11; 1 Chr 22:18) and what the Northern Kingdom of Israel hoped to do to Judah (2 Chr 28:10). The term goes so far as to describe subjecting a person to slavery (Neh 5:5; Jer 34:11, 16).[4] To the degree that this latter term of *subduing* or *subjugating* sheds light on the term for *rule* in Genesis 1, it is clear that the text envisions a task of conquest. Humankind is charged with the job of bringing creation under control. But this could only be the case if creation is conceived of as *still being out of control* in some measure when the humans are created. And indeed, this is precisely what Genesis 1 describes. While the world God creates is declared by its creator to be good, there remains in it a sense of wildness and chaos that must yet be controlled. This is the task entrusted to the humans with the commands to *rule* and *subdue* creation. Chaos has been controlled but not banished; now God charges humankind with taking up the divine mantle of creating and working to push back the boundaries of this chaos still further.

Sadly, humans have often misconstrued the mandate of subduing creation as a license to pillage and plunder the world however they choose. This sort of destructive conquest of creation ignores the fact that the first image the Bible provides of humans interacting with the created world is that of caring for a garden (Gen 2). It also skips casually over the host of biblical commands that mandate care for creation and for God's creatures. The Torah enjoins the observance of the Sabbath not just so that humans can rest but "so that your ox and your donkey may have rest" (Exod 23:12; cf. Deut 5:14). God commands the Israelites not to muzzle an ox while it is treading out the grain so that the laboring ox can enjoy some of the fruits of its work (Deut 25:4). When a donkey or ox has fallen on the road, the Israelites are commanded not to ignore it but to help lift it up (Deut 22:4). Three times they are commanded not to commit the unseemly act of cooking a mother goat's offspring in her own milk (Exod 23:19; 34:26; Deut 14:21).[5] The book of Proverbs praises the righteous as those who "know the needs of their animals" (Prov 12:10). Even trees are given attention in the Scriptures, as the Israelites are forbidden from cutting down trees as a military tactic. Deuteronomy asks, "Are trees of the field humans that they should come under siege from you?" (Deut 20:19). While humans are commanded to subdue creation, they go astray when they forget that the creation they are subduing is one that ultimately belongs to God. Creation is only on loan to humanity.[6]

Tiqqun: *Living Orderly Moral Lives*

If God has entrusted humanity with the task of pushing back the boundaries of chaos, the task of healing creation by living out lives of *tiqqun*, how do the Scriptures suggest we go about this task? One of the chief ways we do this is by *living orderly moral lives*. The same theological circles in Israel that gave us the creation story in Genesis 1 also gave us much of Israel's priestly literature. This is the material in the Torah that is intimately concerned with establishing a sense of order in creation.[7] In Genesis 1, this is evident in the tight structure of the language narrating God's creative work, the four-part structure we examined at length above. It can be seen in the overall structure of the week of creation as Day One pairs with Day Four, Day Two with Day Five, and Day Three with Day Six. It is even evident in the refrain "according to its kind" that accompanies God's creation of each different kind of animal in the story, a sort of taxonomic marker that underscores the orderliness of God's creative work.[8]

The same sense of orderliness found in Genesis 1 is also found in other features of the Torah's priestly literature. In its description of the construction of the tabernacle (Exod 25–31; 35–40), its regulations for the sacrifices (Lev 1–7), its plan for the arrangement of the Israelites' camp in the wilderness (Num 2), and countless other areas, order and organization are the watchwords for the priestly instructions. Israel's priestly literature places the same emphasis on order when it instructs the people on how to live out their daily lives. This strand of the Torah sets boundaries for what the Israelites can eat and what they cannot (Lev 11). It tells them with whom they can have sex and with whom they cannot (Lev 18, 20). It goes so far as to instruct them not to mix their crops by sowing two kinds of seed in the same field, not to breed together two different kinds of animals, and even not to wear clothes made of two different kinds of materials (Lev 19:19).[9]

The purpose of all of these laws was to give the Israelites a sense of order in a time of disorder, to set boundaries that would give them the freedom to walk before God in confidence. Language emphasizing the security that comes from walking in the path of God's commandments is especially prominent in biblical passages that reflect on the Torah. In a psalm like Psalm 119, for example, we find numerous places—far too many to cite here—where this language is deployed:

With all my heart I *seek* you,
    do not let me *stray* from your commandments.

(v. 10)

I *run the way* of your commandments,
    for you enlarge my heart.

(v. 32)

Make me *walk* in the *path* of your commandments,
    for I delight in it.

(v. 35)

I shall *walk about* in a wide path,
    for I have sought your precepts.

(v. 45)

Through your precepts I get understanding;
    therefore I hate every false *way*.
Your word is a *lamp to my feet*
    and a *light to my path*.

(vv. 104–105)

Of particular note is the psalmist's declaration in v. 32: "I *run the way* of your commandments." It is not uncommon, especially in Protestant circles like those in which I move, to hear the Torah's commandments derided as restrictive and burdensome. Six hundred and thirteen commandments! Who could endure such a weight? I confess to being somewhat mystified at these sorts of comments. A great many neighborhoods could give the number 613 a run for its money just in the number of rules included in their subdivision covenants. And this is to say nothing of the thousands of pages of tax laws and health department regulations and cell phone contracts and more that we maneuver through on a daily basis.

    The psalmist found no such sense of restriction or burden in the Torah's laws. On the contrary, the laws of the Torah offered the psalmist the same sense of freedom that guardrails might provide on a mountain road. If you have ever driven on a road that has been repaved but not yet had its lines repainted, you know that the absence of these lines does not make for an easier drive. With no lines to guide us, the uncertainty of where and how we are to drive increases, and the speed of our cars decreases in turn. We see the same dynamic at work in a sport like track and field. Usain Bolt is able to fly through the 100 meters at such astonishing speeds in part because he has a lane that belongs to him and him alone. Take away the lines that mark his lane, force him to start in the same melee of runners that we see at the start of a marathon, and Bolt's records would never have been achieved. There is a safety and confidence that comes from knowing what God asks of us and how we are to live a life pleasing to him.

    We get a taste of this dynamic in the Psalter's first psalm.[10] Even those who cannot read Hebrew will hear the consonance in Psalm 1's first three words, *ʾašrê hāʾîš ʾǎšer*, and see the graphic symmetry in their Hebrew characters: אשרי האיש אשר. These three tightly knit words serve almost as a title for the Psalter. But how to translate this title? Although a number of modern translations continue to render the first word of the psalm as *blessed* (KJV, ESV, NIV), this is not the meaning of the Hebrew term at all. In Hebrew, *blessed* is *bārûḵ*; Psalm 1 begins instead with *ʾašrê*, a word that means *happy*. Indeed, as a plural form, *ʾašrê* conveys an idea difficult to express in English: *happinesses*.[11] Psalm 1 begins with a shout: "O the happinesses of the person who . . . !" It is a psalm concerned above all else with answering the question: What leads human beings to happiness?[12]

The answer Psalm 1 gives to this question is quite unexpected. It responds to the prompt, "O the happinesses of the person who . . . ," with the answer, "*does not . . . , does not . . . , does not . . . .*" In other words, Psalm 1 defines happiness first by what a person *does not do*:

> O the happinesses of the person who
>> *does not walk* in the counsel of the wicked,
>> and in the way of sinners *does not stand*,
>> and in the seat of scoffers *does not sit*.

There is a cadence in the Hebrew of these first lines of the psalm: *lōʾ hālaḵ, lōʾ ʿāmaḏ, lōʾ yāšaḇ*. This drumbeat of *lōʾ, lōʾ, lōʾ* in Hebrew—*no, no, no* (or *not, not, not*) in English—echoes the familiar wording of one of the central passages of the Torah, the Ten Commandments:[13]

> You shall *not* [*lōʾ*] have other gods before me.
> You shall *not* [*lōʾ*] make an idol.
> You shall *not* [*lōʾ*] bow down to them.
> You shall *not* [*lōʾ*] worship them.
> You shall *not* [*lōʾ*] lift up YHWH's name for nothing.
> You shall *not* [*lōʾ*] do any work.
> You shall *not* [*lōʾ*] murder.
> You shall *not* [*lōʾ*] commit adultery.
> You shall *not* [*lōʾ*] steal.
> You shall *not* [*lōʾ*] bear false witness.
> You shall *not* [*lōʾ*] covet.

In Psalm 1:1, the psalmist draws upon the language of the Torah to say that happiness is found in what a person *does not do,* in the options a person cuts off from their life.

A life guided by God's Word is a life that cuts off certain choices from consideration. The reward for our cutting off those choices, though, is the banishment of untold opportunities for chaos to break out in our lives. We have probably all felt the temptation to drive faster than we should; we have enjoyed the satisfaction that comes from zipping around other cars that are not willing to push the boundaries as boldly as we are. But along with that sense of satisfaction comes the reality that our speedy driving opens doors for chaos to break into our routine. A speeding ticket, an accident, an angry response from a driver we have cut off in traffic—all of these moments of chaos lurk in the shadows, ready to break out against us when we say yes, rather than no, to breaking the speeding laws. What is true in an area as seemingly minor as the speed limit is true in areas of greater moral gravity as well. When we say yes rather than no to temptations in the sexual arena, or yes rather than no to the temptations of substance abuse, yes rather than no to the temptation of unrestrained anger, we open the doors for chaos to flood into our lives and overwhelm us.

Psalm 1 extols the happinesses that come to the person who says no to those influences that would tear down our faith rather than build it up. Of course, the psalmist does more than simply focus on the negative. He goes on to say, "On the contrary! Their delight is in the Torah of YHWH, and on his Torah they meditate day and night" (v. 2). Not only do righteous people—those people who would find true happiness—say no to bad influences, they also delight in something good, God's Word. The Hebrew term used here for *meditate, hāgâ*, has a fascinating range of meanings. In other contexts, it is the word used to describe the cooing of a dove (Isa 38:14; 59:11), the growling of a lion (Isa 31:4), the rumbling that comes from one's throat (Job 37:2; Ps 115:7), and even the sigh of those who see their years come to an end (Ps 90:9). At the heart of all of these uses is the sense of a sound that comes from deep within: the coo of a dove, not a whistle; the growl of a lion, not its roar.

When I am lecturing to my students about this Hebrew word, I often illustrate it with a somewhat silly example from a vacation to Disney World. I confess to being a bit of a sucker for Disney. The prices are too high, the lines too long, and the temperatures too hot, but one look at the faces it puts on my kids, and I'm hooked. The first time we took our sons to Disney, they were just eight and six, and I knew they might have some hesitation about a few of the rides. In my attempt to win "Dad of the Year," I told them they had to ride everything, whether they wanted to or not. If they didn't like a ride, they didn't have to ride it a second time; but for that first ride, there were to be no tears and no refusals. My payment for that pronouncement came on a day when our younger son, Elijah, was not feeling well and had to stay back at the hotel with my wife; Samuel and I would have to do the

Magic Kingdom on our own. Having thoroughly mastered the ins and outs of Disney, *conquer* might have been a better term for what we planned to do to the park. We positioned ourselves on the far right of the entrance area at just the right spot, took off through the noodle restaurant as soon as the gates were open, rode Space Mountain when there was no line and got Fast Passes to ride it again when there was, headed to Buzz Lightyear, got the high score, and were off to Fantasy Land. We even had time for that accursed old-timey car ride that Samuel insisted on doing. In Fantasy Land, we clicked off ride after ride and were ready to head over to the Haunted Mansion. That's when Samuel said, "Abba." "Yes Samuel," I replied. "We have to ride it," he said. "Ride what?" I asked. "It's a Small World," Samuel said. "No, no, we don't have to ride *that*." "But you said . . . ," Samuel insisted. I protested, "No, I was talking about roller coasters and such. We don't have to ride that." "But you said . . . ," he reminded me once more.

And so we stepped into the line at my least favorite ride in Disney or any other world. Trudging along in what felt to me like a reenactment of the last pages of *A Tale of Two Cities*, we made our way to the boats. Overhead we could see the forlorn faces peering out from the Pinocchio restaurant as the people waved goodbye to us. I could just make out the sign on the lintel as we passed into the ride: "Abandon Hope, All Ye Who Enter Here," I believe it said. And as we passed from one room to the next, watching one set of animatronic escapees from *Children of the Corn* give way to the next, it was the song, that song, that made things so unbearable. Over and over again, "It's a small world after all; it's a small world after all; it's a small world after all." My nerves were frazzled and my patience nearly spent when finally we reached the white room, the place where all the collective imps and goblins from the ride gather in one place and belt out in a crescendo, "IT'S A SMALL WORLD AFTER ALL!" It was awful, but we were almost done. I knew the end of the ride was just around the corner. *And then, the ride broke down.* Not the musical portion of the ride, mind you, only the boat. For twenty excruciating minutes, we sat motionless in the white room, listening to that song again and again and again. Finally, mercifully, the ride restarted, and we reached the end. We staggered out of the boat, our eyes blinking with hands raised to ward off the now unfamiliar sun. It seemed like it was finally over. Days later, though, that moment would come. I would find myself standing in line at a different ride in a different park and hear myself whistling the tune: "It's a small world after all." They had won. That song was now so deeply embedded in my brain that no power could stop its coming out.

This is the word *meditate* in Psalm 1. It is a word that describes the person who has imbibed from God's Word so deeply that it pours out from their very soul to meet whatever occasion. The person who would see true happiness, the person who would push back the onslaughts of chaos in life, this is the person who says no to those things that are bad and drinks deeply from the streams of God's Word.

Psalm 1 draws a sharp contrast between those who say no to bad influences and yes to God's Word and those who do not. The psalmist compares the righteous person to a tree planted by streams of water, a tree whose leaves never wither, one that always gives its fruit in its season (v. 3). The wicked, on the other hand, are said to be like chaff, the insubstantial husk of a wheat or barley kernel that blows away with the slightest breeze (v. 4). Expressed in the terms of creation and chaos, Psalm 1's righteous person is the one who is able to withstand the winds and waves of storms that are sure to break out in life; in contrast, the one who refuses to be guided by God's Word is sure to be overwhelmed. One of the ways that we live out the ideal of *tiqqun* is by living orderly moral lives, by cutting off those choices that plant the seeds of chaos whose harvest we will inevitably reap. When we live lives guided by God's Word, we take one step toward pushing back the waters and the darkness. We take a step toward healing and repairing the world around us.

Tiqqun: *Helping the Vulnerable*

The second way in which we live out lives of *tiqqun* and thus heal the lingering wounds of creation is by helping those who are vulnerable. While the book of Leviticus, the heart of the same priestly literature to which Genesis 1 belongs, sometimes gets a reputation for being nothing but sacrificial instructions and purification rites, the text actually devotes a great deal of attention to how we interact with other people. Indeed, a commandment that most Christians assume was originally taught by Jesus, "You shall love your neighbor as yourself," is first found in Leviticus 19:18. The same authors who gave us Genesis 1 and who gave Israel laws for living orderly lives when it came to sex and food and even farming and clothing also interspersed among those laws instructions for taking care of their neighbors.

Many of the priestly laws for the ethical treatment of others are concerned simply with fairness and right judgment. They command the Israelites not to steal, deal falsely, lie to one another, or defraud their neighbors (Lev 19:11, 13). They warn against slander or profiting from the death of a neighbor (19:15). They insist that financial transactions must be done fairly: "You shall not do wrong in judgment, in measuring length, weight, or quantity. You shall have honest balances, honest weights, an honest ephah, and an honest hin" (19:35–36).

Other laws go a step beyond simple *justice* and urge the Israelites to give *mercy* to the most vulnerable among them. Leviticus warns against "insulting the deaf" or "putting a stumbling block before the blind" (19:14). It commands, "You shall rise before the gray headed and show honor to the old" (19:32). Knowing the financial vulnerability of a regular worker, the text insists, "You shall not keep the wages of a laborer with you until morning" (19:13). The priestly laws command that an alien must be treated with the same fairness that an Israelite deserves: "When strangers sojourn with you in your land, you shall not oppress them" (19:33). Leviticus also gives particular attention to the plight of the poor. Concerning the harvest, for example, it commands:

> When you reap the harvest of your land, you shall not reap to the very edges of your field, nor shall you gather the gleanings of your harvest. You shall not strip your vineyard bare, nor shall you gather up the fallen grapes of your vineyard. You shall leave them for the poor and the stranger.
>
> (Lev 19:9–10; cf. 23:22)

It gives instructions for caring for relatives who fall into financial distress:

> If any of your kin become impoverished and cannot maintain themselves among you, you shall support them. They shall live with you as though they were a stranger or sojourner. Do not take interest or profit from them, but fear your God. Let them live with you. You shall not lend them your money at interest, nor shall you profit when you give them your food.
>
> (Lev 25:35–37)

Even the year of Jubilee demanded by the priestly system was intended to level the playing field for the poor (Lev 25, 27). Some would inevitably prosper in the land and others founder. The priests envisioned a system, though, that would "reboot" at regular intervals, giving the poor access again to their ancestral lands.

One of the threads that ties together the priestly commands to show mercy to the vulnerable in the Torah is the expression "fear God." While this expression is often used in other places in Scripture to capture a sense of awe or reverence for God, in the Torah's priestly literature, it is exclusively connected with how the Israelites are to treat vulnerable people. When Leviticus commands the Israelites not to insult the deaf or put a stumbling block before the blind, it stipulates that they should do this because "you shall fear your God" (19:14). When it commands them to rise before the gray headed and show honor to the old, it is because "you shall fear your God" (19:32). When it instructs them not to cheat one another, it is because "you shall fear your God" (25:17). When it insists that they not take interest from their poor relatives, make a profit off of them, or force them into slavery over their debts, it is because "you shall fear your God" (25:36–45).

This theme of caring for the vulnerable because of one's fear of God is picked up in other places in the Bible as well. When Joseph has every opportunity to harm his brothers but assures them he will not, he founds his promise on his fear of God: "Do this and you will live, *for I fear God*" (Gen 42:18). The midwives in Exodus 1 refuse to carry out Pharaoh's order to harm the Hebrew babies because "the midwives *feared God*" (Exod 1:17, 21). The people of Amalek are repeatedly cursed in the Torah because they did not show mercy to the vulnerable. In the words of Deuteronomy, "They [the Amalekites] encountered you on the way and attacked those at the rear who were lagging behind when you were faint and weary; *they did not fear God*" (Deut 25:18).[14] Even in the New Testament, the unjust judge who would have ignored the widow's pleas admits, "Though *I fear neither God* nor man, yet because this widow keeps bothering me, I will give her justice, so that she may not weary me by continually coming" (Luke 18:4–5).[15]

When a person fears God, they find opportunities to care for those who are vulnerable. They find a person whose life has been overwhelmed by the chaotic forces of poverty or oppression or even their own sinfulness, and they help to push back the boundaries of that chaos. It is Israel's failure to do this that so incensed a prophet like Amos. As he lays out his indictment against the Northern Kingdom, he declares:

> They sell the righteous for silver,
>   and the needy on account of a pair of sandals,
> those who trample the head of the poor into the dust of the earth,
>   and turn aside the way of the afflicted.
> A man and his father go in to the girl,
>   so that my holy name is profaned.

They stretch themselves out on garments taken in pledge
    beside every altar.
And they drink the wine they have taken as fines
    in the house of their God.

(Amos 2:6b–8)

The litany of charges the prophet lays out against the people is sobering. He accuses them of selling a person into slavery ("they sell the righteous for silver") over a debt as trivial as a pair of sandals. They bully the powerless, stepping on them and pushing them aside. They take advantage of the slave girl who cannot fight back.[16] They take a poor person's garment in pledge for a loan and then use it to pad their fat backsides as they go to worship. They extort fines from those beneath them and use the proceeds to fund their lavish lifestyles. When they find individuals in distress, they exacerbate their troubles rather than relieve them. No wonder the prophet spoke to them in such devastating terms (cf. Amos 3:11–15; 4:1–3, 12)!

We see the very opposite approach in the behavior of those who care for the vulnerable. Moses showed this concern for the vulnerable when he intervened on behalf of the Hebrew who was being beaten by the Egyptian (Exod 2:11–12) and again when he delivered Jethro's daughters from the shepherds who were harassing them at the well in Midian (Exod 2:16–17). As a baby, Moses had himself been the recipient of this same kind of care when Pharaoh's daughter "took pity on him" and brought him into the royal household rather than killing him as Pharaoh had commanded (Exod 2:6). He would receive kind treatment again when Jethro took him into his family as he was fleeing from Egypt (Exod 2:18–22). Examples of this sort of care for the vulnerable are not hard to find in Scripture. This is the behavior of Elijah when he cared for the widow of Zarephath, blessing her both with the miraculous provision of grain and oil and with the resuscitation of her son who had died (1 Kgs 17). This is the same care that Elijah's successor, Elisha, gave first to a widow when he blessed her jar of oil and then to a wealthy woman whose son had died suddenly (2 Kgs 4). It is what Rahab did for the two Hebrew spies when they were pursued by the king of Sodom (Josh 2).

One particularly touching example of this kind of care for the vulnerable is found in the book of Ruth. As the book charts the misfortunes of the women in the story, we are eventually left with just the widows Naomi and her daughter-in-law Ruth as they make their way back from Moab to the land of Israel. With no land of their own and no one to care for them, Ruth puts her own safety at risk by going to glean among the sheaves of grain left behind when harvesters work the fields. Providentially, Ruth made her way to the fields of a wealthy man named Boaz, who was apparently taken with the young woman from Moab the instant he first saw her. When Ruth returned home to Naomi with an excess of barley and revealed how she had gleaned so much, her mother-in-law hatched a plan that she hoped would secure their survival. Unfortunately, though, this plan would put Ruth in terrible danger. Naomi instructed Ruth:

> Wash and anoint yourself, and put on your cloak and go down to the threshing floor, but do not reveal yourself to the man until he has finished eating and drinking. When he lies down, take note of the place where he lies, and go and uncover his feet and lie down. He will tell you what to do.
>
> (Ruth 3:3–4)

Naomi's intentions were plain enough: She was telling her daughter-in-law to offer herself sexually to Boaz.[17] Bathed and perfumed and wearing her best clothes, alone in the dark with a man who had just had his fill of food and drink, lying down next to him, a foreigner with no men to protect her, Ruth was here at her most vulnerable. Boaz could have done anything he wanted to Ruth. He could have set his men loose on her for her brazenness. He could have slept with her and then tossed her away the next morning. She was clearly a beautiful woman, and she was clearly willing; Boaz had every chance to take advantage of her. But instead, he took care of her. At her moment of greatest vulnerability, Boaz lived out the values of *tiqqun*. He pushed back against the chaotic forces of poverty and loneliness in the lives of Ruth and Naomi and created a place of order and safety for them instead.

Tiqvah

When we are faced with a world that often seems so out of control, a world in which the waters and darkness seem always poised to break out again, the Scriptures urge us to heal what is broken in creation by practicing a life of *tiqqun*. The creation story itself records God's intention that humanity should continue to extend his creative labors by subduing the earth and exercising rule over it. In the priestly literature that is linked to Genesis 1, this act of extending creation occurs when we live out lives that promote order and life rather than disorder and death. It commands God's people to live

orderly moral lives and to extend healing and help to those who are vulnerable. Every corner of the Hebrew Bible seems to give voice to these values:

> Wash yourselves; make yourselves clean;
>> put away the evil of your deeds from before my eyes.
> Cease to do evil, learn to do good,
>> seek justice, rebuke the oppressor,
>> give justice to the orphan, defend the widow.
>>> (Isa 1:16–17)

> Those who walk righteously and speak uprightly,
>> who reject the gain of oppression,
> who wave away a bribe rather than taking it,
>> who stop their ears from hearing of bloodshed
>> and who shut their eyes from looking on evil—
> they will dwell on the heights;
>> their refuge will be the strongholds of rocks;
>> their food will be given to them, their water assured.
>>> (Isa 33:15–16)

> He has told you, O mortal, what is good,
>> and what YHWH seeks from you.
> It is to do justice, and to love lovingkindness,
>> and to walk humbly with your God.
>>> (Mic 6:8)

> But let justice roll down like waters,
>> and righteousness like an ever-flowing stream.
>>> (Amos 5:24)

> As for you, return to your God,
>> keep lovingkindness and justice,
>> and wait continually for your God.
>>> (Hos 12:6 [7])

> Open your mouth for the mute,
>> for the rights of all those who are passing away.
> Open your mouth, judge righteously,
>> and defend the poor and needy.
>>> (Prov 31:8–9)

Living orderly moral lives and extending protection to those who are vulnerable can do a great deal to heal the lingering wounds of creation. The problem, of course, is that no matter how righteously we live, no matter how much we reach out to the vulnerable, there will always remain wounds in creation that we cannot heal. Sometimes the darkness falls and the waters overwhelm, and no amount of *tiqqun* will suffice to ward off their blows. This is where our second word of response to the unfinished creation comes in: *tiqvah*, the Hebrew word for *hope*.

Tiqvah *in Psalm 104*

In our consideration of Genesis 1, we have often turned to Psalm 104, perhaps the first commentary on the creation story. As we have noted before, this psalm tracks with the order of creation in Genesis, paraphrasing the story in poetic form. It is particularly interesting to note the way in which Psalm 104 draws to a close. Having reveled throughout the psalm over the blessings God's creation affords to his creatures, the psalmist strikes an odd note in v. 27: "All of these wait for you, to give them their food in its season." Until this moment, the psalm has revolved around nothing but provision and provision and provision: "You are the one who makes the springs gush forth in the wadis" (v. 10); "The earth is satisfied by the fruit of your labors" (v. 13); "You cause the grass to grow for the livestock and plants for people to use" (v. 14); you make "wine to cheer the human heart, oil to make the face shine, and bread to strengthen the human heart" (v. 15). But in v. 27, there is an element of ambiguity: the creatures wait, but will God provide?

The pause in the psalmist's praise is only heightened in the next stanza:

You give to them; they gather up.
   You open your hand; they are well satisfied.
You hide your face; they are terrified.
   You withdraw their breath; they perish,
   and to the dust they return.
You send forth your spirit; they are created.
   And you renew the face of the ground.

(vv. 28–30)

What has been taken for granted in the first twenty-six verses of the psalm—namely, the clockwork-like blessings of creation for God's creatures—is now revealed to be less certain than previously thought. God gives, but he may also take away. He creates, but he may also withdraw his sustaining hand. There is a precariousness to creation's blessings that fits well with the continued presence of the water and darkness in Genesis 1.

In the face of this precariousness, the psalmist purposes to continue to praise God the creator:

> May the glory of YHWH endure forever;
>   may YHWH rejoice in his works.
> He who looks down upon the earth so that it trembles—
>   he touches the mountains, and they smoke.
> I will sing to YHWH while I live;
>   I will sing praise to my God while I remain.
> May my praise [?] to him be pleasing;
>   I will rejoice in YHWH.
> May sinners be consumed from the earth,
>   and may the wicked be no more.
> O my soul, bless YHWH,
>   praise YHWH!
>
> (vv. 31–35)

Even in these words of praise, though, there are resonances of unease. YHWH's rejoicing in his work of creation is not a given; he must be urged through the words of praise to do so (v. 31). Sinners and the wicked remain as an ever-present concern, such that the psalmist must implore God to remove them from the earth (v. 35). Of particular interest is the term the psalmist uses in v. 34 to describe the words he offers up to God, the Hebrew term *śiaḥ*. This term is used in the Hebrew Bible almost exclusively with the sense of a lament or complaint (cf. Pss 55:2 [3]; 64:1 [2]; 102:1; 142:2 [3]; Job 7:13; 9:27; 10:1; 21:4; 23:2).[18] Here, the fact that the psalmist hopes his *śiaḥ* will be pleasing to God suggests a more positive meaning, perhaps *meditation* or *reflection*. Even with this meaning, though, there may yet be a wordplay, an echo of other texts where *śiaḥ* is not so positive. While God's creation is good and full of blessing, it is not yet finished. It requires God's active involvement to sustain its blessings. God's absence spells ruin and death. And so the psalmist laments, or nearly so, saying: God, rejoice in your works and be present with us. Psalm 104 ends with a note of hope, a word necessitated by the tenuousness of the created order.

Tiqvah *in the Prophets*

Set as the preface to the story of Eden in Genesis 2–3, Genesis 1 can hardly avoid striking this same note of hopefulness. Joined to this story of *paradise lost*, it inevitably looks forward with hope toward *paradise regained*. This is the thread the prophets take up in their own descriptions of a paradise still to come. For Ezekiel, himself a writer from the same priestly circles responsible for Genesis 1, that hope for the future is found in his vision of a new temple, cleansed, renewed, and once more home to God's divine presence (Ezek 40–48). His vision extends beyond that of merely a renewed temple, though. Both the people of Israel and the land of Israel will be restored:

> And I will give you a new heart, and a new spirit I will put within you. And I will remove the heart of stone from your flesh and give you a heart of flesh. My spirit I will put within you, and I will make you follow my statutes and be careful to observe my judgments.
>
> (Ezek 36:26–27)

> On the day that I cleanse you from all your iniquities, I will cause the cities to be inhabited and the ruins to be rebuilt. The land that was desolate shall be worked again instead of being the desolation that it was in the eyes of all who passed by. They will say, "This land that was desolate has become *like the garden of Eden*, and the cities, ruined, desolate, and torn down, they will inhabit again as fortified places."[19]
>
> (Ezek 36:33–35)

Here, Ezekiel draws a connection to the creation story as he compares the garden of Eden that once was with the desolate land he hopes will one day be like Eden again.

Other prophets share similar hopes for the future. Isaiah looks forward to the coming of a righteous king who will reign with justice so that all of creation is renewed:

> The wolf shall dwell with the lamb,
>   the leopard shall lie down with the kid,
> the calf and the young lion and the fatling together,
>   and a little child shall lead them.

The cow and the bear shall graze,
>   their young shall lie down together,
>   and the lion shall eat straw like the ox.
The nursing child shall play over the hole of the snake,
>   and the weaned child shall put its hand on the viper's den.
They will not do evil or destroy
>   on all my holy mountain;
for the earth will be full of the knowledge of YHWH
>   as the waters cover the sea.

>   (Isa 11:6–9)

The prophet in the latter chapters of Isaiah goes a step further, promising a new heaven and a new earth:

For I am about to create new heavens
>   and a new earth.
The former things will not be remembered,
>   nor will they come to mind.
But be glad and rejoice forever
>   in what I am creating,
for I am about to create Jerusalem as a joy
>   and its people as a delight.
I will rejoice in Jerusalem
>   and be glad over my people.
No longer shall the sound of weeping be heard in it,
>   or the sound of distress.
No more shall there be in it
>   an infant who lives but a few days,
>   or an old person who does not fill out their days,
for the youth will be one who dies at a hundred years,
>   and one who misses a hundred will be considered accursed.

>   (Isa 65:17–20)

The wolf and the lamb shall graze as one;
>   the lion shall eat straw like the ox;
>   as for the serpent, its food shall be dust!
They shall not do evil or destroy
>   on all my holy mountain,
>   says YHWH.[20]

>   (Isa 65:25)

The Edenic visions found in the Prophets are expressions of hope that the God who began a good work in creation will complete that work in a renewed creation.

This hope for a new creation goes back ultimately even to the odd creation traditions we considered at the outset of this book. While some of these texts praise God for his defeat of the sea and dragon in the primordial past, others apply this same language to the future. As we have already seen, in the section of the book of Isaiah known as the "Little Apocalypse," Isaiah 24–27, the prophet announces:

> *On that day*, YHWH with his hard and great and strong sword will punish Leviathan the fleeing serpent, Leviathan the twisting serpent, and he will kill the dragon that is in the sea.
>
> (Isa 27:1)

The prophet's imagery is drawn from the primordial past. Now, though, he looks forward to a future day when God will defeat those forces once and for all.

Even those odd creation psalms that do not explicitly look for God's defeat of Leviathan in the future are nevertheless psalms built on a foundation of hope. Surrounded by the ruins of Babylon's destruction of Jerusalem, the psalmist who composed Psalm 74 looks back to God's defeat of the sea and Leviathan at creation as a touchstone for hope in God's deliverance of the nation in the future. The psalmist says, in effect, "You are my king; you broke the sea by your might. Now, rise up, O God!" Psalm 89 follows a similar tack. Faced with the collapse of the Davidic monarchy and, seemingly, of God's own promises to the king and the nation, the psalmist remembers God's ancient defeat of the dragon and the sea and says to God, "Remember! Remember!" These are psalms of lament, but psalms of lament are ultimately psalms of hope: they ask God to remember what he did in creation *before* and to *once again* create life and order among his people.[21]

"And there was no more sea"

I confess that the first time I came across one of these passages of hope, I did so entirely by accident. As a young teenager sitting in church, I found myself—I am ashamed to admit it—bored. I am sure that the pastor's sermon was delightful and that my own short attention span was to blame, but the end result was that I was desperate for something to do other than just listen. Unfortunately (or perhaps fortunately, in retrospect), the options for finding "something to do" were somewhat more limited in the days of hoary antiquity when I was a teenager. There are only so many foil gum wrappers you can twist into miniature goblets and only so many offering envelopes you can use for doodling. The great minds of Silicon Valley had not yet invented the cell phone, and my parents would never have let me take a book other than the Bible to church, so I was stuck. As a last resort, I opened my Bible and tried to find something, anything, that was more interesting than what was being preached on that day. There is hardly anything in the Bible more interesting than the book of Revelation, so my fingers made their way there in hopes of some sermonic relief. I could hardly contain my dismay at the words I finally stumbled upon. Tucked away in Revelation 21, I read this: "And I saw a new heaven and a new earth, for the first heaven and the first earth had passed away, and there was no more sea" (v. 1). *And there was no more sea*—my first thought was to ask how God could possibly make a new heaven and a new earth and get rid of the best part of the present earth. I loved the sea, the beach, the wind, the waves. From Jacques Cousteau to the Pirates of the Caribbean, I loved everything about the sea. How could God get rid of that?

It took years before I would come to realize how naively I had first read that incredible verse. The author of Revelation understood the tension of Genesis 1's creation story better perhaps than any other writer in the Bible. In that foundational story of creation, God had controlled the forces of water and darkness but had not banished them entirely. So long as they were still there, they threatened to break out at any moment and overwhelm God's people. The author of Revelation understood this dynamic perfectly, and so, he looked forward to a day when God would finally bring his creative work to completion. The author knew that when he saw the new heavens and the new earth, there would be no more sea. The sea would not just be controlled, it would cease to exist altogether. It is quite interesting to see that the latter verses of this same chapter address the other lingering remnant of creation's chaotic beginnings, darkness. Note the Revelator's words:

> And the city has no need of sun or moon to shine on it, for the glory of God gives it light, and its lamp is the Lamb. The nations will walk by its light, and the kings of the earth will bring their glory into it, and its gates will not be shut by day, *for there will be no night there.*

(Rev 21:23–25)

There will be no night there—at last, not only the sea but the darkness as well will be removed completely.

Set between the banishment of the sea and the darkness are some of the most hopeful words in all of Scripture:

> And I heard a loud voice from the throne saying, "Behold, the tabernacle of God is among humankind. And he will dwell with them, and they will be his peoples, and God himself will be with them. And he will wipe every tear from their eyes. Death will be no more; mourning and crying and pain will be no more, for the first things have passed away." And the one who was seated on the throne said, "Behold, I am making all things new."
>
> (Rev 21:3–5)

It is hard to imagine words more comforting than these for a person of faith. God will be with us. He will wipe every tear from our eyes. Death, crying, and pain will be no more. The Messiah will make all things new.

When faced with the tension of believing in a God who is in control and yet experiencing a world that seems so out of control, God's people are called to practice *tiqqun* and *tiqvah*. While the time remains, we heal what we can. We live orderly moral lives. We help those who are vulnerable. All the while, we know that we will never be able to heal everything. And so, we hope. We hold on to a God whose final work will culminate in the promises of Revelation 21: There will be no more night there and no more sea.

CHAPTER 10

Tiqqun and *Tiqvah* and the Life of Jesus

A discerning reader will note that up until now, our study has focused almost exclusively on the Hebrew Scriptures, that portion of the Bible often referred to as the Old Testament. I openly admit that this has been a deliberate move on my part. The Bible's creation stories are found in the Hebrew Scriptures, and they deserve to be understood on their own terms and in their own times before one moves on to the manner in which they were understood by later communities of faith. For those who read the Bible through the eyes of Christian faith, though, it is important to stress that the values of the Hebrew Bible's creation stories, the very values of *tiqqun* and *tiqvah* that were highlighted in the preceding chapter, are very much in evidence in the New Testament as well. Indeed, I would argue that these two values were the driving force in the ministry of Jesus himself.

Tiqqun in the Life of Jesus

We have previously seen that the idea of *tiqqun*, healing what remains broken in creation, centers around living an orderly moral life and helping those who are vulnerable. What is the life of Jesus if not a visible demonstration of these two ideas?

Living an Orderly Moral Life

Jesus' commitment to living and promoting in others an orderly moral life is particularly evident in the Gospel of Matthew. As Matthew narrates the beginning of Jesus' ministry, he describes first the preaching of John the Baptist (3:1–12), then Jesus' own baptism by John (3:13–17), Jesus' temptation in the wilderness (4:1–11), and finally his move from Nazareth to the village of Capernaum, which would become the base of his ministry (4:12–16). It is at this point in his Gospel that Matthew offers a fascinating, one-sentence summary of the ministry of Jesus: "From that time, Jesus began to proclaim, *'Repent, for the kingdom of heaven has come near!'* " (4:17). It is not uncommon to hear popular characterizations of John the Baptist and Jesus as a sort of good-cop, bad-cop duo. John is cast as the uncompromising preacher of fire and brimstone, while Jesus is portrayed as the figure with the softer touch, the one who only speaks in the positive refrains of "Come unto me, all you who are weary and heavy laden, and I will give you rest" (Matt 11:28). John may have lambasted the people for their sinfulness, but Jesus reassured them with words of "Neither do I condemn you" (John 8:11). Matthew, however, draws no such distinction between the messages of John and Jesus. He captures the *what* of Jesus' preaching in a single word, "Repent!" and the *why* in a single clause, "For the kingdom of heaven has come near!" Matthew would say that living an orderly moral life was at the heart of Jesus' ministry.

This emphasis in Matthew is evident in the extensive attention he gives to Jesus' teaching concerning righteous living. He uses forms of the Greek words for *righteousness, righteous,* and *unrighteous* twenty-six times in his Gospel, far more than any other Gospel and second only to the book of Romans in all the New Testament.[1] Indeed, Jesus' teaching on obeying the Law and living an orderly moral life permeates Matthew's Gospel. In the Beatitudes, Jesus pronounces blessings on "those who hunger and thirst *for righteousness*" (5:6), "the *pure* in heart" (5:8), and "those who are persecuted *for righteousness' sake*" (5:10). When Jesus describes his followers as the light of the world, he instructs them, "Let your light shine before others, so they may *see your good works* and give glory to your Father in heaven" (5:16). This emphasis continues on in the rest of the Sermon on the Mount.

A key theme in this most famous of Jesus' sermons is his commitment to the Law. Jesus declares, "Do not think that I have come to abolish the Law or the Prophets; I have not come to abolish but to fulfill" (5:17). Here, Jesus challenges a belief that was apparently already widespread, namely, that he had come to do away with the Law. Jesus counters that he has not come to get rid of the Law at all. Indeed, he insists, "Until heaven and earth pass away, not one letter, not one stroke of a letter, will pass from the Law until all is fulfilled" (5:18). Jesus urges that a characteristic of kingdom living will be obedience to God's commandments. He says those who break "one of the least of these commandments" will be called "least in the kingdom of heaven" (5:19). He then goes even further, declaring, "Unless your righteousness exceeds that of the scribes and Pharisees, you will never enter the kingdom of heaven" (5:20). Jesus then follows these general statements with specific examples of his own intensification of the Law's requirements. He insists that it is not enough simply to follow the commandment "You shall not murder"; one must not even be angry with a brother or sister or direct insults toward them (5:21–22). It is not enough to check off the box that says, "You shall not commit adultery"; the ethic Jesus espouses demands turning away even from lust (5:27–30). At every turn, Jesus emphasizes the mandate that God's people obey God's commandments and that they obey the spirit of the commandments, not just the letter.[2]

One of the stories Jesus shared with his followers gives particular emphasis to the way an orderly moral life pushes back at the chaos poised to overwhelm us. As the concluding illustration to the Sermon on the Mount, Jesus says that those who follow his words and act on them are like a wise man who builds his house on rock (Matt 7:24–27). When the rains fall and the floods come, when the winds blow and beat on the house, that man's house does not fall. Why? Because it is founded on solid rock. But how different is the experience of those who hear the words of Jesus and fail to act on them! Jesus says that such individuals are like the foolish man who builds his house on the sand. When the rains fall and the floods come, when the winds blow and beat on that house, it is sure to fall. The moral path that Jesus charts is one that is, without question, difficult to follow. It takes work to dig down through the sand to find the rock that will serve as a strong foundation. But Jesus teaches that, when the storms of life come, it is those who have built their moral foundation on the solid ground of God's commandments who will be able to stand when others fall. It is surely noteworthy that Jesus' illustration revolves around waters that threaten to overwhelm us. We push back at the onslaughts of these chaotic waters when we live orderly moral lives.

Taking Care of the Vulnerable

The commitment to care for the vulnerable is equally prominent in the life of Jesus. This is the aspect of Jesus' life and ministry that is especially emphasized in Luke's Gospel. Luke's focus on those outside of the circles of power and influence is evident from the very beginning of his account. He opens his Gospel with the story of Zechariah and Elizabeth, an older couple who remained childless in a culture that set a premium on having children (1:5–25). Luke emphasizes the lowly status of Mary and Joseph as they are forced to take the difficult journey from Nazareth to Bethlehem to satisfy a Roman decree, as Mary is forced to give birth in a place normally reserved for animals, and as they can provide little more than strips of cloth for clothing and a feed trough for a crib for their newborn son (2:1–7). In Luke's Gospel, it is a ragtag band of shepherds who receive the announcement of Jesus' birth, not Matthew's gift-bearing magi (2:8–20). At the temple, it is an old man, Simeon, and an old widow, Anna, who are there to greet the infant Messiah (2:25–38). At every turn, it is the downtrodden, the outcast, and the poor who are emphasized in Luke's account.

This concern for the vulnerable is never far from the surface as Luke narrates the course of Jesus' ministry. As we saw above, Matthew introduces Jesus' ministry with a statement emphasizing his concern for living orderly moral lives: "From that time, Jesus began to proclaim, 'Repent, for the kingdom of heaven has come near!'" (Matt 4:17). Luke begins with a story that underscores Jesus' mission to those who are oppressed. No sooner has Jesus' ministry begun in Luke than he creates a stir in his hometown of Nazareth by standing up in the Sabbath service at the synagogue and reading these words from the prophet Isaiah:

> The Spirit of the Lord is upon me,
>   because he has anointed me
>   to bring good news to the poor.
> He has sent me to proclaim freedom to the captives
>   and recovery of sight to the blind,
>   to let the oppressed go free,
> to proclaim the year of the Lord's favor.
>
>   (Luke 4:18–19; cf. Isa 61:1–2)

Having stood to read the Scriptures, Jesus then sits to deliver his sermon. He says simply, "Today, this scripture has been fulfilled in your hearing." Although this is likely the shortest sermon ever delivered, its single sentence makes extraordinary claims. The Hebrew term for *anointed* in the text Jesus reads is *mašaḥ*, the verb from which the Hebrew noun *māšiaḥ*—which English renders as *messiah*—is derived. When Jesus applies this text to himself, he makes the claim that he himself is Israel's long-awaited Messiah. But note the parameters that define Jesus' messianic role: He claims he has come to proclaim release to captives, sight to the blind, freedom to the oppressed, and God's favor upon humanity. Already in the very first act of Jesus' ministry in Luke, a gauntlet has been thrown down. His ministry will be one of liberation and deliverance. It will be one of helping those who are vulnerable.

Jesus follows up on this initial sermon with a steady drumbeat of support for the poor and downtrodden. His Beatitudes in Luke are much more "earthy" than those in Matthew. He says, "Blessed are you *poor*" (Luke 6:20), rather than, "Blessed are the poor in spirit" (Matt 5:3), and "Blessed are you who are *hungry now*" (Luke 6:21), rather than, "Blessed are those who hunger and thirst after righteousness" (Matt 5:4). In Luke, Jesus' commitment to the poor shames Zacchaeus into restoring to the poor all that he had defrauded from them (and then some), apparently without Jesus' even having to ask him to do so (Luke 19:1–10). In Luke, Jesus tells the parable of the rich man who is sent to a place of torment because he ignored the plight of poor Lazarus at his gate (Luke 16:19–31). In Luke's Gospel, Jesus' focus is constantly on the poor and the outcast.

Jesus' concern with these vulnerable people is central to what is arguably his most famous parable, the story of the Good Samaritan (Luke 10:30–37). When asked by a man skilled in interpreting the Law what a person must do to inherit eternal life, Jesus turns the question back on the man and asks, "What does the Law say?" The man responds by quoting two passages from the Law, Deuteronomy 6:5 and Leviticus 19:18: "You shall love the Lord your God with all your heart and with all your soul and with all your strength and with all your mind, and your neighbor as yourself" (Luke 10:27). Hearing these commands, Jesus affirms that this is indeed the right answer. "Do these, and you will live," he assures the man. But the man then pushes the matter one step further with the question, "Who is my neighbor?" Jesus' response was the parable of the Good Samaritan.

The parable is one that is generally familiar even to those unconnected to Christianity. A man waylaid by bandits is first ignored by the religious functionaries of the day and then aided by the most unlikely of characters, a Samaritan. What is particularly interesting for our purposes is the manner in which the Samaritan's actions accord with the values of *tiqqun*. Behind *tiqqun* is the idea of healing what is broken and pushing back the boundaries of the chaos that still lingers in creation. This is precisely what the Good Samaritan did for the lonely victim in the parable. When the man was wounded, the Samaritan bound him up. When he was abandoned, the Samaritan carried him to safety. When he was left impoverished, the Samaritan paid for his lodging. The Samaritan found a man who had been overwhelmed by the forces of chaos and intervened to repair what that chaos had broken. In a time of disorder and distress, the Samaritan carved out a space of order and life the man could not provide for himself.

One final way in which Jesus showed his concern for pushing back the boundaries of chaos in the lives of the vulnerable is in his constant care for the sick and the dying. Jesus could have let any number of miraculous acts define his ministry. He could have strung together an endless series of death-defying leaps from temples, weddings blessed with miraculous wine, and withered fig trees. Instead, he chose to let healing the sick be the primary way by which he would be known. The lame, the blind, the epileptic, the bleeding, and even the dead would find their recovery in the gentle hands of Jesus. It was in his healing acts that Jesus fully lived out the notion of *tiqqun* as an act of helping those who were vulnerable.

In the subtle tapestry of religious allusions that undergirds J. R. R. Tolkien's *The Lord of the Rings*, it is fascinating to hear echoes of Jesus' ministry in Tolkien's characterization of the exiled king Aragorn. "The hands of the king are the hands of a healer," the women of Minas Tirith repeat to one another, and as if to validate his claim to the throne, Aragorn heals those who are sick within the city's walls. The Gospel writers would agree with Tolkien's description. The hands of the king are indeed the hands of a healer, and it is Jesus himself who most clearly exemplifies this principle. The ministry of Jesus, both in his teaching concerning an orderly moral life and in his reaching out to the vulnerable, was a life of *tiqqun*, a life of healing.

Tiqvah in the Life of Jesus

In those moments when I do not have my head buried in a book or a pack strapped on my back for a trek, I like to think of myself as a small-time art aficionado. As the untold hours of boredom inflicted on my wife and sons could attest, there is little I love more than strolling from gallery to gallery in a museum, musing over the great works of art set on display. While I have a weakness for Van Eyck and Caravaggio—well, it's more than a weakness— my favorite artist is Michelangelo. I confess, though, that while Michelangelo is rightly famous for his work on the ceiling of the Sistine Chapel, his paintings are not my favorite. His *Creation of Adam* is tremendous, and his *Jeremiah* astonishing, but scenes like his *Expulsion from the Garden* and his *Deluge* are average at best. But then, there are his sculptures. No one before or after ever took chisel to rock with the skill of Michelangelo. His

David is unparalleled. His *Moses* is riveting. And his *Pietà*—his *Pietà* is a proof of the spark of divinity God has planted in every human heart.

Michelangelo's *Pietà* is a work of almost indescribable beauty. To chip away one fleck of marble from the sculpture would be to lessen the perfection of the whole. The extraordinary manner in which the lifeless right arm of Jesus hangs toward the ground, the shoulder slightly elevated by the grip of his mother's hand, the gentle curves of his elbow and wrist, the corded muscles that lie beneath the flesh of his arm and leg and torso—these subtle elements betray an absolute mastery of the human form. As moving as the figure of Jesus, though, is the figure of his mother. The myriad folds in Mary's robe have not been matched by another artist working in stone. They are oversized to create the bier on which the slain Messiah lies. They envelop him as the robes of his mother must have done when he was just a child, sleeping on her lap long ago. And then, there is the Madonna's face, perhaps the most serene vision of the female form ever captured by an artist. Superior by far to even the soft look of Leonardo's *Mona Lisa* and the wistful gaze of Botticelli's *Venus* is the visage of Mary beholding her lifeless son. Hers is a look beyond tears, a look that simply asks the question, "How did it come to this? How did my son, my son whose life seemed so full of promise, come to this bitter end?" These are the questions that should haunt anyone reading the Passion Narratives. At sunset on Good Friday, one could be forgiven for thinking that the life of Jesus had been a failure. So much potential, and yet there he was, nailed to a Roman cross like countless others before him. All the *tiqqun* of Jesus' ministry had not been enough to change the course of humanity. He had lived a perfect life. He had helped others to the point of exhaustion. But now, at the end, his healing work had not been enough.

For those who were paying attention, though, this awful and seemingly unexpected end to Jesus' life should not have been unexpected at all. Jesus had repeatedly warned the disciples that his life would come to a bitter end. In Mark's Gospel alone, Jesus warned the disciples three times of the suffering he would endure:

> And he began to teach them that the Son of Man must suffer many things, and be rejected by the elders and the chief priests and the scribes, and be killed.
>
> (Mark 8:31a)

He was teaching his disciples, saying to them, "The Son of Man is to be delivered into the hands of men, and they will kill him."

(Mark 9:31a)

And taking the twelve aside again, he began to tell them what was going to happen to him, saying, "Behold, we are going up to Jerusalem, and the Son of Man will be handed over to the chief priests and the scribes, and they will condemn him to death and hand him over to the gentiles. And they will mock him and spit on him and flog him and kill him."

(Mark 10:32b–34a)

In essence, Jesus had warned the disciples that though he would heal those he met along the way and though he would work to comfort those who were vulnerable, his works of *tiqqun* would be met with a wall of resistance that would stymie his efforts—at least for a time. And so, alongside his works of *tiqqun*, Jesus would also plant seeds of *tiqvah*. That is, alongside his works of *healing*, he would also plant seeds of *hope*.

Resurrection

One of the most important "seeds of hope" Jesus would plant would be his assurance that his death would not be the last act of his life. Just three days later, he would rise again. In each of the three passages noted above in which Jesus warns the disciples of his impending suffering, he concludes with an additional prediction of his resurrection. In Mark 8:31, he warns that the Son of Man must suffer and be killed but then adds that "after three days" he will "rise again." In Mark 9:31, he tells his disciples that though he will be handed over to enemies who will ultimately kill him, "three days after being killed, he will rise again." Again, in Mark 10:34, he assures them that "after three days, he will rise again."

God's raising Jesus from the dead served as the stamp of approval on the way Jesus conducted his life and ministry. Throughout his public work, Jesus had sided with those on the outskirts of proper society. The disciples he called to himself were a band of "uneducated and ordinary men" (Acts 4:13).[3] They were regarded as uncouth and unclean by Jesus' opponents (Mark 7:2; cf. Matt 15:2; Luke 11:38), and they were regularly chastised by Jesus himself for their inability to understand his teaching (Mark 4:13; 8:17, 21; 9:19; Matt 16:23). In a time when women were widely regarded as second-class citizens, Jesus' wider circle of followers included a great many women—the various Marys, including Mary Magdalene, who was said to have once been possessed by seven demons (Luke 8:2), Salome, Martha, and others. He created a scandal by dining with tax collectors and sinners (Matt 9:10; 11:19; Mark 2:15; Luke 5:30; 7:34; 15:1–2). He risked ritual uncleanness by touching lepers (Matt 8:3; Mark 1:41; Luke 5:13) and the dead (Matt 9:25; Mark 5:41; Luke 7:14). He constantly surrounded himself with the blind, the lame, the mute, and the possessed (Matt 8:16; 9:6, 27–30, 32–33; 11:5; 12:22; 15:30–31; 20:30–34; 21:14; Mark 1:32–34; 2:10–11; 7:37; 8:22–26; 9:25–27; 10:46–52; Luke 7:21–22; 9:42; 11:14; 13:11–13; 18:35–43; John 4:50; 5:8; 9:1–41). He reached out to gentiles: the Syro-Phoenician woman whose daughter was possessed by a demon (Matt 15:21–28; Mark 7:24–30), the Gerasene demoniac (Matt 8:28–32; Mark 5:1–13; Luke 8:26–35) and the crowds who later came to see what Jesus had done for him (Matt 15:30–31), the centurion's servant (Matt 8:5–13; Luke 7:2–9), and the Samaritan woman at the well (John 4:5–42). Even on the cross, Jesus comforted the criminal who was being crucified alongside him (Luke 23:40–43).

The death Jesus died was one that continued to embrace the status of the oppressed and outcast. From the perspective of Rome, Jesus was just another rabble-rouser bent on stirring up political trouble by setting himself up as king. From the perspective of the religious leaders of the day, Jesus was just another false claimant to the role of messiah and a threat to the temple system. For both Rome and the religious leaders, crucifixion was precisely the punishment needed to quash these aspirations. For Rome, the cross was the instrument used to put down political insurrection. Nailed to a cross, the victim would learn the lesson of what happened to those who resisted Rome's power and would teach others that same lesson in the process. One could not be king and be crucified. For the religious leaders, the cross was a demonstration of rejection by God himself. As the book of Deuteronomy insists, "Anyone hung on a tree is under God's curse" (Deut 21:23). One could not be messiah and be crucified.

When Jesus died such an ignoble death, it seemed that the final nail had been driven into the coffin of his messianic claims. He had entered Jerusalem like a conquering hero on Palm Sunday, but less than a week later, his broken body and his lofty aspirations lay dead in a tomb. It was the resurrection that shattered this logic. When God raised Jesus from the dead, he announced that the death Jesus died and thus the life he had lived were, in fact, pleasing to God. Jesus had lived and finally died among the oppressed. By raising him from the dead, God gave the ultimate fulfillment of his earlier words, "This is my beloved son with whom I am well pleased"

(Matt 3:17; 12:18; 17:5). With his various predictions of his resurrection, Jesus was laying down the first markers of hope—*tiqvah*—for the disciples. In the dark times that were yet to come, he encouraged them to hang on; new light would come with the dawn.

Return

The resurrection of Jesus would serve as the basis for the future hope to come, but it was not the only hopeful note Jesus struck in his ministry. The bookend to Jesus' resurrection would be his return. In his conversations with his disciples, Jesus repeatedly assured them that in time they would see the kingdom of God manifest on earth. One of the most touching of these scenes is found on the heels of the story of the rich young ruler (Matt 19:16–26). After witnessing the young man turn away from Jesus because he was unwilling to part with his many possessions, Peter—it had to be Peter—turned to Jesus and asked, "Look, we have left everything and followed you. What then will we have?" (v. 27). Ordinarily, we might have expected Jesus to issue a rebuke to Peter for his question, to chastise him for setting his mind on earthly things rather than heavenly things (cf. Matt 16:23). Here, though, Jesus does just the opposite. He seems to recognize in Peter's question an element of truth: The disciples had left everything behind—their families, their occupations, their possessions. They were committed to following Jesus. But to what end? Where was all of this headed? Jesus' encouragement to Peter and the other disciples was this:

> Truly, I say to you, at the renewal of all things, when the Son of Man is seated on his glorious throne, you who have followed me will also sit on twelve thrones, judging the twelve tribes of Israel. And everyone who has left houses or brothers or sisters or father or mother or children or fields for my name's sake shall receive a hundredfold and inherit eternal life.
>
> (Matt 19:28–29)

Jesus assured the disciples that the day would come when he would return, when they would see the kingdom come, when their hopes would be fulfilled, and when they would be rewarded for all they had given up to follow him.

This language of hope for the coming kingdom permeates Jesus' teaching. It is there in his warning concerning the day when he will judge the nations, separating the sheep and the goats (Matt 25:31–46). It is there in the apocalyptic sermon he delivered concerning the destruction of the temple and the coming times of the gentiles (Matt 24:1–51; Mark 13:1–37; Luke 21:5–28). It is there in the parables he told about the bridesmaids who failed to bring their oil (Matt 25:1–13), the talents entrusted to the master's servants (Matt 25:14–30; Mark 13:34–37; Luke 19:11–27), the watchful slaves (Matt 24:42–51; Luke 12:35–40), and the fig tree (Luke 21:29–32).

Interestingly, it is the language of the coming kingdom that lays the foundation for the story of the Mount of Transfiguration. In each of the synoptic Gospels—Matthew, Mark, and Luke—the passage preceding the transfiguration account follows a similar pattern: Jesus asks the disciples who they say he is, and they at last recognize him as the Messiah (Matt 16:13–20; Mark 8:27–30; Luke 9:18–21). He begins to warn them of the suffering he must endure and of the suffering they will also face (Matt 16:21–26; Mark 8:31–38; Luke 9:22–26). Then, immediately before he reveals his true nature on the mountain, he tells the disciples that they will not taste death until they see the kingdom of God:

> Truly, I say to you, there are some standing here who will not taste death before they see the Son of Man coming in his kingdom.
>
> > (Matt 16:28)

> And he said to them, "Truly, I say to you, there are some standing here who will not taste death until they see that the kingdom of God has come with power."
>
> > (Mark 9:1)

> But I tell you truly, there are some standing here who will not taste death until they see the kingdom of God.
>
> > (Luke 9:27)

The language of the Gospels differs somewhat, in keeping with the different understandings of the end times each holds. What they share in common, though, is the belief that the vision of Jesus transfigured on the mountain is a foretaste of the kingdom that is to come. There will be suffering to come, but in the midst of their suffering, the disciples should remember the person whose true glory they have seen, and they should hold on in hope for the time when they will see that glory again.

Jesus and the Sea

As Jesus taught his followers, he often gave them assurances of the future hope that lay ahead at the end of the dark days they now faced. As important as those assurances in his *teaching*, though, were his symbolic *actions* that dramatized that future hope. Many of these actions center on the sea. It was, perhaps, inevitable that the sea would figure prominently in the ministry of Jesus once he moved to Capernaum—a village located on the north shore of the Sea of Galilee—and made it his base of operations (Matt 4:13). At least four of Jesus' disciples—Peter, Andrew, James, and John—were fishermen from the area (vv. 18, 21), and Jesus determined to put their sailing skills to the test during his time with them. On a regular basis, Jesus pushed them to go "to the other side of the sea."

From a first-century Jewish perspective, the *other side* of the sea was gentile territory. In the years following Alexander the Great's conquest of the region in 323 BCE, a number of Greek cities were founded in the area that today comprises parts of northwestern Jordan and southwestern Syria (Scythopolis, located just on the west side of the Jordan River, is the lone exception). These cities came to be known as the Decapolis and served as outposts for Hellenistic life and culture in this frontier area. In time, the cities of the Decapolis would come under Roman rule, but whether Greek or Roman, they posed the same challenge to the Jews of the land of Israel. Their morality and culture were contrary to the values of the Jewish Law, their pantheon of gods was inimical to Jewish monotheism, and their military might was beyond the ability of the Jewish political leaders to combat. The safest course of action for most Jews was simply to avoid the area and leave its gentile inhabitants to their own devices. Yet, Jesus repeatedly instructed the disciples to venture right over to this gentile side of the sea.

Perhaps the most harrowing story of the disciples' time on the other side of the sea is found in the account of the Gerasene demoniac (Matt 8:28–34; Mark 5:1–20; Luke 8:26–39). Mark's version of the incident is particularly riveting as he describes the man's condition:

> And they came to the other side of the sea, to the country of the Gerasenes. And when he [Jesus] had gotten out of the boat, immediately a man out of the tombs with an unclean spirit confronted him. He had his dwelling among the tombs, and no one could restrain him anymore, even with a chain. For he had often been bound with shackles and

chains, but the chains had been wrenched apart and the shackles broken in pieces, and no one had the strength to subdue him. Night and day among the tombs and on the mountains he was crying out and gashing himself with stones.

(Mark 5:1–5)

One can scarcely imagine the scene as the man emerges from the tombs, naked perhaps (as the text will later emphasize that he is clothed; cf. v. 15), broken fetters still dangling from his wrists, and scarred and bleeding from gashes he had inflicted upon himself with stones.[4] The disciples were rightly terrified. Indeed, there is not a shred of evidence in the text to suggest that they ever got out of the boat at all. Verse 2 mentions only Jesus as it says, "When *he* got out of the boat," and v. 18 refers only to Jesus again when it says, "As *he* was getting in the boat." Between these verses, *only Jesus* speaks to the unclean spirits and the man they possessed, and it is only *to Jesus* that these spirits, the man, and the nearby townspeople speak themselves. The disciples are nowhere to be seen in the story, because they never set foot on the land.[5]

It is hard to blame the disciples for their reticence to join the fray on this occasion. For pious Jews like the disciples, the place where their boat had landed was simply beyond the pale. A gentile area set among the pagan cities of the Decapolis, a place of tombs haunted by a demoniac, a place of swine and their swineherds—the very thought of setting foot in such a ritually defiled place was more than the disciples could bear! But Jesus would bring the disciples back here once again later in his ministry. When Jesus cast the unclean spirits into the swine, the swineherds and the people from the area begged him to leave their region (v. 17). The man who had been released from their torments begged for something else, however. He implored Jesus to let him return with him (v. 18). Somewhat surprisingly, Jesus refused. He told him instead, "Go home to your friends, and tell them how much the Lord has done for you and how he has had mercy on you" (v. 19). Mark records that the man did just as Jesus had commanded him: "And he went away and began to proclaim in the Decapolis how much Jesus had done for him, and everyone marveled" (v. 20). It was the freed demoniac's preaching that set the stage for the disciples' return trip to the other side.

After some time had passed, Jesus and his disciples returned to Galilee from a time of rest in Tyre and Sidon. Their return brought them to the east side of the sea, once again to the region of the Decapolis (Matt 15:29; Mark 7:31). This time, Jesus did not encounter a wild demoniac shouting among the tombs. He did not find a group of swineherds and their neighbors begging him to leave their neighborhood. What he found instead was a group looking to him for help. In the words of Matthew:

> And great crowds came to him, having with them the lame, the blind, the crippled, the mute, and many others. They lay them at his feet, and he healed them, so that the crowd marveled when they saw the mute speaking, the crippled whole, the lame walking, and the blind seeing. And they praised the God of Israel.
>
> (Matt 15:30–31)

What could account for this profound difference in how Jesus was received? Put simply, it was the effectiveness of the demoniac's preaching among his gentile neighbors. Jesus had commanded him to tell others about the mercy God had shown to him, and he apparently did so with abandon, so much so that crowds now came out to embrace Jesus rather than to warn him away.

Jesus had asked a great deal of the disciples when he instructed them to make their way to the "other side" of the sea. Something more than just the force of his personality would be needed to assure them that there was a method behind this seeming madness. That something came in the form of two confrontations between Jesus and the sea. The first of these confrontations took place as Jesus and his disciples were sailing east to their initial encounter with the Gerasene demoniac. As Mark recounts the story (4:35–41), along their way across the sea, a terrible storm arose and began to batter the disciples' boat with waves that threatened to swamp it. Jesus, meanwhile, was fast asleep in the stern of the boat. Nearly at their breaking point, the disciples confronted Jesus, rousing him from sleep and asking, "Teacher, do you not care that we are perishing?" When Jesus awoke, he commanded the sea, "Peace! Be still!" As the winds ceased and the waves calmed, Jesus demanded of the disciples, "Why are you afraid? Do you still have no faith?" It is the question raised by the disciples, though, that is especially interesting: "What manner of man is this that even the winds and the sea obey him?" *What manner of man is this that even the winds and the sea obey him?* Even in Mark, the Gospel that so dramatically highlights the failings of Jesus' followers, the disciples stumble upon the question that defines the essence of Jesus' ministry. What manner of man could control the winds and waves? No ordinary man at all, surely! Only God had ever mastered the sea. This was just what Jesus' actions were intended to convey. In the person of Jesus, the disciples were not dealing with any ordinary man.

The one who controlled the winds and the waves, the one who controlled the sea, was the one who bore a connection to the God of Genesis 1 like no other. The one whom the disciples followed was the one who had controlled the sea long ago in creation and who would do so again completely in the age to come. He was the one worthy of their hope.

The second account of Jesus' confrontation with the sea is found in the familiar story of his walking on the water (Matt 14:22–36; Mark 6:45–52). The Gospel writers tell us that after he had fed the five thousand, Jesus compelled his disciples to get in the boat and make their way back to Capernaum.[6] Once the disciples had made their getaway, he then dismissed the crowds and was left alone on the land. It seems clear from the text that Jesus was setting the stage for what was about to happen. While he was praying on the top of a mountain, Jesus looked out toward the sea and saw his disciples struggling against a storm. Mark notes, "He saw that they were straining to make headway because the wind was against them" (6:48), and Matthew adds, "By this time the boat, battered by the waves, was far away from the land, because the wind was against them" (14:24–25). It was at this moment that Jesus left the mountain and went out to rescue the disciples.

It is important not to miss the symbolism that permeates this move. Jesus was alone on the mountain in prayer, but he was willing to interrupt this moment of intimacy and communion with the Father because he saw that his followers were in trouble. The sea had reared its winds and waves against the disciples. They were in danger of being overwhelmed. But then, in that desperate moment, Jesus marched straight out onto the stormy seas to deliver them. It is hard not to hear in this account echoes of Paul's description of Jesus' ultimate act of rescue:

> Let the same mind be in you that was in Christ Jesus, who, though being in the form of God, did not regard equality with God as something to cling to, but emptied himself, taking the form of a slave, being born in human likeness. And being found in human form, he humbled himself, becoming obedient to the point of death—even death on a cross.
>
> (Phil 2:5–8)

Here, Paul describes a similar scene of Jesus' interrupting his perfect communion with the Father to come down the mountain, as it were, and intervene to rescue his people.

Like the previous story of Jesus' calming the winds and the waves, the story of his walking on the water is one that is pregnant with *tiqvah*. This is especially evident in Matthew's description of Peter's own moment on the sea with Jesus (14:26–32). When the disciples saw Jesus walking on the sea, they were understandably terrified and cried out in fear. Jesus sought to allay these fears, saying, "Have courage! It is I, do not be afraid." Ever the boldest of Jesus' followers, Peter replied, "Lord, if it is you, command me to come to you on the water." Jesus answered, "Come." In what must have been one of the bravest acts of his entire life, Peter got out of the boat and started walking on the water toward Jesus. Ultimately, the storm proved to be too sore a test for Peter. Matthew tells us, "Seeing the strong wind, he became frightened, and beginning to sink, he cried out, saying, 'Lord, save me!'" What Jesus did and said in response to Peter's outcry captures perfectly the note of hope he wanted to leave with his followers. When Peter could not support himself, Jesus "immediately reached out his hand and caught him." Then he said to him, "You of little faith, why did you doubt?" Jesus said to him in essence, "Peter, you can trust me. I've got this." His assurance was that though the seas might rage and threaten, though the storm winds might howl and blow, the disciples could put their hope in the one they were following; Jesus was master even of the sea.

In their own very different ways, both the disciples and creation itself voiced their affirmation of Jesus' mastery of the sea. The sea did so as its threatening winds immediately ceased to blow. For the disciples, this affirmation took the form of an exclamation, one that seemed to answer the question they had raised when Jesus last showed his control of the sea. When he awoke from sleep to calm the winds and the waves, the disciples had asked, "What manner of man is this that even the winds and the sea obey him?" (Matt 8:27). Having seen him control the sea once more, they seemed to answer their own question: "Truly, you are the Son of God" (Matt 14:33).

It cannot be a coincidence that the Gospel writers chose to include these stories of Jesus' mastery over the sea in their accounts of his life. Jesus' control of the sea was a marker that would have resonated deeply with his followers. It was an act that placed him in a stream of creation traditions that ranged from Genesis to Job to the Psalms and the Prophets. It was an act that announced that though he now healed only in part (*tiqqun*), his followers' hopes that he would one day do so completely would not be disappointed (*tiqvah*). He had controlled the sea at creation; he had controlled the sea while he was with the disciples; he would control the sea again in the world to come. Indeed, in that day he would finally bring to pass the words "And there was no more sea."

Notes

Note to the Introduction

1. Unless otherwise indicated, all translations of biblical and extrabiblical texts in this book are my own. Biblical texts are cited throughout according to their English versification. Where the underlying Hebrew versification differs, the Hebrew reference follows in brackets.

Notes to Chapter 1

1. Whether Copernicus took holy orders is a matter of some debate. See Edward Rosen, "Galileo's Misstatements about Copernicus," *Isis* 49 (1958): 319–20.

2. J. L. E. Dreyer, ed., *Tychonis Brahe Dani opera omnia* (Copenhagen: Libraria Gyldendaliana, 1913–29), 4:156, lines 114–118. Translated in Owen Gingerich and James R. Voelkel, "Tycho Brahe's Copernican Campaign," *Journal for the History of Astronomy* 29 (1998): 23–24.

3. Concerning the issues involved in the Church's response to the scientific developments of this period, see Jules Speller, *Galileo's Inquisition Trial Revisited* (Frankfurt am Main: Lang, 2008).

4. Luther's comments were preserved by his recorders in two versions. The first, from Johann Aurifaber, is found in *Tischreden* (Weimar ed.) I:419 no. 855, and the second, from Anton Lauterbach, in IV:412–13 no. 4638 (Martin Luther, *D. Martin Luthers Werke: Kritische Gesamtausgabe* [Weimar: Hermann Böhlaus Nachfolger, 1883]). Noting that Luther is said to have labeled the unnamed Copernicus a "fool" (*Narr*) only in Aurifaber's transcript but not Lauterbach's, Wilhelm Norlind argues that Luther did not use the term *Narr* at all and that his comment "He has to make something of his own" was meant as praise. See Norlind, "Copernicus and Luther: A Critical Study," *Isis* 44 (1953): 273–76. Both suggestions are highly unlikely, as both Edward Rosen and Heinrich Meyer note (Rosen, "Galileo's Misstatements," 324n29; Meyer, "More on Copernicus and Luther," *Isis* 45 [1954]: 99). Luther's comments date from 1539, four years before Copernicus published his *De revolutionibus*,

attesting to the fact that word of Copernicus' views had spread widely even before they were put in print.

5. Philipp Melanchthon, "Initia doctrinae physicae," in *Philippi Melanthonis opera quae supersunt omnia*, ed. Karl Gottlieb Bretschneider, Corpus Reformatorum 1–28 (Halle: C. A. Schwetschke & Son, 1834–60), 13:216–17. The translation here is from Andrew Dickson White, *A History of the Warfare of Science with Theology in Christendom* (New York: D. Appleton, 1896), 1:126–27.

6. Melanchthon, "Letter 2391, to Burcardo Mithobio," in *Philippi Melanthonis opera quae supersunt omnia*, 4:679. The translation is from Rosen, "Galileo's Misstatements," 324.

7. The genesis and subsequent promulgation of this apocryphal quote are traced by Rosen in "Calvin's Attitude toward Copernicus," *JHI* 21 (1960): 431–41.

8. John Calvin, *Commentary on the Book of Psalms*, trans. James Anderson (Edinburgh: Calvin Translation Society, 1845–49; repr. Grand Rapids: Baker, 1996), 4:6–7.

9. Calvin, *Commentaries on the Book of Joshua*, trans. Henry Beveridge (Edinburgh: Calvin Translation Society, 1854; repr., Grand Rapids: Baker, 1996), 153.

10. Calvin, *Ioannis Calvini opera quae supersunt omnia*, ed. Wilhelm Baum, Edward Cunitz, and Eduard Reuss, Corpus Reformatorum 29–87 (Braunschweig: C. A. Schwetschke & Son, 1863–1900), 49:677. Translated by Robert White, "Calvin and Copernicus: The Problem Reconsidered," *CTJ* 15 (1980): 236–37.

11. The circumstances of Galileo's trial and its aftermath are discussed at length in Maurice A. Finocchiaro, *Retrying Galileo, 1633–1992* (Berkeley: University of California Press, 2005).

12. Whether it was his intention to do so or not, in his *Dialogue on the Two Chief World Systems, Ptolemaic and Copernican* (1632) Galileo appeared to cast himself as *Salviati*, a sage Copernican scientist, and Pope Urban VIII as *Simplicio*, a simpleton dogmatically committed to the geocentric view.

13. Finocchiaro, *Retrying Galileo*, 194–98.

14. John Polkinghorne, "The Universe as Creation," in *Intelligent Design: William A. Dembski and Michael Ruse in Dialogue*, ed. Robert B. Stewart (Minneapolis: Fortress, 2007), 166.

15. Galileo Galilei, "Letter to the Grand Duchess Christina," in *Discoveries and Opinions of Galileo*, trans. Stillman Drake (Garden City, NY: Doubleday, 1957), 173–216. The quotations that follow in this and the subsequent paragraphs are found on pp. 179–85, 194.

16. From Augustine, *De Genesi ad litteram*, 2.9. Rehearsing similar arguments from Augustine, Jerome, and Aquinas, Galileo argued in his letter to the grand duchess that the biblical authors spoke in the language of the common people on matters of science lest the people's inability to grasp a confusing scientific point lead them to reject a more important theological tenet. Thus, he held that the biblical authors knew that the world is spherical, that the heavens are not a void but are full of air, and that the sun remains at rest while the earth moves. He insisted that "not only respect for the incapacity of the vulgar, but also current opinion in those times, made the sacred authors accommodate themselves (in matters unnecessary

to salvation) more to accepted usage than to the true essence of things" (*Discoveries and Opinions of Galileo*, 200). He maintained that some scientific matters could perhaps have been explained, "yet the holy scribes forbore to attempt it" (ibid., 201).

17. A helpful discussion of the importance of discerning genre in biblical interpretation is available in Richard F. Carlson and Tremper Longman III, *Science, Creation, and the Bible: Reconciling Rival Theories of Origins* (Downers Grove, IL: InterVarsity Press, 2010), 56–69.

18. George Plimpton, "The Curious Case of Sidd Finch," *Sports Illustrated*, April 1, 1985.

19. *The Blair Witch Project* (1999) and *Paranormal Activity* (2007) are notable examples. Concerning the largely legendary tales of panic over Welles' *War of the Worlds*, see A. Brad Schwartz, *Broadcast Hysteria: Orson Welles's War of the Worlds and the Art of Fake News* (New York: Hill & Wang, 2015).

20. The Hebrew form is generally the noun (*a man, two men, a vineyard*) followed by a form of the verb **hyh* "to be." The key phrase in Greek is *anthrōpos tis*, "a certain man." As the examples above demonstrate, this phrase is especially common in Luke's parables, lending even greater weight to the suggestion that Luke's story of the Rich Man and Lazarus is a parable.

21. So Henry, Barnes, Ellicott, Jamieson-Fausset-Brown, Maclaren, Barclay, Walvoord and Zuck, and others too numerous to mention.

22. Interestingly, although Calvin regarded the story of the Rich Man and Lazarus as a historical account, he emphasized that understanding the theological message of the story was what was most important: "Some look upon it as a simple parable; but, as the name Lazarus occurs in it, I rather consider it to be the narrative of an actual fact. But that is of little consequence, provided that the reader comprehends the doctrine which it contains." See Calvin, *Commentary on a Harmony of the Evangelists, Matthew, Mark, and Luke*, trans. William Pringle (Edinburgh: Calvin Translation Society, 1845; repr., Grand Rapids: Baker, 1996), 2:184.

23. The same Greek verb, *peirazō*, is used by James to say God *cannot be tempted* (Jas 1:13) and by the author of Hebrews to say Jesus *was tempted* (Heb 4:15).

24. Concerning the Ebionites and the Docetists, see James D. G. Dunn, *Unity and Diversity in the New Testament: An Inquiry into the Character of Earliest Christianity*, 2nd ed. (London: SCM, 1990), 28, 240–45, 298–305.

25. These issues are explored at length in Peter Enns, *Inspiration and Incarnation: Evangelicals and the Problem of the Old Testament* (Grand Rapids: Baker Academic, 2005) and Kenton L. Sparks, *Sacred Word, Broken Word: Biblical Authority and the Dark Side of Scripture* (Grand Rapids: Eerdmans, 2012).

Notes to Chapter 2

1. Concerning Paul's language in this passage, see ch. 7 below.

2. Galileo ("Letter to the Grand Duchess," 189–90) offers a withering critique of some who, even in his day, suggested on the basis of this biblical text that the moon must give off its own light and not merely reflect the light of the sun.

3. Nicole Kiefert, "Astronomers Just Discovered the Smallest Star Ever," July 12, 2017, http://www.astronomy.com/news/2017/07/tiny-new-star. By way of comparison, Saturn is 760 times larger than the earth.

4. Concerning the size of some of the largest stars yet discovered, see ch. 7 below.

Notes to Chapter 3

1. The first creation account in Genesis extends from Gen 1:1–2:3. For the sake of convenience, I will generally refer to this account simply as "Genesis 1."

2. There is little in the text to support a connection with the exodus from Egypt rather than creation. Verse 13 refers to breaking or shattering the sea, not—as Exod 14 does—to splitting it (see the discussion below). Further, vv. 14–15 bear little resemblance to the provision of water and food during the sojourn in the wilderness. As J. A. Emerton notes, it is more likely that the reference to *splitting open springs* in the first half of v. 14 has to do with making openings to drain away the chaotic waters, thus leading to God's *drying up ever-flowing rivers* in the second half of the verse. See Emerton, "'Spring and Torrent' in Psalm LXXIV 15," in *Volume du Congrès: Genève, 1965*, ed. P. A. H. de Boer, VTSup 15 (Leiden: Brill, 1966), 122–33. The references to creation in vv. 16–17, on the other hand, are quite clear. See further Marvin E. Tate, *Psalms 51–100*, ed. David A. Hubbard and Glenn W. Barker, WBC 20 (Dallas: Word, 1990), 250–52; John Day, *God's Conflict with the Dragon and the Sea: Echoes of a Canaanite Myth in the Old Testament* (Cambridge: Cambridge University Press, 1985), 23–24; and André Lelièvre, "YHWH et la mer dans les Psaumes," *RHPR* 56 (1976): 256–63.

3. David Tsumura argues convincingly that the Hebrew verb **prr* found in v. 13 should be understood as *break* or *break up* rather than *divide*, as most translations have it. As we will see below, his coordinate suggestion that Ps 74 does not involve the *Chaoskampf* motif is unconvincing. See Tsumura, "The Creation Motif in Psalm 74:12–14? A Reappraisal of the Theory of the Dragon Myth," *JBL* 134 (2015): 547–51. Tsumura's arguments concerning the absence of the *Chaoskampf* in the psalm are convincingly addressed in Nathaniel E. Greene, "Creation, Destruction, and a Psalmist's Plea: Rethinking the Poetic Structure of Psalm 74," *JBL* 136 (2017): 90–100.

4. Although the MT renders the term as plural, the parallel with the singular "Leviathan" may suggest that it was originally singular with an enclitic *mem*. See Mark S. Smith and Wayne T. Pitard, *The Ugaritic Baal Cycle*, vol. 2, *Introduction with Text, Translation and Commentary of KTU/CAT 1.3–1.4*, VTSup 114 (Leiden: Brill, 2009), 256.

5. *HALOT* regards the reading *lᶜmlṣy ym*, "for the creatures of the sea," as much more likely than the MT's inscrutable *lᶜm lṣyym*, "for the people of the wilderness." In the context of the passage, a reference to the sea makes much better sense. See further Herbert Donner, "Ugaritismen in der Psalmenforschung," *ZAW* 79 (1967): 338n103. Day (*God's Conflict*, 22n57) remains skeptical, however. See also Wayne

T. Pitard, "The Binding of Yamm: A New Edition of the Ugaritic Text *KTU* 1.83," *JNES* 57 (1998): 280.

6. The KJV, RSV, NRSV, and NAB have "dragons." The ASV, NASB, HCSB, ESV, and JPS (1917) have "sea monsters." The NIV and NJPS (1985) have "monsters." The NKJV has "sea serpents."

7. Concerning the Hebrew term *peṯen*, "asp," see Deut 32:33; Job 20:14, 16; Pss 58:4 [5]; 91:13; Isa 11:8.

8. Hebrew poetry exhibits a brevity of style in which definite articles and various other grammatical elements are often omitted. Such is the case in this verse for both *sea* and *tannîn*, making it unclear whether Job refers to "a *tannîn*" or "the *tannîn*."

9. The connection between the *tannîn* and the sea is further emphasized in Ps 148:7: "Praise YHWH from the earth, you *tannînîm* and all deeps." Though the *tannînîm* are here enjoined to praise God, they are normally cast as God's opponents. See also Gen 1:21.

10. See Edward Lipiński, "לִוְיָתָן *liwyāṯān*," *TDOT* 7:504–9.

11. An extended discussion of Isa 27:1 is available in Bernhard W. Anderson, "The Slaying of the Fleeing, Twisting Serpent: Isaiah 27:1 in Context," in *Uncovering Ancient Stones: Essays in Memory of H. Neil Richardson*, ed. Lewis M. Hopfe (Winona Lake, IN: Eisenbrauns, 1994), 3–15.

12. There are hints of crocodilian imagery in the use of *tannîn* in two passages in Ezekiel. In Ezek 29:3, the prophet describes Pharaoh as "the great dragon lying in the midst of its channels, saying, 'My Nile is my own; I made it for myself.' " Later, in Ezek 32:2, he adds, "You consider yourself a lion among the nations, but you are like a dragon in the seas; you thrash about in your streams, trouble the water with your feet, and foul their rivers." The language of sprawling in the Nile, thrashing about, and troubling the water with its feet echoes the actions of the crocodiles that inhabit the Nile even today. Even here, though, it is clear that no mere crocodile would suffice to satisfy the full extent of the prophet's description. Concerning the insufficiency of the various proposals for identifying the Leviathan with a natural creature—crocodile, whale, dolphin, etc.—see Day, *God's Conflict*, 65–72.

13. See the Ugaritic text *KTU* 1.5 I, 1–3, 27–30, and the depiction of the dragon on the famous Tel Asmar seal. Concerning the latter, see Gary A. Rendsburg, "*UT* 68 and the Tell Asmar Seal," *Or* 53 (1984): 448–52.

14. Note that the dragon with seven heads appears again in the New Testament, in Rev 12:3 and 13:1.

15. Concerning the hunting of both whales and crocodiles in antiquity, see Day, *God's Conflict*, 65–67.

16. Like many other verses that appear to countenance the presence of other gods, this verse has suffered a great deal from scribal "corrections." See the discussion in Emanuel Tov, *Textual Criticism of the Hebrew Bible* (Minneapolis: Fortress, 1992), 64–67, 267–69. Tov notes various other examples, in passages such as Deut 32:8; 2 Sam 2:8; 3:8; 4:4, 5; 5:16; 9:6; 11:21; 16:1; 19:25; 21:7; 23:8; Ps 96:7.

17. Renderings of *Leviathan* using forms of *drakōn* are found in Job 41:1 [40:25]; Pss 74:14; 104:26; and Isa 27:1 [3x]. Only Job 3:8 differs, as Leviathan is translated as

to mega kētos, "the great sea monster" or "the great fish." Forms of *drakōn* are found in the New Testament in Rev 12:3, 4, 7, 9, 13, 16, 17; 13:2, 4, 11; 16:13; 20:2.

18. See *KTU* 1.5 I, 1–3; 1.3 III, 39–42.

19. Cf. Exod 7:9–10, 12; Deut 32:33; Job 7:12; Pss 74:13; 91:13; 148:7; Isa 27:1; Jer 51:34; Ezek 29:3; 32:2.

20. The phrase translated here as "divine beings" is in Hebrew *banê ʾēlîm*, literally, *sons of (the) gods*. Tate suggests that *the heavens* who praise YHWH in v. 5 should be understood metonymically as a reference to *those in the heavens* (*Psalms 51–100*, 409).

21. The etymology of the Hebrew term **rhb* is notoriously difficult. It seems likely that it is connected with the Akkadian verb *raʾābu*, meaning *to rage* or *tremble*. See U. Rüterswörden, "רָהַב *rāhaḇ*," *TDOT* 13:351–57; *CAD* 14:1–3.

22. Reading *kēseh*, "full moon," for the MT's *kissēh*, apparently "throne." The Hebrew term for "throne," *kissēʾ*, is spelled only twice with a final *heh* rather than final *aleph*, both times in a single verse, 1 Kgs 10:19.

23. Alongside the language of *pillars*, the biblical authors often refer to the *foundations* of the heavens or earth. Cf. 2 Sam 22:16 (// Ps 18:15 [16]); Ps 82:5; Prov 8:29; Isa 24:18; 40:21; 48:13; 51:13, 16; Jer 31:37; Mic 6:2. Although 2 Sam 22 and Ps 18 are nearly identical, it is interesting that Ps 18:8 has "foundations of the mountains" and 2 Sam 22:8 has "foundations of the heavens."

24. As has already been noted, the language of God's combat against the dragon will be deployed again in the book of Revelation, a book whose powerful symbolism is steeped in the creation traditions of the Hebrew Bible. See especially Rev 12–13.

Notes to Chapter 4

1. *Jaws* is, of course, more famous as the movie by Steven Spielberg than the novel by Peter Benchley. Though the movie, like the book, continues to echo *Moby-Dick*, there are interesting differences in the treatment of Hooper's character by Spielberg and Benchley. Spielberg's Hooper is far more likable than Benchley's, making him more like Melville's Queequeg. Unlike Benchley (and Melville), though, Spielberg has Hooper survive the expedition to kill the shark. This was not the movie's original intent, however. To incorporate a particularly well-done bit of footage in which a great white attacked the empty shark cage, the screenplay had to be significantly modified to allow for Hooper to survive the incident.

2. Any study that intends to consider parallels between biblical and extrabiblical materials must avoid falling into the trap of what Samuel Sandmel has derisively called "parallelomania" (Sandmel, "Parallelomania," *JBL* 81 [1962]: 1–13). At the same time, the fact that some scholars have been overexuberant in their pursuit of parallels does not negate the evidence for the many such parallels that do exist. A more reasoned approach is that described by William Hallo as the "contextual approach": "The goal of the contextual approach is fairly modest. It is not to find the key to every biblical phenomenon in some ancient Near Eastern precedent, but rather to silhouette the biblical text against its wider literary and cultural environ-

ment and thus to arrive at a proper assessment of the extent to which the biblical evidence reflects that environment or, on the contrary, is distinctive and innovative over against it." See Hallo, "Compare and Contrast: The Contextual Approach to Biblical Literature," in *The Bible in Light of Cuneiform Literature*, ed. William W. Hallo, Bruce William Jones, and Gerald L. Mattingly (Lewiston, NY: Mellen, 1990), 1–30; the quoted material is found on p. 3.

3. Helpful introductions to the discovery of Ugarit and the discoveries it has produced can be found in William M. Schniedewind and Joel H. Hunt, *A Primer on Ugaritic: Language, Culture, and Literature* (New York: Cambridge University Press, 2007), and Michael Patrick O'Connor, "Ugarit and the Bible," in *Backgrounds for the Bible*, ed. Michael Patrick O'Connor and David Noel Freedman (Winona Lake, IN: Eisenbrauns, 1987), 151–64. An extensive review of the progress and literature of Ugaritic studies from 1928 to 1999 is available in Mark S. Smith, *Untold Stories: The Bible and Ugaritic Studies in the Twentieth Century* (Peabody, MA: Hendrickson, 2001).

4. Cuneiform refers to the wedge-shaped style of writing first developed by the Sumerians in Mesopotamia and subsequently adapted for the Akkadian language spoken by the Semitic populations that replaced them. A variety of cuneiform scripts were developed for the two main dialects of Akkadian, Babylonian and Assyrian, but all of these scripts differed from the native script found at Ugarit in that they were based on the use of logograms (one symbol = one word) and syllabograms (one symbol = one syllable). The cuneiform script at Ugarit, by contrast, was an alphabetic script in which one symbol represented one consonant (or, in three cases, one consonant—namely, *aleph*—plus a vowel). The excavations at Ugarit have also unearthed a variety of texts written in languages and scripts other than Ugaritic (Akkadian, Hurrian, Hittite, Egyptian, etc.), suggesting the city was host to a thriving scribal culture.

5. Apart from a hiatus in 1939–47 due to World War II, the excavations at Ugarit continued under Schaeffer's direction on an annual basis from 1929 to 1970 and in subsequent decades under his successors.

6. The Baal Cycle is generally regarded as consisting of six tablets. By most scholars' reckoning, the first two tablets describe Baal's conflict with Yamm, the third and fourth are concerned with the construction of a palace for Baal, and the fifth and sixth return to the theme of conflict, this time between Baal and the god Mot. These issues are addressed in painstaking detail in Mark S. Smith, *The Ugaritic Baal Cycle*, vol. 1, *Introduction with Text, Translation and Commentary of KTU 1.1–1.2*, VTSup 55 (Leiden: Brill, 1994), 2–25, and Smith and Pitard, *Ugaritic Baal Cycle*, 9–10. More accessible versions of the text are available in Michael D. Coogan and Mark S. Smith, *Stories from Ancient Canaan*, 2nd ed. (Louisville: Westminster John Knox, 2012), 97–153; and "The Baʿlu Myth," trans. Dennis Pardee, *COS* 1.86:241–74.

7. For the sake of clarity, I have simplified the spelling of Ugaritic names, omitting case vowels and certain diacritical marks. The name *baʿlu*, for example, I have rendered simply as *Baal*, *yammu* as *Yamm*, *kôṯaru wa-ḫasīsu* as *Kothar-wa-Hasis*, and so forth.

8. The Baal cycle contains a great deal of repetition from one tablet to the next. In Tablet III, Anat confronts El and secures his permission to have Kothar-wa-Hasis

build a palace for Baal. In Tablet IV, an almost identical set of steps is taken to enlist the help of El's wife, Asherah, who then confronts El and secures his permission all over again.

9. The Baal Cycle goes on in Tablets V and VI to recount the tale of Baal's battle against the Canaanite god of death, Mot. While this element of the story does not bear directly on our discussion here, it does relate to other biblical texts. The story of Elijah's contest with the prophets of Baal in 1 Kgs 18 echoes elements of the story, as do passages such as Hos 13:14.

10. The Ugaritic and Hebrew nouns for "sea" are for all intents and purposes identical even though they are sometimes spelled slightly differently from one another. The root from which the noun is derived in both languages, *ymm, is classified as a *geminate* because it ends with two identical consonants. In words without suffixes, Hebrew retains only one of these consonants. Thus, the singular form for "sea" is *yām*, but the plural (bearing the plural suffix *-îm*) is *yammîm*, "seas." In this plural form, the second *m*, which we see in the Ugaritic form *yamm* or *yammu*, is restored.

11. As noted previously, the Baal Cycle consists of three movements. In the first, Baal battles against Yamm, the god of the sea. In the second, Baal's palace is constructed on the heights of Mount Zaphon. In the third, Baal battles against Mot, the god of death, who is often identified with the desert to the east of the Levant. These three movements may well derive from the natural movement of storms from west to east in the region. In the west, storm (Baal) and sea (Yamm) appear to battle in the Mediterranean. Victorious, the storm (Baal) then moves east to the heights of the mountains (Baal's palace), where it sends fructifying rains down to the earth below. Finally, the storm (Baal) moves off to the east, where its rains are finally spent and come to an end over the eastern deserts (Mot). The fact that the Baal Cycle appears to describe Baal's death, or at least disappearance, as part of his battle with Mot only serves to underscore this potential connection. See further Paul G. Mosca, "Ugarit and Daniel 7: A Missing Link," *Bib* 67 (1986): 505–8.

12. Anat's claims here are part of a larger section in which she also boasts of defeating "Desire, Beloved of El," "Rebel, Calf of El," "Fire, Dog of El," and "Flame, Daughter of El." Scholars have debated not only the number and nature of the enemies envisioned by the author here, but also how Anat's claims in the passage can be squared with the rest of the Baal Cycle. Elsewhere in the account, the defeat of the sea and the dragon are attributed to Baal, not Anat. Anat's claims here may suggest either that the author has drawn upon a separate, Anat-centered tradition without attempting to reconcile it fully with the Baal traditions or that the broken sections of the cycle once contained a description of Anat's own combat against these enemies. Further discussion of the passage is available in Smith and Pitard, *Ugaritic Baal Cycle*, 247–65.

13. A helpful starting point for the connections between Hebrew and Ugaritic poetry is found in Wilfred G. E. Watson, *Classical Hebrew Poetry: A Guide to Its Techniques*, JSOTSup 26 (Sheffield: JSOT Press, 1984), and Watson, *Traditional Techniques in Classical Hebrew Verse*, JSOTSup 170 (Sheffield: Sheffield Academic, 1994). Watson compares examples of Hebrew and Ugaritic poetry throughout these

studies. See also Mark S. Smith, "Canaanite Backgrounds to the Psalms," in *The Oxford Handbook of the Psalms*, ed. William P. Brown (Oxford: Oxford University Press, 2014), 43–56.

14. As Smith and Pitard note, "Usually a character is named in the first line of a bi- or tricolon, then referred to in the next line or two with epithets" (*Ugaritic Baal Cycle*, 251–52). They note a similar example in the tricolon found in *KTU* 1.3 III, 29–31: "In the midst of my mountain, Divine Saphon, / In the holy mountain of my heritage, / In the beautiful hill of my might" (translation by Smith and Pitard, ibid., 252). Here, the first part of the poetic line refers to Baal's mountain, "Divine Saphon" (the name "Saphon" being simply a spelling variation for "Zaphon"). The next two cola then use the epithets "holy mountain of my heritage" and "beautiful hill of my might" to extend the description of Saphon (Zaphon).

15. See further Pitard, "Binding of Yamm," 279–80.

16. Rendsburg, "*UT* 68 and the Tell Asmar Seal," 448–52.

17. Hebrew *bārīaḥ* for Ugaritic *bāriḥa* ("fleeing") and *ʿāqallātôn* for *ʿaqallatāna* ("twisting").

18. Michael Fishbane traces the continuing echoes of this imagery into the rabbinic period. See Fishbane, *Biblical Myth and Rabbinic Mythmaking* (Oxford: Oxford University Press, 2003), 112–31.

19. Psalms 93, 95–99 are generally considered to form a collection focused on YHWH's divine kingship. Concerning the background of these psalms, see Tate, *Psalms 51–100*, 474–79, and, more recently, Shawn W. Flynn, *YHWH Is King: The Development of Divine Kingship in Ancient Israel*, VTSup 159 (Leiden: Brill, 2014), 36–46.

20. See Kevin Chau, "The Poetry of Creation and Victory in the Psalms," in *Inner Biblical Allusion in the Poetry of Wisdom and Psalms*, ed. Mark J. Boda, Kevin Chau, and Beth LaNeel Tanner, LHBOTS 659 (London: T&T Clark, 2019), 70–71.

21. Smith, *Ugaritic Baal Cycle*, 83.

22. Attempts to identify cosmogonic elements in the Baal Cycle (and to connect those creative actions with Baal) are found in Loren Fisher, "Creation at Ugarit and in the Old Testament," *VT* 15 (1965): 313–24; Richard J. Clifford, "Cosmogonies in the Ugaritic Texts and in the Bible," *Or* 53 (1984): 183–201; Frank Moore Cross, "The 'Olden Gods' in Ancient Near Eastern Creation Myths," in *Magnalia Dei, the Mighty Acts of God: Essays on the Bible and Archaeology in Memory of G. Ernest Wright*, ed. Frank Moore Cross, Werner E. Lemke, and Patrick D. Miller Jr. (Garden City, NY: Doubleday, 1976), 333–35; and Cross, *Canaanite Myth and Hebrew Epic: Essays in the History of the Religion of Israel* (Cambridge: Harvard University Press, 1973), 39–43, 120. Arvid Kapelrud offers a compelling rebuttal to these arguments. See Kapelrud, "Creation in the Ras Shamra Texts," *ST* 34 (1980): 1–11. Further discussion of the weaknesses of the cosmogonic approach to the Cycle is available in Smith, *Ugaritic Baal Cycle*, 75–87.

23. See Miller, "El, the Creator of Earth," in *Israelite Religion and Biblical Theology: Collected Essays*, JSOTSup 267 (Sheffield: Sheffield Academic, 2000), 45–50; and Jon D. Levenson, *Creation and the Persistence of Evil: The Jewish Drama of Divine Omnipotence* (Princeton: Princeton University Press, 1994), 9–10.

24. Day (*God's Conflict*, 17) argues that the strong connection between creation and the battle against sea and dragon in the Bible provides evidence that these two must also have been connected among the Canaanites: "The fact that the Old Testament so frequently uses the imagery of divine conflict with the dragon and the sea in association with creation, when this imagery is Canaanite, leads one to expect that the Canaanites likewise connected the two themes." As I will argue, however, the more likely source of the link between the sea conflict and creation is to be found in Mesopotamia.

25. The name *Enuma Elish* derives from the first words of the epic, Akkadian *enūma eliš*, meaning "When on high . . . ."

26. Scholars have debated which moment in Babylon's rise provides the most likely setting for the composition of the epic. In the decades immediately following the discovery of the epic, it was quite common to see arguments connecting it with the Old Babylonian period and specifically Hammurapi's establishment of Babylon as his capital. In recent years, however, the most widely held view of the text's composition has been the one advanced by the great Assyriologist W. G. Lambert, who argued that the text was composed during the reign of Nebuchadnezzar I (1126–1105 BCE) in response to pressures Babylon faced during the Kassite period. Shawn Flynn argues for a date roughly a century earlier than that proposed by Lambert, making the case that the threats from Assyria during the reign of Tukulti-Ninurta I (1244–1208 BCE) were even more significant than those posed by the Kassites. Discussions of the relevant issues are available in Lambert, "The Reign of Nebuchadnezzar I: A Turning Point in the History of Ancient Mesopotamian Religion," in *The Seed of Wisdom: Essays in Honour of T. J. Meek*, ed. W. S. McCullough (Toronto: University of Toronto Press, 1964), 3–13; Lambert, *Babylonian Creation Myths*, MC 16 (Winona Lake, IN: Eisenbrauns, 2013), 439–65; and Flynn, *YHWH Is King*, 103–18.

27. A thorough discussion of the dynamics of creation in Enuma Elish is available in Andrea Seri, "The Role of Creation in Enūma eliš," *JANER* 12 (2012): 4–29.

28. Thorkild Jacobsen ("The Battle between Marduk and Tiamat," *JAOS* 88 [1968]: 107–8) has argued that the tradition of a god battling the sea was at home in the west, where storms battering the coast were a regular occurrence, rather than in the dry interior of Mesopotamia. Lambert (*Babylonian Creation Myths*, 449–52) makes the case instead for an indigenous Mesopotamian background for Enuma Elish in the story of Ninurta's battle against the Anzû bird. The prominence of the sea in Canaanite traditions and in Enuma Elish, as well as the corresponding absence of the sea in the Anzû Epic, lends support to Jacobsen's proposal. As Enuma Elish is clearly eclectic in its use of antecedent traditions, however, it is hardly necessary to choose between Jacobsen's and Lambert's positions. Mark Smith notes that a second-millennium letter from Mari mentions the battle between Adad (= Akkadian *Haddu*, Ugaritic *Baal*) and *tâmtum* (i.e., Tiamat), confirming the presence of the tradition west of Babylon from a very early period. See Smith, *The Early History of God: Yahweh and the Other Deities in Ancient Israel*, 2nd ed., BRS (Grand Rapids: Eerdmans, 2002), 94–95.

29. Anu is said to give winds to Marduk: "Anu created four winds, he gave birth to them. He set them in his hand: 'My son, let them whirl!' He formed dust and let a storm drive it; he made a wave and it roiled Tiamat" (I.105–108). When Marduk

goes to battle, he rides the storms (II.151). His weapons include "the Storm-flood, his great weapon" and every manner of wind: "He stationed the four winds so that no part of her might escape: South Wind, North Wind, East Wind, West Wind. He fastened at his side the net, a present from his father, Anu. He formed Evil Wind, Storm, Dust Storm, Four-fold Wind, Seven-fold wind, Severe Wind, Irresistible Wind. He set out the winds he had made, seven of them" (IV.42–47). He rides into battle on a "chariot of irresistible storm" (IV.50).

30. This is not to suggest that nets were used only for maritime activities. As Lambert notes (*Babylonian Creation Myths*, 450), nets were a staple of military weaponry from Sumerian times, and a net was used by Ninurta to capture the Anzû bird in the epic that formed one of the main sources for Enuma Elish.

31. Concerning the iconographic representations of Tiamat, see Othmar Keel, *The Symbolism of the Biblical World: Ancient Near Eastern Iconography and the Book of Psalms*, trans. Timothy J. Hallett (New York: Seabury, 1978), 47–56.

32. The foundational study of the Mesopotamian influences on Gen 1 is Hermann Gunkel's *Schöpfung und Chaos in Urzeit und Endzeit*, originally published in 1895 and now available in English as *Creation and Chaos in the Primeval Era and the Eschaton: A Religio-Historical Study of Genesis 1 and Revelation 12*, trans. K. William Whitney Jr., BRS (Grand Rapids: Eerdmans, 2006). It is fair to say that most scholars no longer see a direct literary connection between Enuma Elish and the biblical account(s) of creation. See, importantly, W. G. Lambert, "A New Look at the Babylonian Background of Genesis," in *"I Studied Inscriptions from before the Flood": Ancient Near Eastern, Literary, and Linguistic Approaches to Genesis 1–11*, ed. Richard S. Hess and David Toshio Tsumura, SBTS (Winona Lake, IN: Eisenbrauns, 1994), 96–113. Even among the scholars who hold this view, however, it is generally admitted that the account in Gen 1 responds at least to ideas or traditions of creation that were broadly shared in ancient Israel's cultural matrix. As I believe the arguments that follow demonstrate, there remains a strong case to be made for a more direct dependence on Enuma Elish in Gen 1. See further, Kenton Sparks, "*Enūma Elish* and Priestly Mimesis: Elite Emulation in Nascent Judaism," *JBL* 126 (2007): 625–48; Bernard F. Batto, *Slaying the Dragon: Mythmaking in the Biblical Tradition* (Louisville: Westminster John Knox, 1992), 73–101; and Batto, "The Combat Myth in Israelite Tradition Revisited," in *Creation and Chaos: A Reconsideration of Hermann Gunkel's Chaoskampf Hypothesis*, ed. JoAnn Scurlock and Richard H. Beal (Winona Lake, IN: Eisenbrauns, 2013), 217–36, esp. 232–36.

33. Day (*God's Conflict*, 17) rightly notes that the language of the biblical accounts is Canaanite. The connection these texts make between creation and combat with the sea/dragon, however, is Mesopotamian.

34. See *KTU* 1.3 VI, 12–20.

35. See *KTU* 1.2 III, 18; 1.6 I, 63–67. Athtar plays an interesting role in the Baal Cycle as a deity who aspires to ultimate kingship but is ultimately unable to attain it. In various quarters in the ancient Near East, Athtar appears to have been regarded as an astral deity and may have been specifically connected with the planet Venus. The relative orbital movements of the Earth and Venus that cause Venus to appear to rise higher and higher in the evening or morning sky before reversing course

and descending again may well lie behind this depiction of Athtar as a deity who ascends toward kingship but cannot maintain it. Aspects of this belief likely form part of the backdrop to the descriptions of the king of Tyre in Ezek 28 and the king of Babylon in Isa 14 (see esp. vv. 12–15). There is also evidence for connecting Athtar with the provision of water for farming, particularly via irrigation. In a setting like Ugarit, which received ample rainfall each year, it would not be surprising to see a deity connected with rain (Baal) supplant one connected with irrigation (Athtar). That Athtar received greater veneration to the east, where irrigation was more important, only serves to support this notion. For a more in-depth discussion of Athtar and his role in the Baal Cycle, see Smith, *Ugaritic Baal Cycle*, 240–50.

36. See *KTU* 1.6 VI, 28–29.

37. The distinctions between the kingship of Baal, El, and Marduk are considered in Smith, *Ugaritic Baal Cycle*, 95–114, 296. See also Levenson, *Creation and the Persistence of Evil*, 9–10.

38. Enuma Elish depicts the earliest gods as emerging from the matrix of Apsu and Tiamat as deities similar to the Titans of Greek mythology. They are antecedent to the other gods both in terms of antiquity and authority. Key to Marduk's rise to the kingship is the fact that even these ancient deities confer their authority on Marduk and submit to him.

39. In an attempt to make Qingu king of the gods, Tiamat had given him the so-called Tablets of Destiny and declared his command to be the greatest of the gods'. When Tiamat has been defeated, Marduk strips Qingu of the tablets and takes them for himself (V.69–70).

40. Concerning the meteorological elements of the Baal Cycle and specifically the connection between Mot and the desert, see note 11 above.

41. Lambert (*Babylonian Creation Myths*, 204–5) suggests that Ninurta's restraining the waters that threatened the land stands in the background of Marduk's actions in Enuma Elish.

42. See Ps 96:4–5 as well: "For great is YHWH, and greatly to be praised; he is to be feared above all gods. For all the gods of the peoples are idols, but YHWH made the heavens." The mention of the sea in v. 11 of this psalm ("Let the heavens be glad, and let the earth rejoice; *let the sea roar, and all that fills it*") may be yet another example of God's kingship being tied to his rule over the sea.

Notes to Chapter 5

1. The Gospel of Luke and the Book of Acts form a two-volume work by the same author, traditionally held to be the physician Luke (cf. Col 4:14; 2 Tim 4:11; Phlm 24). As both books fail to specify their authors, it may be that they were written by someone other than Luke, so I refer to Luke here merely as a matter of convenience. To what degree the sentiments in Acts 17 derive ultimately from Paul, as opposed to Luke, is a matter of extensive debate. A brief but helpful introduction is available in C. K. Barrett, *On Paul: Aspects of His Life, Work and Influence in the Early Church* (London: T&T Clark, 2003), 139–54.

2. The word I have translated here as "babbler" is *spermologos*, a term describing birds that "pick up seeds." Its meaning is quite pejorative and is apparently meant to suggest Paul is an unoriginal thinker who is merely passing off as his own scraps of thought he picked up from another. Unfortunately, no English term quite captures this meaning.

3. Joshua Jipp argues that Luke presents Paul as, in essence, a Socrates redivivus. See Jipp, "Paul's Areopagus Speech of Acts 17:16–34 as Both Critique and Propaganda," *JBL* 131 (2012): 569–74. As Jipp notes, the parallels between the two are quite striking. Socrates was famous, or perhaps better, infamous for his constant arguments with the Athenian philosophers in the agora; Luke presents Paul in precisely the same light. Socrates was charged with the serious offense of introducing foreign deities into Athens; Paul is questioned by the Areopagus for just the same reason. Socrates was famously tried by the Athenians; Luke presents Paul's own appearance before the Areopagus as a sort of trial. Jipp emphasizes the fact that Paul is compelled to appear before the Areopagus, the members of which pronounce their right to know what he is teaching about new divinities (p. 573).

4. Areopagus is Greek for "hill of Ares." The translation "Mars Hill," familiar from the King James Version, reflects the fact that Mars was the Roman equivalent of the Greek deity Ares. Metonymically, the Areopagus also referred to the Athenian tribunal, the Council of the Areopagus. Luke's description of Paul's stance in vv. 22a and 33 suggests that when Luke refers to the Areopagus in the former verse, he has in mind the tribunal and not necessarily the hill.

5. More extensive surveys of the allusions in Paul's speech, both to Hellenistic and to Jewish sources, are available in Jipp, "Paul's Areopagus Speech," 567–88, and C. K. Barrett, *A Critical and Exegetical Commentary on the Acts of the Apostles*, ICC 30–31 (Edinburgh: T&T Clark, 1994–98), 2:839–55.

6. Translation from H. W. Attridge, *First-Century Cynicism in the Epistles of Heraclitus*, HTS 29 (Missoula, MT: Scholars Press, 1976), 58–59.

7. Various scholars have suggested that the allusion is to a poem by Epimenides. See the discussion in John B. Polhill, *Acts*, NAC 26 (Nashville: Broadman, 1992), 375–76.

8. The translation here is by Jipp, "Paul's Areopagus Speech," 584. Scholars remain divided over the potential allusion to Cleanthes in the text. Barrett (*Acts*, 2:848) notes that Paul's quotation is definitely from Aratus, though he concedes that the apostle may have been influenced by Cleanthes' words as well. Polhill (*Acts*, 376) suggests Aratus may himself have been quoting Cleanthes' hymn, perhaps explaining Paul's consequent reference to "some of your *poets*." See also Mark J. Edwards, "Quoting Aratus: Acts 17,28," *ZNW* 83 (1992): 266–69.

9. Note, for example, Paul's subtle allusion in Acts 17:24–25 ("the God who made the world and everything in it . . . himself gives to all mortals life and breath") to the Septuagint of Isa 42:5 ("Thus says the Lord God, who made the heaven and established it, who settled the earth and the things in it and gives breath unto the people on it"). The remainder of the address contains other echoes of Scripture as well: vv. 25 (cf. Ps 50:12; Job 12:10); 26 (cf. Deut 32:8); 27 (cf. Deut 4:7; Jer 23:23); 29 (cf. Isa 40:18–25; 46:5–9); 30 (cf. Jer 16:19); 31 (cf. Ps 96:13).

10. See further Mark S. Smith, "Biblical Narrative between Ugaritic and Akkadian Literature: Part I: Ugarit and the Hebrew Bible: Consideration of Comparative Research," *RB* 114 (2007): 5–29.

11. See Mordechai Cogan, "Judah under Assyrian Hegemony: A Reexamination of *Imperialism and Religion*," *JBL* 112 (1993): 403–14, esp. 410–13; and Sparks, "Priestly Mimesis," 625–27, 642–48.

12. This component of the Baal Cycle begins in Tablet IV, column 7, and continues through the end of Tablet VI (*KTU* 1.4 VII – 1.6 VI). Translations are available in Coogan and Smith, *Stories from Ancient Canaan*, 136–53, and Pardee, "The Baʿlu Myth."

13. Concerning Sheol as the netherworld, see, for example, Deut 32:22; Isa 14:9; Ps 139:8.

14. Concerning the dynamics of personification and mythology in the biblical authors' references to foreign deities, see the present author's "Let the Day Perish: The Nexus of Personification and Mythology in Job 3," *JSOT* 43 (2018): 247–69. Note that in 1 Cor 15:55 the apostle Paul turns Hosea's language of judgment here into the language of victory over death through Christ's resurrection.

15. Following the common emendation of *brothers* (ʾaḥîm) to *rushes* (ʾāḥû).

16. There may be another allusion to Mot in the first verse of ch. 13. The phrase that concludes v. 1 sounds innocuous enough in English: "He incurred guilt by Baal and he died." In Hebrew, however, it ends with *babbaʿal wayyāmōt*. Given the other allusions in the book, it would not be surprising to find a deliberate echo of Mot's name in the word *wayyāmōt* alongside the reference to Baal in *babbaʿal*. Another possible allusion is found in Hos 14:8 [9]. Here the statement "I answer, and I look after him" appears quite unremarkable in English. In Hebrew, however, it is ʾănî ʿāniṯî waʾăšûrennû, a phrase that may well mimic the names of the Canaanite goddesses Anat (ʿănāṯ) and Asherah (ʾăšērâ).

17. Jipp ("Paul's Areopagus Speech," 576–78) argues that Paul's supposed commendation of the Athenians in Acts 17:22 for their piety ("Men of Athens, I observe how very religious you are in every way") is actually a subtle jibe at them for being superstitious. In the remainder of his speech, Paul will demonstrate that though the Athenians pride themselves on their disdain for others' superstitious beliefs, their own beliefs are cast as "inferior superstition when compared to the philosophically superior and consistent Christian movement" (p. 578). This is observed also by Hans-Josef Klauck, who argues that Paul's statement is sufficiently ambiguous as to be rendered, "Your superstition is especially striking." Klauck draws a distinction between the manner in which the phrase would have been understood by Paul's audience of hearers (as a compliment) and by Luke's audience of readers (as a criticism). See Klauck, *Magic and Paganism in Early Christianity: The World of the Acts of the Apostles*, trans. Brian McNeil (Edinburgh: T&T Clark, 2000), 81–82.

18. On the Bible's depictions of YHWH's sparring with Baal, see further John Day, *Yahweh and the Gods and Goddesses of Canaan*, JSOTSup 265 (Sheffield: Sheffield Academic, 2000), 68–90.

19. Note the *rain* language the prophet uses of YHWH: "Let us know, let us press on to know YHWH; like the dawn, his appearing is sure; *he will come to us like the showers, like the spring rains that water the earth*" (Hos 6:3); "Sow for yourselves

righteousness; reap steadfast love; break up your fallow ground; for it is time to seek YHWH, that he may come and *rain righteousness upon you*" (Hos 10:12).

20. Devotion to Baal is evident in the names of Jezebel and her father. Ethbaal appears to mean "Baal is with him." Jezebel means "Where is the prince?" and is apparently connected to the mourning rites associated with (Prince) Baal's disappearance in the Baal Cycle.

21. Because *b* and *p* are similar consonants from a linguistic perspective (both are what linguists call "labials" because they are articulated using the lips), they often interchange in the Semitic languages. Thus, the word for "soul, life" is *npš* in Hebrew but *nbš* in Ugaritic; the word for "iron" is *brzl* in Hebrew but *przl* in Aramaic. In the example cited here—ʿ*rbt* in Hebrew, ʿ*rpt* in Ugaritic—the same phenomenon is evident. The allophones *b* and *p* interchange, but the words are the same.

22. Unfortunately, the last colon of this poetic line is extraordinarily difficult and may well have become corrupted through the process of scribal transmission. For a discussion of the difficulties it poses, see Tate, *Psalms 51–100*, 166.

23. This same kind of language is found in Psalm 18 as well. As the psalmist recalls his deliverance from distress in vv. 9–10 [10–11], he describes the coming of the God of Israel in this fashion: "He bowed the heavens and came down, / and darkness was beneath his feet. // He rode on a cherub and flew; / and he swooped down on the wings of the wind." The similarities between this language and the description of Baal as the "cloud rider" are obvious.

24. The cedar tree is nearly synonymous with Lebanon. The modern flag of Lebanon is emblazoned with a cedar tree, for example, and a recent political movement in the country was given the name "the Cedar Revolution." In the Gilgamesh Epic, the setting for Gilgamesh and Enkidu's battle against Humbaba is thought to be set in Lebanon because of the story's reference to cedar trees (see Tablet II). And King Solomon was forced to negotiate with King Hiram of Tyre (a city located in Phoenicia/Lebanon) to get cedars for his palace (1 Kgs 5–6).

25. The Canaanite background of the psalm was first proposed by H. L. Ginsberg in 1935. See "A Phoenician Hymn in the Psalter," in *Atti del XIX Congresso Internazionale degli Orientalisti: Roma, 23–29 Settembre 1935* (Rome: Tipografia del Senato, 1935), 472–76. A number of subsequent studies have extended Ginsberg's initial insight. See, for example, Theodor H. Gaster, "Psalm 29," *JQR* 37 (1946): 55–65; Frank Moore Cross, "Notes on a Canaanite Psalm in the Old Testament," *BASOR* 117 (1950): 19–21; Cross, *Canaanite Myth and Hebrew Epic*, 151–56; and F. Charles Fensham, "Psalm 29 and Ugarit," *OTWSA* 6 (1963): 84–99. Peter Craigie expresses reservations over the idea that the psalm derives from a Canaanite/Phoenician original but acknowledges that "there are sufficient parallels and similarities to require a Canaanite background to be taken into account in developing the interpretation of the psalm." See Craigie, *Psalms 1–50*, WBC 19 (Waco, TX: Word, 1983), 243–46 (quoted text on p. 245), and Craigie, "The Poetry of Ugarit and Israel," *TynBul* 22 (1971): 15–19.

26. For a more in-depth consideration of imagery related to YHWH and Baal, see Smith, *Early History of God*, 43–47, 80–91; Cross, *Canaanite Myth and Hebrew Epic*, 147–77; and Day, *Yahweh and the Gods and Goddesses of Canaan*, 91–127.

27. Despite its unfortunate spelling, the name *Sîn* for the Mesopotamian moon god is not related to "sin" in the sense of transgression or error. In Sumer, the god was known as *Nanna*; in Akkadian, he was known as *Suen*, which eventually came to be pronounced *Sîn*.

28. Adapted from "Cyrus Cylinder," trans. Mordechai Cogan, *COS* 2.124:315.

29. Noted as early as Rudolf Kittel, "Cyrus und Deuterojesaja," *ZAW* 18 (1898): 149–62. Joseph Blenkinsopp makes a compelling case for seeing in Isa 40–48 a polemic against Enuma Elish and the Babylonian Akītu festival. See Blenkinsopp, "The Cosmological and Protological Language of Deutero-Isaiah," *CBQ* 73 (2011): 506–10.

30. Concerning the role of rhetoric in the Psalms generally, see Davida Charney, *Persuading God: Rhetorical Studies of First-Person Psalms* (Sheffield: Sheffield Phoenix, 2015).

31. The underlying text of v. 5 is notoriously difficult and appears to have suffered scribal corruption early on (the Septuagint, for example, appears to have been at a loss as to how to translate the verse). The translation here follows that found in the NRSV, though the reader is encouraged to consult the relevant commentaries for a full accounting of the textual problems involved.

32. The Hebrew text includes the expression "to the earth/ground" (translated above as "in the dust") in its description of the manner in which the sanctuary was profaned or defiled. The English expression of "dragging one's name through the mud/dirt" is similar, though it fails to capture the fact that the psalmist's temple has been both spiritually profaned and physically brought down to the ground.

Notes to Chapter 6

1. Not surprisingly, the Apollo astronauts drew upon the venerable King James Version of the Bible for their reading.

2. There are only a handful of biblical texts that move further in the direction of creation *ex nihilo*. In the Hebrew Bible, only Prov 8:23–29 does so, as it describes wisdom's creation as "at the first, from the beginnings of the earth," and envisions a time when there were no depths or springs, mountains or hills, earth, fields, dust, or heavens. The author's mention of a time "when there were no depths" (v. 24; cf. v. 28) is particularly interesting. Note also 2 Macc 7:28, from the second century BCE: "I ask you, O child, to look up at the heaven and the earth and behold everything that is in them. Know that God did not make them from things that existed." In the New Testament, Heb 11:3 insists, "By faith we understand that the worlds were prepared by the word of God, so that what is seen was made from things that are not visible." Genesis 1's description of creation differs significantly from these texts, however.

3. See, for example, Brevard Childs (*Myth and Reality in the Old Testament* [London: SCM, 1960], 30), who observes, "It is rather generally acknowledged that the suggestion of God's first creating a chaos is a logical contradiction and must be rejected"; and Gerhard von Rad (*Genesis: A Commentary*, trans. John H. Marks, rev. ed., OTL [Philadelphia: Westminster, 1972], 48), who notes, "The notion of a created chaos is itself a contradiction."

4. See the extended discussion of the syntax of vv. 1–3 in Claus Westermann, *Genesis 1–11*, trans. John J. Scullion, CC (Minneapolis: Fortress, 1994), 93–98. Westermann contends that v. 1 is a complete sentence and serves as a heading for the account that follows. Mark Smith (*The Priestly Vision of Genesis 1* [Minneapolis: Fortress, 2010], 43–49) argues just as forcefully that v. 1 should be regarded as a dependent clause along the lines of "When at first God created the heavens and the earth . . . ." As I note, it is unlikely that a definitive verdict will be reached on the grammar of this first verse of Scripture. What should be clear, however, is that the verse does not narrate the first act of creation; this occurs in v. 3 with God's decree "Let there be light." Verse 1 serves as either a heading (should the verse be regarded as an independent clause) or as the temporal subordinate to v. 2 (should the verse be regarded as a dependent clause).

5. As Westermann (*Genesis 1–11*, 94) argues, "The sentence in 1:1 is not the beginning of an account of creation, but a heading that takes in everything in the narrative in one single sentence."

6. See E. A. Speiser, *Genesis*, AB 1 (New York: Doubleday, 1962), 9–11; Westermann, *Genesis 1–11*, 96–97.

7. The final -*at* in *ti'āmat* is the feminine ending in Akkadian. The word is not marked for gender in Hebrew, but the verbal and adjectival forms connected with it show that it was construed as feminine in some contexts (Gen 7:11; 49:25; Deut 33:13; Ps 36:6 [7]; Isa 51:10; Ezek 31:4; Amos 7:4) and masculine in others (Job 28:14; Ps 42:7 [8]; 104:6; Jonah 2:6; Hab 3:10).

8. David Tsumura, supported by Gary Rendsburg, argues at length that the word *təhōm* in Gen 1:2 is not "borrowed" from the name of the goddess Tiamat. See Tsumura, *The Earth and the Waters in Genesis 1 and 2: A Linguistic Investigation*, JSOTSup 83 (Sheffield: JSOT Press, 1989), 45–65; and Rendsburg's review in *JBL* 110 (1991): 137. Tsumura's argument relies far too heavily, however, on linguistic concerns that would have been unintelligible to an ancient audience. He insists, for example, that because *təhōm* is only etymologically cognate to Tiamat's name (both terms deriving from the Semitic root *thm), and not an actual loanword from Akkadian, the goddess Tiamat cannot stand as part of the mythological background of the Hebrew term (p 47). This sort of argument grossly underestimates the range of possibilities for allusion and echo available to an ancient (or modern) author. Just as biblical characters regularly supply explanations for Hebrew names that make perfect sense on a popular level but would rightly be regarded as scandalous from a technical and linguistic point of view (e.g., the explanations for the name of Jacob in Gen 25:26 and the names of his various sons in Gen 29–30), the author of Genesis 1 was perfectly capable of echoing the Babylonian creation account with only modest regard for the technicalities of modern linguistics.

9. Cross ("Olden Gods," 335) is certainly correct in his assessment that "there is in the Genesis creation story no element of cosmogonic *conflict*" (emphasis mine). The numerous echoes of the Babylonian creation account remain, however, suggesting the biblical author has interacted with these traditions in a way that differs from the rehearsals of the *Chaoskampf* in texts like Pss 74 and 89.

10. I discuss the relationship between this psalm and Gen 1 in greater detail in "Identifying Subtle Allusions: The Promise of Narrative Tracking," in *Subtle Citation, Allusion, and Translation in the Hebrew Bible*, ed. Ziony Zevit (Sheffield: Equinox, 2017), 99–105.

11. Among the translations that render the phrase "Spirit of God" are the English Revised Version (1885), the American Standard Version (1901), the Revised Standard Version (1952), the New American Standard Bible (1971), the New King James Version (1972), the New International Version (1978, 1984, 2011), the English Standard Version (2001), the Holman Christian Standard Bible (2004), and the Christian Standard Bible (2017). "A wind from God" is found in the New Revised Standard Version (1989) and the Jewish Publication Society Tanakh (1985). "A mighty wind" is found in the New American Bible (1970) and "a divine wind" in the New Jerusalem Bible (1985). It is interesting to note the change from "the spirit of God" in the 1917 Jewish Publication Society version to "a wind from God" in the 1985 Jewish Publication Society Tanakh and the change from "the Spirit of God" in the 1952 Revised Standard Version to "a wind from God" in the 1989 New Revised Standard Version.

12. Verse 11 is notable for the fact that, unlike the rest of the book of Jeremiah, it is written in Aramaic, not Hebrew. While this is often used as the basis for treating the verse as secondary, Garnett Reid makes the case that v. 11 serves as "the architectural axis of the unit" and that its Aramaic rendering was crucial since it was intended as "a polemical summary of the Hebrews' theology, designed as a kerygmatic challenge they are to deliver to their Babylonian captors proclaiming Yahweh as the true God." See Reid, "'Thus You Will Say to Them': A Cross-Cultural Confessional Polemic," *JSOT* 31 (2006): 221–38, esp. 237–38.

13. See Batto, "Combat Myth," 236.

14. So the NRSV, for example. The ESV translates this as "an exceedingly great city," and the NIV as "a very large city."

15. Other superlative uses of divine epithets include Gen 23:6 ("prince of God" = mighty prince); Pss 36:6 [7] ("mountains of God" = mighty mountains); 80:10 [11] ("cedars of God" = mighty cedars); Isa 14:13 ("stars of God" = mighty stars). To this list, we might also add Ps 50:10, the final phrase of which may refer to "mountains of God," not "a thousand mountains." It is possible that the same superlative meaning is intended in the use of the divine name YHWH in Gen 10:9, "Nimrod was a hero of hunters *before YHWH*." If so, the sense would be that Nimrod was an *exceedingly* mighty hunter.

16. To these, we might also add God's separation of water from land on Day Three (vv. 9–10), though the language used in reference to this day does not include the Hebrew term *hibdîl*.

17. See the discussion in Lambert, *Babylonian Creation Myths*, 171.

18. Concerning the Hebrew term *rāqîaʿ*, variously translated as *dome, expanse, firmament*, and *vault*, see ch. 7. For the time being, I have simply used the Authorized Version's *firmament*.

19. Vern Poythress ("Biblical Studies: Three Modern Myths in Interpreting Genesis 1," *WTJ* 76 [2014]: 321–50) attempts to demonstrate that Marduk's manipulation of Tiamat's body in Tablet IV of Enuma Elish cannot be interpreted as

a "materialistic" description of the physical world. He argues, for example, that if Tiamat is water, "Where is the alleged solid barrier that holds up the heavenly sea?" The answer to his question is readily available and, indeed, mentioned in his own footnote on p. 337 of his article. As he notes, the translations of Benjamin Foster (*COS* 1.111:398) and Wayne Horowitz (*Mesopotamian Cosmic Geography* [Winona Lake, IN: Eisenbrauns, 1998], 112) describe Marduk as stretching out the hide/skin of Tiamat, which, to use Poythress' own language, "might serve as a solid barrier for her internal waters." Poythress chides both Foster and Horowitz for offering no explanation for their translations, however, and insists that the object in question in the text is a *bar* or *bolt* and not a *skin*, *hide*, or *dome*. Poythress' error lies in his assuming the underlying Assyrian word derives from *parku*, "bar, bolt" (for which he cites *CAD* 12:188 B, which makes no reference to the present text). While the cuneiform sign in question can be rendered *pár*, in this case Assyriologists now recognize the preferred reading to be *maš*. As a result, the underlying Assyrian term is not *parku* but *mašku*, meaning "skin" or "hide." This reading should be obvious, since *mašku* is the object of the verb *šadādu*, which means "to pull taut, stretch" (as *CAD* 17.1:21, which does cite our text, confirms). It is worth noting that the translations Poythress cites in favor of reading the word as "bar" or "bolt" date from 1902, 1921, and 1923. Modern translations such as those of Foster (1996), Horowitz (1998), and, even more recently, Lambert (2013) recognize the reference to Tiamat's hide. A much larger problem in Poythress' overall argument lies in his unwillingness to recognize that ancient peoples seem to have been quite comfortable with the notion that their gods could simultaneously exist as anthropomorphic characters and physical numina (e.g., Šamaš and the sun) and that physical entities could simultaneously be physical entities and gods (e.g., the sun and Šamaš). However illogical such a view might seem in the light of orthodox belief, it remains the view of the ancient Mesopotamians (and other ancient peoples).

20. John H. Walton, *The Lost World of Genesis One: Ancient Cosmology and the Origins Debate* (Downers Grove, IL: InterVarsity Press, 2009), 72–77. See also Levenson, *Creation and the Persistence of Evil*, 78–99. Nathaniel Greene ("Creation, Destruction, and a Psalmist's Plea," 90–100) observes similar dynamics in Ps 74:12–17 as well.

21. It is noteworthy that Marduk rests twice, first after defeating Tiamat (IV.135) and then when he takes up residence in his temple. Genesis 1 needs no such initial rest because it deliberately omits any notion of a battle between God and Tiamat. The *təhōm* in Gen 1:2 does not resist. See further Bernard F. Batto, "The Sleeping God: An Ancient Near Eastern Motif of Divine Sovereignty," *Bib* 68 (1987): 162–66.

Notes to Chapter 7

1. See Luis I. J. Stadelmann, *The Hebrew Conception of the World: A Philological and Literary Study*, AnBib 39 (Rome: Pontifical Biblical Institute, 1970), 56–61; von Rad, *Genesis*, 53–54; Westermann, *Genesis 1–11*, 117; Paul H. Seely, "The Firmament and the Water Above: Part I: The Meaning of *raqiaʿ* in Gen 1:6–8," *WTJ* 53 (1991):

227–40; Seely, "The Firmament and the Water Above: Part II: The Meaning of 'The Water above the Firmament' in Gen 1:6–8," *WTJ* 54 (1992): 31–46. Concerning the conception of the universe described in Enuma Elish, see Horowitz, *Mesopotamian Cosmic Geography*, 107–29.

2. In a similar usage, David boasts in 2 Sam 22:43 of beating, crushing, and *stamping* his enemies like dust. Ezekiel 6:11 and 25:6 also refer to clapping one's hands and *stamping* one's feet.

3. The remaining three uses of *rāqîaʿ* in the Hebrew Bible are less explicit in their description of a dome-like structure but in no way contradict this understanding. Cf. Pss 19:1 [2]; 150:1; Dan 12:3.

4. C. John Collins' attempt to argue against the biblical descriptions of a solid dome is unconvincing on several counts (see Collins, "Inerrancy Studies and the Old Testament: 'Ancient Science' in the Hebrew Bible," *Presb* 44 [2018]: 54–59). First, he derides as a "literalistic etymological argument" (p. 54) the connection between the action of the verb **rqʿ* (which he acknowledges refers to "stamping out," "spreading out," or "beating out") and the sense of the noun *rāqîaʿ* as something akin to a product that is stamped, spread, or beaten out. Scholars have not depicted the *rāqîaʿ* as a solid structure solely based on etymology, however; they have done so because the *rāqîaʿ* is, in fact, depicted as such a solid structure in the various biblical and postbiblical texts noted here. Second, he insists without really arguing the point that *rāqîaʿ* has "the sense of 'surface,' with the context identifying what kind of surface. Hence, the conventional 'expanse' suits the word just fine" (p. 55). Apart from the fact that a "surface" and an empty "expanse" are conceptually incompatible with one another, the preceding discussion has demonstrated that this notion of an empty expanse fits neither the etymology of the term nor its actual description by the biblical authors. Third, Collins argues that since it is clear that the ancient Israelites understood rain to come from clouds, "therefore they might be counted on to realize that the description in Genesis is a poetic portrayal" (p. 58). He continues, "It seems highly unlikely that any of this ideal audience would have taken Genesis as offering a physical description to compete with their already utilitarian perception of the rain and sky." The flaw in Collins' argument is his assumption that the notions of rain coming from clouds and of the existence of a celestial body of water would have been thought by an ancient person to be *competing* notions at all. Rain was, of course, normally connected with clouds, but this experience neither contradicted the ancient cosmological understanding of a solid sky supporting celestial waters nor denied moments when these celestial waters were unleashed (along with their subterranean counterparts), usually in the service of divine judgment (cf. Gen 7:11; 8:2; Isa 24:18). Poythress' objections are even less convincing, since he simply assumes his conclusion without demonstrating it (see Poythress, "Biblical Studies: Rain Water versus a Heavenly Sea in Genesis 1:6–8," *WTJ* 77 [2015]: 181–91). He insists: "In Gen 1 as a whole and in Gen 1:6–8 in particular God speaks of acts of creation that not only evoke praise but have practical interest to human beings. Thus Gen 1:6–8 is speaking about water above, such as Israelites received from clouds. The alleged heavenly sea is irrelevant, and so it must be rejected as an incorrect interpretation of 1:6–8" (p.

190). This is mere assertion, not argument. There is no reason at all to assume that the biblical authors were prevented from describing a heavenly sea merely because such a structure would not have been of "practical interest to human beings." Poythress consistently treats as straightforward descriptions of nature biblical statements that accord with science and dismisses as poetic or phenomenological statements that do not.

5. The phrase typically rendered "birds of the air" in English translations is actually "birds of the heavens" and occurs more than one hundred times in the Hebrew Bible. Note also expressions such as those found in Deut 4:17; Ps 8:9; Jer 8:7; and Lam 4:19. Concerning clouds in the heavens, see, for example, 1 Kgs 18:45; Job 20:6; 35:5; Pss 57:10; 108:4; Dan 7:13.

6. See, for example, Deut 26:15; 1 Kgs 8:30, 39; Isa 63:15; 66:1; Pss 2:4; 11:4; 20:7; 102:19; 115:3, 16; Lam 3:41.

7. In the case of Ps 29, the "flood" mentioned by the psalmist may refer to the waters of the Mediterranean rather than the heavenly waters supported by the *rāqîaʿ*. As noted above (see ch. 5), the psalm draws heavily upon the imagery of Baal's defeat of Yamm, the Canaanite god of the sea, and his subsequent enthronement in a cloud-palace over the sea.

8. See Calvin R. Schoonhoven, *The Wrath of Heaven* (Grand Rapids: Eerdmans, 1966), 64; Philip Edgcumbe Hughes, *Paul's Second Epistle to the Corinthians: The English Text with Introduction, Exposition and Notes* (Grand Rapids: Eerdmans, 1962), 432–34; and Ralph P. Martin, *2 Corinthians*, WBC 40 (Waco, TX: Word, 1986), 401–7.

9. The nomenclature related to 2 Esdras is quite complicated. The book is composed of three separate works, which scholars generally label 5 Ezra (chs. 1–2 of the book), 4 Ezra (chs. 3–14), and 6 Ezra (chs. 15–16). To make matters worse, in the Slavonic Bible, 2 Esdras is called 3 Esdras, and in the Vulgate it appears as 4 Esdras. The text cited above derives from the third century CE and, though it only survives in Latin, it is believed to have been originally composed in Greek.

10. In Ezekiel's case, the additional use of terms such as "sapphire" and "amber" in the context may point toward a crystalline structure for the *rāqîaʿ*. Note also the pavement of sapphire described in the theophany found in Exod 24:10. By way of contrast, Josephus seems to draw a connection between the dome and the production of moisture, rain, and dew. This may suggest that he envisions the dome as an icy structure that supplies these waters as it melts.

11. Although our atmosphere thins gradually so that there is no abrupt division between air and space, many scientists have settled upon the so-called Kármán line of 100 km (62 miles) above sea-level as the boundary for space, while the U.S. Air Force and NASA mark the boundary at 50 miles (80 km).

12. Asterisms are familiar groupings of stars that are not full constellations themselves but rather parts of large constellations. Thus, for example, the Big Dipper is not a constellation but an asterism found within the constellation Ursa Major (the "Great Bear").

13. Robert Alter, *The Pleasures of Reading in an Ideological Age* (New York: Simon & Schuster, 1989), 116.

14. Concerning Ps 78, see further the present author's "Identifying Inner-Biblical Allusions: Psalm 78 as a Test Case," *JBL* 127 (2008): 241–65.

15. In his important study of textual dependence in the book of Isaiah, Benjamin Sommer outlines various reasons for which one text might allude to another. Along with *exegesis, influence, revision, allusion,* and *echo,* Sommer argues that texts may evoke other texts for *polemical* purposes. See *A Prophet Reads Scripture: Allusion in Isaiah 40-66* (Stanford: Stanford University Press, 1998), 22–31.

16. The relevant Hebrew expressions in the golden calf episode and in Jeroboam's proclamation are virtually identical: Exod 32:4, 8—*'ēlleh 'ĕlōhĕkā yiśrā'ēl 'ăšer he'ĕlûkā mē'ereṣ miṣrāyim;* 1 Kgs 12:28—*hinnēh 'ĕlōhĕkā yiśrā'ēl 'ăšer he'ĕlûkā mē'ereṣ miṣrāyim.*

17. The allusions here are similar to those found in Paul's speech at the Areopagus in Acts 17 (see the discussion above in ch. 5). Paul echoes the language of the philosophers ultimately to polemicize against them.

18. The polemical nature of Genesis 1 vis-à-vis the traditions (not necessarily the text) of Enuma Elish is discussed at length by Gerhard F. Hasel, "The Polemic Nature of the Genesis Cosmology," *EvQ* 46 (1974): 81–102. See also Peter Enns in *The Evolution of Adam: What the Bible Does and Doesn't Say about Human Origins* (Grand Rapids: Brazos, 2012), 40–43.

19. "Kein Wort gibt es in den Kosmogonien anderer Völker, das diesem ersten Wort der Bibel gleichkäme." See Hermann Gunkel, *Genesis,* 7th ed. (Göttingen: Vandenhoeck & Ruprecht, 1966), 101.

20. Westermann, *Genesis 1–11,* 97.

21. See the discussion above in ch. 6.

22. Highlighted also by Hasel, "Polemic Nature," 82–85.

23. Gerhard Hasel ("Polemic Nature," 87) makes the important observation that the Hebrew verb *bārā',* "to create," which is attributed solely to God in the Bible, appears in v. 21's description of the creation of the *tannînīm* for the first time *since v. 1.* It is hard to avoid the conclusion that the author wanted to emphasize that the *tannînīm* existed at God's good pleasure and not independently of him.

24. Throughout the chapter, the creative decrees are expressed in Hebrew in one-word jussive forms that require longer and less elegant translations in English: *yəhî,* "let there be" (vv. 3, 6, 14); *yiqqāwû,* "let them be gathered" (v. 9); *taḏšē',* "let it sprout" (v. 11); *yišrəṣû,* "let them swarm" (v. 20); *yīreḇ,* "let it multiply" (v. 22); *tôṣē',* "let it bring forth" (v. 24).

25. It is worth noting that the depiction of God's effortless creation in Gen 1 stands out even among biblical texts. The battle-connected creation traditions in Pss 74 and 89 are certainly more graphic in their depiction of divine activity than Gen 1 and even, for that matter, than the very earthy picture of divine creation found in Gen 2. Unlike the characterization of God in the first chapter of Genesis, YHWH God in Gen 2 makes the man from dust and breathes life into his nostrils (v. 7), plants a garden and puts the man in it (v. 8), forms animals from the ground, brings them to the man, and waits to see what the man will call them (v. 19); and finally, he puts the man to sleep, takes one of his ribs, forms the woman from it, and brings the woman to the man (vv. 21–22). By contrast, so effortless is God's

creation in Gen 1 that it actually raises questions about the nature of God's rest on Day Seven (Gen 2:1–3). The incongruity between this rest and God's creation by merely speaking lends support to Walton's conclusion that the divine rest is connected with God's taking up residence in his cosmic temple (see Walton, *Lost World of Genesis One*, 72–86).

26. "Let there be light," and its Latin translation, *Fiat Lux*, is the motto for a great many schools, including those specifically mentioned above, namely, UCLA (and, indeed, the rest of the University of California system) and the University of Liverpool.

27. Noted by J. Gerald Janzen, "On the Moral Nature of God's Power: Yahweh and the Sea in Job and Deutero-Isaiah," *CBQ* 56 (1994): 464.

28. Following Lambert's translation. The Akkadian form of the name *Marduk*, ^dAMAR.UTU, presented certain theological challenges to ancient Babylonian scribes. Lambert (*Babylonian Creation Myths*, 163–64) notes that the most obvious etymology of the name would be "Bull-calf of Utu" (Utu was the Sumerian god of the sun). The problem, however, is that Marduk seems not to have had any connection with the sun god. Lambert argues that the author of Enuma Elish cleverly sidestepped this problem by clarifying that Marduk was the sun god *of the gods* (*māri* ^d*šamši^{ši}* ^d*šamši^{ši} ša ilāni*), thereby differentiating him from the regular sun god, Shamash. See also the discussion in Lambert's "The Historical Development of the Mesopotamian Pantheon: A Study in Sophisticated Polytheism," in *Unity and Diversity: Essays in the History, Literature, and Religion of the Ancient Near East*, ed. Hans Goedicke and J. J. M. Roberts, JHNES (Baltimore: Johns Hopkins University Press, 1975), 193–95.

29. Smith (*Priestly Vision of Genesis 1*, 96–97) argues against the notion that the sun and moon are polemicized against in Gen 1. Importantly, though, he appears not to take into account either the delay in their creation or the creation of light without their aid.

30. Sumerian uses the same asterisk-shaped symbol to write the word DINGIR (*god*), AN (*Anu*, head of the gods), and AN (*heaven*, Anu's abode). Akkadian, the name given to the Babylonian and Assyrian dialects together, maintained these conventions when it adopted the Sumerian script. One of the most common uses in Akkadian of this DINGIR sign, as scholars often call it, is as a *determinative* signifying that the character in question is a god. That is, just as our signs $ or % or ° tell us that a number is to be understood as *dollars*, *percent*, or *degrees*, so a star in Akkadian (the DINGIR sign) indicated that an ancient figure was divine.

31. Charles Q. Choi, "Earth's Sun: Facts about the Sun's Age, Size and History," November 14, 2017, https://www.space.com/58-the-sun-formation-facts-and-characteristics.html.

32. Jack J. Lissauer and Imke de Pater, *Fundamental Planetary Science: Physics, Chemistry, and Habitability* (New York: Cambridge University Press, 2013), 4.

33. Eye-crossingly technical explanations are available in M. Wittkowski et al., "Fundamental Properties and Atmospheric Structure of the Red Supergiant VY Canis Majoris based on VLTI/AMBER Spectro-interferometry," *Astronomy and Astrophysics* 540 (2012): 1; and B. Arroyo-Torres et al., "The Atmospheric Structure

and Fundamental Parameters of the Red Supergiants AH Scorpii, UY Scuti, and KW Sagittarii," *Astronomy and Astrophysics* 554 (2013): 9.

34. The circumference of the sun is estimated to be 2.7 million miles. A 747 flying at 570 miles per hour would take 197.4 days to make this journey. By comparison, UY Scuti, assuming a radius of 1708 solar radii, would have a circumference of 4.6 billion miles.

35. It is actually quite difficult to give an accurate count of the stars in our galaxy, in part because it is not possible to count the stars individually. Most estimates attempt to determine the mass of the galaxy and then divide that figure by the mass of an "average" star. If it is assumed that the sun is an average-sized star, then the figure comes out to be approximately 100 billion stars. Other scientists, using different assumptions, have come out with estimates ranging as high as 400 billion. A discussion of the subject can be found in Maggie Masetti, "How Many Stars in the Milky Way?," July 22, 2015, https://asd.gsfc.nasa.gov/blueshift/index .php/2015/07/22/how-many-stars-in-the-milky-way/.

36. In the so-called "Great Debate" held on April 26, 1920, Harlow Shapley and Heber Curtis argued over whether the universe was one big galaxy (Shapley) or a combination of multiple galaxies (Curtis). An excellent summary of the circumstances, arguments, and outcomes of the debate is available in Virginia Trimble, "The 1920 Shapley-Curtis Discussion: Background, Issues, and Outcome," 1995, https://apod.nasa.gov/diamond_jubilee/papers/trimble.html.

37. On the estimate that the number of galaxies in the universe reaches as high as 2 trillion, see Ethan Siegel, "This Is How We Know There Are Two Trillion Galaxies in the Universe," October 18, 2018, https://www.forbes.com/sites /startswithabang/2018/10/18/this-is-how-we-know-there-are-two-trillion-galaxies -in-the-universe/#64c991485a67; and, from a more technical standpoint, Christopher J. Conselice et al., "The Evolution of Galaxy Number Density at $z < 8$ and Its Implications," *The Astrophysical Journal* 830 (Oct. 20, 2016), 1.

38. The complex issues surrounding the composition of the Torah lie beyond the scope of the present study. A helpful introduction to these issues is available in Richard Elliott Friedman, *Who Wrote the Bible?* (New York: Simon & Schuster, 2019).

39. Piotr Michalowski argues compellingly that the elevation of Marduk in Enuma Elish reflects a Babylonian response to political and cultural pressures from its northern neighbor and rival, Assyria. See Michalowski, "Presence at the Creation," in *Lingering over Words: Studies in Ancient Near Eastern Literature in Honor of William L. Moran*, ed. Tzvi Abusch, John Huehnergard, and Piotr Steinkeller (Atlanta: Scholars Press, 1990), 381–96, esp. 389–96. Whereas Marduk had traditionally been regarded only as the patron deity of the city of Babylon, in Assyria the god Aššur (Assur) was the head of a national pantheon. Michalowski notes: "To assert the primacy of Marduk, the Babylonians had to make their pantheon homologous to that of Assyria. The central act in this reform was the exaltation of the city god of Babylon to the status of a national deity, an exaltation that provided a direct counterpart to Assur" (p. 390). A quite similar case is advanced by Flynn (*YHWH Is King*, 92–118), who goes on to argue that similar sorts of cultural pressures contributed

to Israel's growing attribution to YHWH of a universal kingship rooted in his role as creator (pp. 121–35). Kenton Sparks, who adduces extensive parallels between Israel's priestly literature and Enuma Elish and its accompanying rites in the Akītu festival, also suggests that cultural pressures from Assyria and Babylonia played a role in shaping these Israelite traditions. See Sparks, "Priestly Mimesis," 642–48.

40. The twelve-day ceremony held each spring during the month of Nisannu was known as the Akītu Festival. A brief introduction to the festival and its connection with the battle between Marduk and Tiamat is found in Lambert, "The Great Battle of the Mesopotamian Religious Year: The Conflict in the Akītu House," *Iraq* 25 (1963): 189–90. More in-depth studies are available in Thorkild Jacobsen, "Religious Drama in Ancient Mesopotamia," in Goedicke and Roberts, *Unity and Diversity*, 72–77; Jeremy A. Black, "The New Year Ceremonies in Ancient Babylon: 'Taking Bel by the Hand' and a Cultic Picnic," *Religion* 11 (1981): 39–59; Mark E. Cohen, "The *Akītu* Festival," in *The Cultic Calendars of the Ancient Near East* (Bethesda, MD: CDL, 1993), 400–453; and Benjamin D. Sommer, "The Babylonian Akitu Festival: Rectifying the King or Renewing the Cosmos?," *JANES* 27 (2000): 81–95.

41. The so-called "Hubble Deep Field" is actually the combination of a series of studies that began with the original Hubble Deep Field North in 1995 and extended to the Hubble Ultra Deep Field in 2004 and the Hubble Ultra Deep Field Infrared in 2009. The Hubble eXtreme Deep Field, produced in 2012, was based on the combination of the exposures that had been taken previously. The results of this combined analysis of the Deep Field efforts are available in a technical article by G. D. Illingworth et al., "The *HST* Extreme Deep Field (XDF): Combining All ACS and WFC3/IR Data on the HUDF Region into the Deepest Field Ever," *Astrophysical Journal Supplement Series* 209 (2013).

Notes to Chapter 8

1. The MT's *yôrḏê hayyām* is likely an error for *yir'am hayyām*.

2. Later, Jeremiah uses the same language to describe the judgment that will be visited in turn on Babylon (cf. Jer 50:42).

3. Along with the passages noted here, see Pss 32:6; 124:2–5; 144:7.

4. To highlight the word connections in the passage, I have listed only the relevant Hebrew verbal roots, not the full forms in which they appear in the biblical text.

5. Unlike the description of Day Five (vv. 20–23), Day Six will finally refer to *fish* (vv. 26, 28). It may be that fish are mentioned on Day Six because they fall among the sorts of animals over which humans—who are also created on Day Six—will have dominion.

6. Cf. 2 Chr 20:35–37, which presents a somewhat different version of the event.

7. One of the commissions entrusted to Herod the Great by Rome was the construction of a suitable harbor. The remains of this harbor and the city that was built along with it, Caesarea Maritima, can still be visited today.

8. Fabrice De Backer, "Fragmentation of the Enemy in the Ancient Near East during the Neo-Assyrian Period," in *Ritual Dynamics and the Science of Ritual*, vol. 3, *State, Power, and Violence*, ed. Margo Kitts (Wiesbaden: Harrassowitz, 2010), 393–412.

9. For examples of Egypt and Mesopotamia (especially Assyria) set as opposite geographical poles, see Isa 7:18; 19:23; 27:13; Jer 2:18; Hos 7:11; 9:3; 11:5, 11; 12:1; Mic 7:12; Zech 10:10. For examples of fleeing to Egypt, see 1 Kgs 11–12; 2 Kgs 25:26; Isa 30:2; 31:1; Jer 24:8; 26:21; 41:17; 42–44. For examples of relying on Egypt to resist Mesopotamia, see 2 Kgs 17:4; 18:21; Isa 36:6–9.

10. It is only after the waters have been further restrained on Day Three in order that the land can appear that God will finally declare this aspect of creation to be good (cf. v. 10).

11. The tension between the goodness and imperfection of God's creation is explored in Terence E. Fretheim, *Creation Untamed: The Bible, God, and Natural Disasters* (Grand Rapids: Baker Academic, 2010), 9–37.

12. On Day Two God produces two elements of creation, seas and sky, and on Day Five he fills these two realms with fish and birds, respectively. In both cases, though, these pairs of created things (seas and sky; fish and birds) are created in tandem, with only one instance of the four-part structure discussed above used to narrate the creation of the two together. Only on Days Three and Six are God's creative acts described via two separate instances of the four-part structure.

13. *Cease from* or *cease to (do)* is the predominant meaning of the Qal form of *šābat* + *min* elsewhere in the Bible. In Job 32:1, Job's friends *ceased to answer him* when it was clear he would not concede that he was guilty. In Jer 31:36, the prophet speaks of the impossibility of Israel's *ceasing to be* his chosen people. Lamentations 5:14 mourns that elders have *ceased from* the gate and young men have *ceased from* their music. Hosea 7:14 refers to a baker who *ceases to stir* the fire. Joshua 5:12 has a somewhat different construction but still uses *šābat* to refer to ceasing: *the manna ceased from the day after they ate the produce of the land.* Earlier traditions in the Torah portray the God of Israel in more anthropomorphic terms than does the relatively late Gen 1:1–2:3. Thus, Exod 20:11 does say that YHWH *rested* (from the verb *nûaḥ*) on the seventh day, and Exod 31:17 goes further, saying that YHWH *rested* (*šābat* without *min*) and *was refreshed* (from the verb *nāpaš*). As noted previously, the sense in which *rest* does appear in Gen 2:1–3 is not that of God's resting due to fatigue but that of his taking up his place in his cosmic temple (see 2 Chr 6:41; Ps 132:8; Exod 20:11; 31:17).

14. Levenson, *Creation and the Persistence of Evil*, 17–18.

Notes to Chapter 9

1. The prophet Jeremiah asks a similar question as he laments to God: "*Why did I come forth from the womb to see toil and sorrow, and spend my days in shame?*" (Jer 20:18).

2. In his consideration of Ps 74, Levenson (*Creation and the Persistence of Evil*, 19) argues: "The psalmist refuses to deny the evidence of his senses in the name of

faith, to pretend that there is some higher or inner world in which these horrific events are unknown. But he also refuses to abandon the affirmation of God's world-ordering mastery, his power to defeat even the primeval personifications of chaos and to fashion the world as he sees fit."

3. The word *tiqqûn* has a rich (and complicated) etymological history. The nominal form derives from the verb *tqn*, which is itself a by-form of *tkn*. The variant *tqn* is more commonly found in eastern Semitic dialects (e.g., Akkadian *taqānu*) and is found in Biblical Hebrew only in Qoh 1:15, 7:13, and 12:9, and in an Aramaic passage in Dan 4:36 [33]. The western form *tkn* is more common in the Bible (cf. 1 Sam 2:3; 2 Kgs 12:12; Job 25:25; Ps 75:3 [4]; Prov 16:2; 21:2; 24:12; Isa 40:12, 13; Ezek 18:25 [3x], 29 [3x]; 33:17 [3x], 20 [3x]). The phrase *tiqqûn ʿôlām*, which refers to *fixing* (or *repairing*) *the world*, does not appear in the Bible itself. The earliest use of the term found thus far is in the so-called *Aleinu* prayer, which may date from as early as the second to third centuries CE. The phrase appears occasionally in early Jewish interpretive texts (midrashim) and in the Talmud. It has developed into a major tenet of modern and especially progressive Judaism, however.

4. In Mic 7:19 and Zech 9:15, *kābaš* is used in the sense of *treading down* something. This is an apt illustration of the sort of subjugation the term envisions.

5. This is, of course, the genesis of the prohibition on mixing meat and dairy that occupies such a prominent place in Judaism's kosher laws.

6. Christopher Southgate offers an elegant treatment of these issues in the chapter "The Call of Humanity" in his book *The Groaning of Creation: God, Evolution, and the Problem of Evil* (Louisville: Westminster John Knox, 2008), 92–115. See also the chapter "The Role of Humanity" in Sean M. McDonough, *Creation and New Creation: Understanding God's Creation Project* (Peabody, MA: Hendrickson, 2016), 179–202.

7. Israel's priestly literature shows an interest in order far beyond the story of creation. This strand of literature in the Torah is responsible for nearly all of the dates, ages, itineraries, lists, and censuses that tie together and organize the Pentateuchal traditions. See the discussion in S. R. Driver, *An Introduction to the Literature of the Old Testament* (New York: Scribner's Sons, 1891; repr. Gloucester, MA: Peter Smith, 1972), 126–31. For a general introduction to the priestly source, see Jacob Milgrom, "Priestly ("P") Source," *ABD* 5:454–61.

8. Tikva Frymer-Kensky carefully charts the connections between the Bible's cosmology and the role humans are to play in maintaining its cosmic order. See her essay "Biblical Cosmology" in *Backgrounds for the Bible*, ed. Michael Patrick O'Connor and David Noel Freedman (Winona Lake, IN: Eisenbrauns, 1987), 231–40.

9. On the precedent set by Gen 1 for *separation* in other aspects of Israelite religion, see Edward L. Greenstein, "Presenting Genesis 1, Constructively and Deconstructively," *Prooftexts* 21 (2001): 5–8.

10. The delightful study of this psalm by Nahum Sarna ("Psalm 1: The Moral Individual—The Immoral Society") wends its way through the manifold nuances the song has to offer. See Sarna, *On the Book of Psalms: Exploring the Prayers of Ancient Israel* (New York: Schocken Books, 1993), 25–47.

11. Another way of understanding *ʾašrê* would be as a *plural of intensification*, in which case the line might be rendered, "O the *indescribable happiness* of the person who . . . ." See GKC §124e.

12. Note the similar language in the opening verses of Ps 119: "O the happinesses of those whose way is blameless, those who walk in the Law of YHWH. O the happinesses of those who observe his decrees and seek him with their whole heart" (vv. 1–2).

13. Cf. Exod 20; Deut 5.

14. The underlying Hebrew text here refers to the Amalekites metonymically as "Amalek." For the sake of clarity, I have rendered the text using the plural, "Amalekites," and correspondingly plural pronouns.

15. See also Gen 20:11; 2 Sam 23:3; 2 Chr 19:7, 9–10; Neh 5:15; Job 6:14; Isa 11:2–4; Luke 23:40.

16. The exact nature of the offense in the prophet's charge "A man and his father go in to the girl, so that my name is profaned" is debated. Some suggest that the "girl" (Hebrew, *naʿărâ*) in the passage is a cultic prostitute, and thus the sin that is committed is one of illicit worship. All of the other charges in the passage, however, have to do with mistreating the poor and the oppressed; this suggests that the girl here is also being mistreated and taken advantage of. The odd description of those who go in to her as "a man and his father" appears to be the equivalent of the English expression "every Tom, Dick, and Harry." In this case, the text apparently decries the fact that everyone is having their way with a girl who cannot fight back, presumably a slave girl.

17. As if the nature of Naomi's instructions were not clear enough, the language of the passage includes additional sexual innuendos. The term for *uncover* (Hebrew *gālâ*) is regularly used euphemistically in the context of sexual activity (cf. Lev 18; 20; Deut 23:1; 27:20). Further, the term *feet* is used in Hebrew as a euphemism for male genitalia. For example, it is likely Moses' genitals, not his feet, that Zipporah touches with the foreskin of her son in Exod 4:25. It is the genitals of the captive Israelites, not their feet, that, as Isaiah warns, the Assyrians will shave (Isa 7:20). The "water of their feet" in 2 Kgs 18:27 and Isa 36:12 is the urine (parallel to *dung*) the Rabshakeh threatens the besieged Israelites will have to drink. It may also be the genitalia of the seraphim and not their feet that two wings cover in Isaiah's famous vision of the divine throne room (Isa 6:2), though here it is difficult to be certain.

18. The verb *śyh (not the noun) is used more often with positive connotations (cf. Ps 105:2 // 2 Chr 16:9; Pss 145:5; 119 [6x]). Many of these uses are still quite reflective rather than exuberant, however, and other uses of the verb are tied directly to lament (cf. Pss 55:17 [18]; 77:3, 6 [4, 7]; Job 7:11).

19. Cf. Ezek 11:17–20; Jer 31:31–34.

20. Cf. Isa 66:22–23.

21. The Hebrew Scriptures are filled with similar expressions of hope built on God's past mastery of the sea. In Ps 33, the psalmist first (in vv. 6–9) praises God for his creative works and his control of the sea: "He gathered the waters of the sea as in a bottle; he put the deeps in storehouses" (v. 7). This then (in vv. 16–22) becomes

the basis of his hope in God's deliverance: "We hope in you" (v. 22). Cf. also Pss 46:1–5 [2–6]; 96:5, 10–13; Dan 7:2–3, 13–14; Hab 3:8–16; Hag 2:6–9.

Notes to Chapter 10

1. Concerning Matthew's use of the terms *lawlessness* and *righteousness*, see Dunn, *Unity and Diversity*, 246–51.

2. This emphasis is evident elsewhere in Matthew and in the other Gospels as well. Cf. Matt 13:41–43; 15:18–20; 19:16–24; Mark 7:6–15; 9:43–48; 10:17–23; Luke 3:3; 10:25–29; John 3:19–21; 5:45–47.

3. The underlying Greek text labels them *agrammatoi* and *idiōtai*. The first term means literally *unlettered* or *illiterate*. The second is the source of our English word *idiot*, though the sense of the Greek is somewhat less pejorative.

4. The Greek term used to describe what the man did to himself with stones is *katakoptō*, a term that refers to *making rough cuts* or *lacerating*, not bruising.

5. The accounts of this story in Matthew and Luke are equally deliberate in noting that only Jesus, not the disciples, ever got out of the boat (cf. Matt 8:28–34; Luke 8:26–37).

6. Concerning the differences between the feeding of the five thousand and the four thousand, see Donald A. Hagner, *Matthew 14–28*, WBC 33B (Dallas: Word, 1995), 447–52.

Bibliography

Alter, Robert. *The Pleasures of Reading in an Ideological Age*. New York: Simon & Schuster, 1989.

Anderson, Bernhard W. "The Slaying of the Fleeing, Twisting Serpent: Isaiah 27:1 in Context." Pages 3–15 in *Uncovering Ancient Stones: Essays in Memory of H. Neil Richardson*. Edited by Lewis M. Hopfe. Winona Lake, IN: Eisenbrauns, 1994.

Arroyo-Torres, B., M. Wittkowski, J. M. Marcaide, and P. H. Hauschildt. "The Atmospheric Structure and Fundamental Parameters of the Red Supergiants AH Scorpii, UY Scuti, and KW Sagittarii." *Astronomy and Astrophysics* 554 (2013).

Attridge, H. W. *First-Century Cynicism in the Epistles of Heraclitus*. HTS. Missoula, MT: Scholars Press, 1976.

Barrett, C. K. *A Critical and Exegetical Commentary on the Acts of the Apostles*. ICC 30–31. 2 vols. Edinburgh: T&T Clark, 1994–98.

———. *On Paul: Aspects of His Life, Work and Influence in the Early Church*. London: T&T Clark, 2003.

Batto, Bernard F. "The Combat Myth in Israelite Tradition Revisited." Pages 217–36 in *Creation and Chaos: A Reconsideration of Hermann Gunkel's Chaoskampf Hypothesis*. Edited by JoAnn Scurlock and Richard H. Beal. Winona Lake, IN: Eisenbrauns, 2013.

———. *Slaying the Dragon: Mythmaking in the Biblical Tradition*. Louisville: Westminster John Knox, 1992.

———. "The Sleeping God: An Ancient Near Eastern Motif of Divine Sovereignty." *Bib* 68 (1987): 153–77.

Black, Jeremy A. "The New Year Ceremonies in Ancient Babylon: 'Taking Bel by the Hand' and a Cultic Picnic." *Religion* 11 (1981): 39–59.

Blenkinsopp, Joseph. "The Cosmological and Protological Language of Deutero-Isaiah." *CBQ* 73 (2011): 493–510.

Brown, William P. *The Seven Pillars of Creation: The Bible, Science, and the Ecology of Wonder.* Oxford: Oxford University Press, 2010.

Calvin, John. *Commentaries on the Book of Joshua.* Translated by Henry Beveridge. Edinburgh: Calvin Translation Society, 1854; repr., Grand Rapids: Baker, 1996.

——. *Commentary on a Harmony of the Evangelists, Matthew, Mark, and Luke.* Translated by William Pringle. Edinburgh: Calvin Translation Society, 1845; repr., Grand Rapids: Baker, 1996.

——. *Commentary on the Book of Psalms.* Translated by James Anderson. Edinburgh: Calvin Translation Society, 1845–49; repr. Grand Rapids: Baker, 1996.

——. *Ioannis Calvini opera quae supersunt omnia.* Edited by Wilhelm Baum, Edward Cunitz, and Eduard Reuss. Corpus Reformatorum 29–87. Braunschweig: C. A. Schwetschke & Son, 1863–1900.

Carlson, Richard F., and Tremper Longman III. *Science, Creation, and the Bible: Reconciling Rival Theories of Origins.* Downers Grove, IL: InterVarsity Press, 2010.

Charney, Davida. *Persuading God: Rhetorical Studies of First-Person Psalms.* Sheffield: Sheffield Phoenix, 2015.

Chau, Kevin. "The Poetry of Creation and Victory in the Psalms." Pages 65–83 in *Inner Biblical Allusion in the Poetry of Wisdom and Psalms.* Edited by Mark J. Boda, Kevin Chau, and Beth LaNeel Tanner. LHBOTS 659. London: T&T Clark, 2019.

Childs, Brevard S. *Myth and Reality in the Old Testament.* London: SCM, 1960.

Choi, Charles Q. "Earth's Sun: Facts about the Sun's Age, Size and History." Published electronically on November 14, 2017. https://www.space.com /58-the-sun-formation-facts-and-characteristics.html.

Clifford, Richard J. "Cosmogonies in the Ugaritic Texts and in the Bible." *Or* 53 (1984): 183–201.

Cogan, Mordechai. "Judah under Assyrian Hegemony: A Reexamination of *Imperialism and Religion*." *JBL* 112 (1993): 403–14.

Cohen, Mark E. "The *Akītu* Festival." Pages 400–453 in *The Cultic Calendars of the Ancient Near East.* Bethesda, MD: CDL, 1993.

Collins, C. John. "Inerrancy Studies and the Old Testament: 'Ancient Science' in the Hebrew Bible." *Presb* 44 (2018): 42–66.

Conselice, Christopher J., Aaron Wilkinson, Kenneth Duncan, and Alice Mortlock. "The Evolution of Galaxy Number Density at $z < 8$ and Its Implications." *The Astrophysical Journal* 830 (2016): 1–17.

Coogan, Michael D., and Mark S. Smith. *Stories from Ancient Canaan.* 2nd ed. Louisville: Westminster John Knox, 2012.

Craigie, Peter C. "The Poetry of Ugarit and Israel." *TynBul* 22 (1971): 3–31.

——. *Psalms 1–50.* WBC 19. Waco, TX: Word, 1983.

Cross, Frank Moore. *Canaanite Myth and Hebrew Epic: Essays in the History of the Religion of Israel.* Cambridge: Harvard University Press, 1973.

———. "Notes on a Canaanite Psalm in the Old Testament." *BASOR* 117 (1950): 19–21.

———. "The 'Olden Gods' in Ancient Near Eastern Creation Myths." Pages 328–38 in *Magnalia Dei, the Mighty Acts of God: Essays on the Bible and Archaeology in Memory of G. Ernest Wright.* Edited by Frank Moore Cross, Werner E. Lemke, and Patrick D. Miller Jr. Garden City, NY: Doubleday, 1976.

Day, John. *God's Conflict with the Dragon and the Sea: Echoes of a Canaanite Myth in the Old Testament.* Cambridge: Cambridge University Press, 1985.

———. *Yahweh and the Gods and Goddesses of Canaan.* JSOTSup 265. Sheffield: Sheffield Academic, 2000.

De Backer, Fabrice. "Fragmentation of the Enemy in the Ancient Near East during the Neo-Assyrian Period." Pages 393–412 in *Ritual Dynamics and the Science of Ritual,* vol. 3, *State, Power, and Violence.* Edited by Margo Kitts. Wiesbaden: Harrassowitz, 2010.

Donner, Herbert. "Ugaritismen in der Psalmenforschung." *ZAW* 79 (1967): 322–50.

Dreyer, J. L. E., ed. *Tychonis Brahe Dani opera omnia.* Copenhagen: Libraria Gyldendaliana, 1913–29.

Driver, S. R. *An Introduction to the Literature of the Old Testament.* New York: Scribner's Sons, 1891; repr. Gloucester, MA: Peter Smith, 1972.

Dunn, James D. G. *Unity and Diversity in the New Testament: An Inquiry into the Character of Earliest Christianity.* 2nd ed. London: SCM, 1990.

Edwards, Mark J. "Quoting Aratus: Acts 17,28." *ZNW* 83 (1992): 266–69.

Emerton, J. A. "'Spring and Torrent' in Psalm LXXIV 15." Pages 122–33 in *Volume du Congrès: Genève, 1965.* Edited by P. A. H. de Boer. VTSup 15. Leiden: Brill, 1966.

Enns, Peter. *The Evolution of Adam: What the Bible Does and Doesn't Say about Human Origins.* Grand Rapids: Brazos, 2012.

———. *Inspiration and Incarnation: Evangelicals and the Problem of the Old Testament.* Grand Rapids: Baker Academic, 2005.

Epictetus. *Epictetus: The Discourses as Reported by Arrian, the Manual, and Fragments.* Translated by W. A. Oldfather. 2 vols. LCL. Cambridge: Harvard University Press, 1925–61.

Fensham, F. Charles. "Psalm 29 and Ugarit." *OTWSA* 6 (1963): 84–99.

Finocchiaro, Maurice A. *Retrying Galileo, 1633–1992.* Berkeley: University of California Press, 2005.

Fishbane, Michael A. *Biblical Myth and Rabbinic Mythmaking.* Oxford: Oxford University Press, 2003.

Fisher, Loren. "Creation at Ugarit and in the Old Testament." *VT* 15 (1965): 313–24.

Flynn, Shawn W. *YHWH Is King: The Development of Divine Kingship in Ancient Israel.* VTSup 159. Edited by Christl M. Maier. Leiden: Brill, 2014.

Fretheim, Terence E. *Creation Untamed: The Bible, God, and Natural Disasters.* Grand Rapids: Baker Academic, 2010.

Friedman, Richard Elliott. *Who Wrote the Bible?* New York: Simon & Schuster, 2019.

Frymer-Kensky, Tikva. "Biblical Cosmology." Pages 231–40 in *Backgrounds for the Bible.* Edited by Michael Patrick O'Connor and David Noel Freedman. Winona Lake, IN: Eisenbrauns, 1987.

Galilei, Galileo. "Letter to the Grand Duchess Christina." Pages 173–216 in *Discoveries and Opinions of Galileo.* Translated by Stillman Drake. Garden City, NY: Doubleday, 1957.

Gaster, Theodor H. "Psalm 29." *JQR* 37 (1946): 55–65.

Gingerich, Owen, and James R. Voelkel. "Tycho Brahe's Copernican Campaign." *Journal for the History of Astronomy* 29 (1998): 1–34.

Ginsberg, H. L. "A Phoenician Hymn in the Psalter." Pages 472–76 in *Atti del XIX Congresso Internazionale degli Orientalisti: Roma, 23–29 Settembre 1935.* Rome: Tipografia del Senato, 1935.

Goedicke, Hans, and J. J. M. Roberts, eds. *Unity and Diversity: Essays in the History, Literature, and Religion of the Ancient Near East.* JHNES. Baltimore: Johns Hopkins University Press, 1975.

Greene, Nathaniel E. "Creation, Destruction, and a Psalmist's Plea: Rethinking the Poetic Structure of Psalm 74." *JBL* 136 (2017): 85–101.

Greenstein, Edward L. "Presenting Genesis 1, Constructively and Deconstructively." *Prooftexts* 21 (2001): 1–22.

Gunkel, Hermann. *Creation and Chaos in the Primeval Era and the Eschaton: A Religio-Historical Study of Genesis 1 and Revelation 12.* Translated by K. William Whitney Jr. BRS. Grand Rapids: Eerdmans, 2006. Translation of *Schöpfung und Chaos in Urzeit und Endzeit: Eine religionsgeschichtliche Untersuchung über Gen. 1 und Ap. Jon 12.* Göttingen: Vandenhoeck & Ruprecht, 1895, 1921.

———. *Genesis.* 7th ed. Göttingen: Vandenhoeck & Ruprecht, 1966.

Hagner, Donald A. *Matthew 14–28.* WBC 33B. Dallas: Word, 1995.

Hallo, William W. "Compare and Contrast: The Contextual Approach to Biblical Literature." Pages 1–30 in *The Bible in Light of Cuneiform Literature.* Edited by William W. Hallo, Bruce William Jones, and Gerald L. Mattingly. Lewiston, NY: Mellen, 1990.

Hasel, Gerhard F. "The Polemic Nature of the Genesis Cosmology." *EvQ* 46 (1974): 81–102.

Horowitz, Wayne. *Mesopotamian Cosmic Geography.* Winona Lake, IN: Eisenbrauns, 1998.

Hughes, Philip Edgcumbe. *Paul's Second Epistle to the Corinthians: The English Text with Introduction, Exposition and Notes.* Grand Rapids: Eerdmans, 1962.

Illingworth, G. D., D. Magee, P. A. Oesch, R. J. Bouwens, I. Labbé, M. Stiavelli, P. G. van Dokkum, et al. "The *HST* Extreme Deep Field (XDF): Combining All ACS and WFC3/IR Data on the HUDF Region into the Deepest Field Ever." *Astrophysical Journal Supplement Series* 209 (2013).

Jacobsen, Thorkild. "The Battle between Marduk and Tiamat." *JAOS* 88 (1968): 104–8.

———. "Religious Drama in Ancient Mesopotamia." Pages 65–77 in *Unity and Diversity: Essays in the History, Literature, and Religion of the Ancient Near East.* Edited by Hans Goedicke and J. J. M. Roberts. JHNES. Baltimore: Johns Hopkins University Press, 1975.

Janzen, J. Gerald. "On the Moral Nature of God's Power: Yahweh and the Sea in Job and Deutero-Isaiah." *CBQ* 56 (1994): 458–78.

Jipp, Joshua W. "Paul's Areopagus Speech of Acts 17:16–34 as Both Critique and Propaganda." *JBL* 131 (2012): 567–88.

Kapelrud, Arvid S. "Creation in the Ras Shamra Texts." *ST* 34 (1980): 1–11.

Keel, Othmar. *The Symbolism of the Biblical World: Ancient Near Eastern Iconography and the Book of Psalms.* Translated by Timothy J. Hallett. New York: Seabury, 1978.

Kiefert, Nicole. "Astronomers Just Discovered the Smallest Star Ever." Published electronically on July 12, 2017. http://www.astronomy.com/news/2017/07/tiny-new-star.

Kittel, Rudolf. "Cyrus und Deuterojesaja." *ZAW* 18 (1898): 149–62.

Klauck, Hans-Josef. *Magic and Paganism in Early Christianity: The World of the Acts of the Apostles.* Translated by Brian McNeil. Edinburgh: T&T Clark, 2000.

Lambert, W. G. *Babylonian Creation Myths.* MC. Winona Lake, IN: Eisenbrauns, 2013.

———. "The Great Battle of the Mesopotamian Religious Year: The Conflict in the Akītu House." *Iraq* 25 (1963): 189–90.

———. "The Historical Development of the Mesopotamian Pantheon: A Study in Sophisticated Polytheism." Pages 191–99 in *Unity and Diversity: Essays in the History, Literature, and Religion of the Ancient Near East.* Edited by Hans Goedicke and J. J. M. Roberts. JHNES. Baltimore: Johns Hopkins University Press, 1975.

———. "A New Look at the Babylonian Background of Genesis." Pages 96–113 in *"I Studied Inscriptions from before the Flood": Ancient Near Eastern, Literary, and Linguistic Approaches to Genesis 1–11.* Edited by Richard S. Hess and David Toshio Tsumura. SBTS. Winona Lake, IN: Eisenbrauns, 1994.

———. "The Reign of Nebuchadnezzar I: A Turning Point in the History of Ancient Mesopotamian Religion." Pages 3–13 in *The Seed of Wisdom: Essays in Honour of T. J. Meek*. Edited by W. S. McCullough. Toronto: University of Toronto Press, 1964.

Lelièvre, André. "YHWH et la mer dans les Psaumes." *RHPR* 56 (1976): 253–76.

Leonard, Jeffery M. "Identifying Inner-Biblical Allusions: Psalm 78 as a Test Case." *JBL* 127 (2008): 241–65.

———. "Identifying Subtle Allusions: The Promise of Narrative Tracking." Pages 91–113 in *Subtle Citation, Allusion, and Translation in the Hebrew Bible*. Edited by Ziony Zevit. Sheffield: Equinox, 2017.

———. "Let the Day Perish: The Nexus of Personification and Mythology in Job 3." *JSOT* 43 (2018): 247–69.

Levenson, Jon D. *Creation and the Persistence of Evil: The Jewish Drama of Divine Omnipotence*. Princeton: Princeton University Press, 1994.

Lissauer, Jack J., and Imke de Pater. *Fundamental Planetary Science: Physics, Chemistry, and Habitability*. New York: Cambridge University Press, 2013.

Luther, Martin. *D. Martin Luthers Werke: Kritische Gesamtausgabe*. Weimar: Hermann Böhlaus Nachfolger, 1883.

Martin, Ralph P. *2 Corinthians*. WBC 40. Waco, TX: Word, 1986.

Masetti, Maggie. "How Many Stars in the Milky Way?" Published electronically on July 22, 2015. https://asd.gsfc.nasa.gov/blueshift/index.php/2015/07/22/how-many-stars-in-the-milky-way/.

McDonough, Sean M. *Creation and New Creation: Understanding God's Creation Project*. Peabody, MA: Hendrickson, 2016.

Melanchthon, Philipp. "Initia doctrinae physicae." In *Philippi Melanthonis opera quae supersunt omnia*. Edited by Karl Gottlieb Bretschneider. Corpus Reformatorum 1–28. Halle: C. A. Schwetschke & Son, 1834–60.

Meyer, Heinrich. "More on Copernicus and Luther." *Isis* 45 (1954): 99.

Michalowski, Piotr. "Presence at the Creation." Pages 381–96 in *Lingering over Words: Studies in Ancient Near Eastern Literature in Honor of William L. Moran*. Edited by Tzvi Abusch, John Huehnergard, and Piotr Steinkeller. Atlanta: Scholars Press, 1990.

Miller, Patrick D. *Israelite Religion and Biblical Theology: Collected Essays*. JSOTSup 267. Sheffield: Sheffield Academic, 2000.

Mosca, Paul G. "Ugarit and Daniel 7: A Missing Link." *Bib* 67 (1986): 496–517.

Norlind, Wilhelm. "Copernicus and Luther: A Critical Study." *Isis* 44 (1953): 273–76.

O'Connor, Michael Patrick. "Ugarit and the Bible." Pages 151–64 in *Backgrounds for the Bible*. Edited by Michael Patrick O'Connor and David Noel Freedman. Winona Lake, IN: Eisenbrauns, 1987.

Pitard, Wayne T. "The Binding of Yamm: A New Edition of the Ugaritic Text *KTU* 1.83." *JNES* 57 (1998): 261–80.

Polhill, John B. *Acts*. NAC. Nashville: Broadman, 1992.

Polkinghorne, John. "The Universe as Creation." Pages 166–78 in *Intelligent Design: William A. Dembski and Michael Ruse in Dialogue*. Edited by Robert B. Stewart. Minneapolis: Fortress, 2007.

Poythress, Vern S. "Biblical Studies: Rain Water versus a Heavenly Sea in Genesis 1:6–8." *WTJ* 77 (2015): 181–91.

——. "Biblical Studies: Three Modern Myths in Interpreting Genesis 1." *WTJ* 76 (2014): 321–50.

Rad, Gerhard von. *Genesis: A Commentary*. Translated by John H. Marks. Rev. ed. OTL. Philadelphia: Westminster, 1972.

Reid, Garnett. " 'Thus You Will Say to Them': A Cross-Cultural Confessional Polemic." *JSOT* 31 (2006): 221–38.

Rendsburg, Gary A. "Review of David Toshio Tsumura, *The Earth and the Waters in Genesis 1 and 2: A Linguistic Investigation*." *JBL* 110 (1991): 136–38.

——. "*UT* 68 and the Tell Asmar Seal." *Or* 53 (1984): 448–52.

Rosen, Edward. "Calvin's Attitude toward Copernicus." *JHI* 21 (1960): 431–41.

——. "Galileo's Misstatements about Copernicus." *Isis* 49 (1958): 319–30.

Sandmel, Samuel. "Parallelomania." *JBL* 81 (1962): 1–13.

Sarna, Nahum M. *On the Book of Psalms: Exploring the Prayers of Ancient Israel*. New York: Schocken Books, 1993.

Schniedewind, William M., and Joel H. Hunt. *A Primer on Ugaritic: Language, Culture, and Literature*. New York: Cambridge University Press, 2007.

Schoonhoven, Calvin R. *The Wrath of Heaven*. Grand Rapids: Eerdmans, 1966.

Schwartz, A. Brad. *Broadcast Hysteria: Orson Welles's War of the Worlds and the Art of Fake News*. New York: Hill & Wang, 2015.

Seely, Paul H. "The Firmament and the Water Above: Part I: The Meaning of *raqia'* in Gen 1:6–8." *WTJ* 53 (1991): 227–40.

——. "The Firmament and the Water Above: Part II: The Meaning of 'The Water above the Firmament' in Gen 1:6–8." *WTJ* 54 (1992): 31–46.

Seneca. *Seneca ad Lucilium Epistulae Morales*. Translated by Richard M. Gummere. 3 vols. LCL. London: Heinemann, 1925.

Seri, Andrea. "The Role of Creation in Enūma eliš." *JANER* 12 (2012): 4–29.

Siegel, Ethan. "This Is How We Know There Are Two Trillion Galaxies in the Universe." Published electronically on October 18, 2018. https://www.forbes.com/sites/startswithabang/2018/10/18/this-is-how-we-know-there-are-two-trillion-galaxies-in-the-universe/#64c991485a67.

Smith, Mark S. "Biblical Narrative between Ugaritic and Akkadian Literature: Part I: Ugarit and the Hebrew Bible: Consideration of Comparative Research." *RB* 114 (2007): 5–29.

——. "Canaanite Backgrounds to the Psalms." Pages 43–56 in *The Oxford Handbook of the Psalms*. Edited by William P. Brown. Oxford: Oxford University Press, 2014.

————. *The Early History of God: Yahweh and the Other Deities in Ancient Israel*. 2nd ed. BRS. Grand Rapids: Eerdmans, 2002.

————. *The Priestly Vision of Genesis 1*. Minneapolis: Fortress, 2010.

————. *The Ugaritic Baal Cycle*, vol. 1, *Introduction with Text, Translation and Commentary of KTU 1.1–1.2*. VTSup 55. Leiden: Brill, 1994.

————. *Untold Stories: The Bible and Ugaritic Studies in the Twentieth Century*. Peabody, MA: Hendrickson, 2001.

Smith, Mark S., and Wayne T. Pitard. *The Ugaritic Baal Cycle*, vol. 2, *Introduction with Text, Translation and Commentary of KTU/CAT 1.3–1.4*. VTSup 114. Leiden: Brill, 2009.

Sommer, Benjamin D. "The Babylonian Akitu Festival: Rectifying the King or Renewing the Cosmos?" *JANES* 27 (2000): 81–95.

————. *A Prophet Reads Scripture: Allusion in Isaiah 40–66*. Stanford: Stanford University Press, 1998.

Southgate, Christopher. *The Groaning of Creation: God, Evolution, and the Problem of Evil*. Louisville: Westminster John Knox, 2008.

Sparks, Kenton L. "*Enūma Elish* and Priestly Mimesis: Elite Emulation in Nascent Judaism." *JBL* 126 (2007): 626–48.

————. *Sacred Word, Broken Word: Biblical Authority and the Dark Side of Scripture*. Grand Rapids: Eerdmans, 2012.

Speiser, E. A. *Genesis*. AB 1. New York: Doubleday, 1962.

Speller, Jules. *Galileo's Inquisition Trial Revisited*. Frankfurt am Main: Lang, 2008.

Stadelmann, Luis I. J. *The Hebrew Conception of the World: A Philological and Literary Study*. AnBib. Rome: Pontifical Biblical Institute, 1970.

Tate, Marvin E. *Psalms 51–100*. WBC 20. Dallas: Word, 1990.

Tov, Emanuel. *Textual Criticism of the Hebrew Bible*. Minneapolis: Fortress, 1992.

Trimble, Virginia. "The 1920 Shapley-Curtis Discussion: Background, Issues, and Outcome." Published electronically in 1995. https://apod.nasa.gov /diamond_jubilee/papers/trimble.html.

Tsumura, David Toshio. "The Creation Motif in Psalm 74:12–14? A Reappraisal of the Theory of the Dragon Myth." *JBL* 134 (2015): 547–55.

————. *The Earth and the Waters in Genesis 1 and 2: A Linguistic Investigation*. JSOTSup 83. Sheffield: JSOT Press, 1989.

Walton, John H. *The Lost World of Genesis One: Ancient Cosmology and the Origins Debate*. Downers Grove, IL: InterVarsity Press, 2009.

Watson, Wilfred G. E. *Classical Hebrew Poetry: A Guide to Its Techniques*. JSOTSup 26. Sheffield: JSOT Press, 1984.

————. *Traditional Techniques in Classical Hebrew Verse*. JSOTSup 170. Sheffield: Sheffield Academic, 1994.

Westermann, Claus. *Genesis 1–11*. Translated by John J. Scullion. CC. Minneapolis: Fortress, 1994.

White, Andrew Dickson. *A History of the Warfare of Science with Theology in Christendom*. 2 vols. New York: D. Appleton, 1896.

White, Robert. "Calvin and Copernicus: The Problem Reconsidered." *CTJ* 15 (1980): 233–43.

Wittkowski, M., P. H. Hauschildt, B. Arroyo-Torres, and J. M. Marcaide. "Fundamental Properties and Atmospheric Structure of the Red Supergiant VY Canis Majoris based on VLTI/AMBER Spectro-interferometry." *Astronomy and Astrophysics* 540 (2012).

Index of Ancient Sources